MW00681221

ADVANCES IN MERGERS AND ACQUISITIONS

ADVANCES IN MERGERS AND ACQUISITIONS

Series Editors: Sydney Finkelstein and Cary L. Cooper

Recent Volumes:

Volumes 1–2:   Edited by Cary L. Cooper and Alan Gregory
Volumes 3–14:   Edited by Sydney Finkelstein and Cary L. Cooper

ADVANCES IN MERGERS AND ACQUISITIONS
VOLUME 15

ADVANCES IN MERGERS AND ACQUISITIONS

EDITED BY

SYDNEY FINKELSTEIN
*Tuck School of Business, Dartmouth College,
Hanover, NH, USA*

CARY L. COOPER
*Manchester Business School, University of Manchester,
Manchester, UK*

United Kingdom – North America – Japan
India – Malaysia – China

Emerald Group Publishing Limited
Howard House, Wagon Lane, Bingley BD16 1WA, UK

First edition 2016

Copyright © 2016 Emerald Group Publishing Limited

Reprints and permissions service
Contact: permissions@emeraldinsight.com

British Library Cataloguing in Publication Data
A catalogue record for this book is available from the British Library

ISBN: 978-1-78635-394-8
ISSN: 1479-361X (Series)

Printed and bound by CPI Group (UK) Ltd, Croydon, CR0 4YY

ISOQAR certified
Management System,
awarded to Emerald
for adherence to
Environmental
standard
ISO 14001:2004.

Certificate Number 1985
ISO 14001

INVESTOR IN PEOPLE

CONTENTS

LIST OF CONTRIBUTORS

Anjali Bansal	Mudra Institute of Communications Ahmedabad (MICA), Ahmedabad, India
Olivier Bertrand	SKEMA Business School, Paris, France; Université Lille Nord de France, Lille, France
Nina Bertschy	University of Fribourg, Fribourg, Switzerland
Marie-Ann Betschinger	University of Fribourg, Fribourg, Switzerland; National Research University Higher School of Economics, Moscow, Russia
Daniel R. Denison	International Institute for Management Development, Lausanne, Switzerland
Cynthia E. Devers	Texas A&M University, College Station, TX, USA
Isabel Estrada	University of Groningen, Groningen, The Netherlands
David R. King	Iowa State University, Ames, IA, USA
Ia Ko	Denison Consulting, LLC, Ann Arbor, MI, USA
Jingyu Li	Texas A&M University, College Station, TX, USA
Killian McCarthy	University of Groningen, Groningen, The Netherlands
Gerry McNamara	Michigan State University, East Lansing, MI, USA
Olimpia Meglio	University of Sannio-DEMM, Benevento, Italy

Florian Noseleit	University of Groningen, Groningen, The Netherlands
Pankaj C. Patel	Ball State University, Muncie, IN, USA
Roman Shidlauskas	National Research University Higher School of Economics, Moscow, Russia
Adam Steinbach	Michigan State University, East Lansing, MI, USA
Peter Stokes	University of Chester, Chester, UK
Mahima Thakur	University of Delhi, New Delhi, India
Martin Weiss	University of Erlangen-Nürnberg, Nürnberg, Germany

INTRODUCTION

This volume brings together eight diverse, and compelling, chapters on mergers and acquisitions. Once again, as is always the case when we put together a new collection of chapters on mergers and acquisitions, the variety of context, question, methodology, and result is remarkable. We are happy to bring this collection to our readers, and excited for the potential that much of this work holds to suggest new ways of thinking about what works, and what doesn't, when it comes to this central method of growth for companies around the world.

The chapter by Mahima Thakur, Anjali Bansal, and Peter Stokes, investigates the correlates and predictors of employees' psychological outcomes during mergers and acquisitions (M&As) in the context of India. This study examines the role of different types of training initiatives (awareness training, human capital development training, and cross-cultural training) on building employees' feeling of psychological empowerment and thriving.

The chapter by Olivier Bertrand, Marie-Ann Betschinger, Nina Bertschy, and Roman Shidlauskas focuses on the determinants of the choice between international joint ventures and acquisitions when entering emerging countries. The key question here is whether sub-regional variation in political regimes matters for the entry mode decision of foreign investors.

The chapter by Daniel R. Denison and Ia Ko takes stock of the existing research and practice in the area of cultural due diligence and evaluates the strengths and limitations. They offer a set of due diligence strategies that are designed to overcome what they see as the limitations of existing approaches. The final product is an integrated overall framework of the cultural due diligence process.

The chapter by Isabel Estrada, Florian Noseleit, and Killian McCarthy tackles transitional governance (TG) in mergers and acquisitions. The key storyline here is about how the basic premises of economic geography can inform the field of TG. This chapter suggests some really interesting topics for researchers interested in moving this topic forward.

The chapter by Olimpia Meglio takes a much-needed look at acquisition performance from both a shareholder and a stakeholder perspective. As readers know, M&A literature has been dominated by a concern for how shareholders make out in a deal, yet there are other key constituencies that bear on whether a deal is actually "good" or not. This chapter brings these competing interests to the fore.

Next, Pankaj C. Patel and David R. King examine how the globalization of knowledge has driven an increased emphasis on cross-border, high technology acquisitions. When a target firm in a technology industry is acquired by a firm in another nation, integration challenges are even tougher than usual. These authors find that learning depends on similarity of knowledge, and that similarity can be provided by either technology or culture.

Adam Steinbach, Cynthia E. Devers, Gerry McNamara, and Jingyu Li review recent work on the influence of individual executive characteristics on acquisition behavior. They are particularly interested in situations where managers pursue their private interests rather than that of their shareholders. This is a great summary chapter as well of upper echelons research and methodology and how it all can inform M&A research.

In the last chapter Martin Weiss takes on the high priest of M&A research in strategy-relatedness. Ever since Dick Rumelt highlighted the importance of relatedness in M&A research when he did his dissertation, this construct has been central to the field. Weiss takes a fresh look at the phenomenon and how it affects our understanding of the diversification-performance linkage. A fitting last chapter to another fine collection of chapters that make up this volume of *Advances in Mergers and Acquisitions*.

Sydney Finkelstein
Cary L. Cooper
Editors

THE ROLE OF THRIVING AND TRAINING IN MERGER SUCCESS: AN INTEGRATIVE LEARNING PERSPECTIVE

Mahima Thakur, Anjali Bansal and Peter Stokes

ABSTRACT

This empirical investigation studies the correlates and predictors of employees' psychological outcomes during mergers and acquisitions (M&As) in the context of India. This study examined the role of different types of training initiatives (awareness training, human capital development training, and cross-cultural training) on building employees feeling of psychological empowerment and thriving. Further, second-order attitudes were studied in the form of employee satisfaction and commitment. A cross-sectional research design was adopted where quantitative and qualitative data were collected to investigate the interplay between the variables. Data were collected on an adapted standardized questionnaire from the employees of a public sector organization (N = 117) which had merged with a software company to deliver its IT services. Descriptive analysis, multiple correlational analysis, and stepwise regression analysis have assisted in exploring the different relationships amongst the variables. This study produces a prescriptive

Advances in Mergers and Acquisitions, Volume 15, 1−35
ISSN: 1479-361X/doi:10.1108/S1479-361X20160000015001

framework for merger success based on the model of growth and thriving (Spreitzer & Porath, 2012). Broadly, the results point towards the facilitative role of training in developing feelings of psychological empowerment, thriving, commitment and satisfaction with the merger, however qualitative data identified significant cultural undercurrents.

Keywords: Mergers and acquisitions; training; thriving; psychological empowerment; satisfaction; commitment

INTRODUCTION

Mergers and acquisitions (M&As) have been a key strategy for companies to consolidate and grow (Ellis & Lamont, 2004). In recent times, resurgence in the M&A activity shows their increasing importance in the developing economies like India. The recent trends of M&A activities in India suggest that the volume of M&A transactions in India has increased to approximately 67.2 billion USD in 2010 from 21.3 billion USD in 2009. Contemporaneously, M&A activity is witnessing a major increase in deals and recorded a 270% increase in the first quarter of the financial year, 2013. This increase is mainly attributed to the rise in cross-border M&A transactions. However, many researchers (Mitleton-Kelly, 2005; Weber, Rachman-Moore, & Tarba, 2012) report very high rates of M&A failure despite these being ostensibly used as growth strategies. The substantial economic and emotional costs resulting from failures in mergers make it important to understand the fundamental factors that relate to both corporate merger success and failure (Cartwright & Cooper, 1992; Dean, 2007; Thakur & Bansal, 2015). Several reasons have been put forward to explain the phenomena of M&A failure by M&A researchers, however, a commonly identified issue concerns ignorance of the human resource issues of the merged organization (Bansal & Thakur, 2013; Dass, 2008; Haspeslagh & Jemison, 1991; Mirc, 2014; Weber & Tarba, 2010). Even though there is growing acceptance of the pivotal role of human issues during a merger, companies frequently fail to give due attention to integration of cultures (Rottig, Reus, & Tarba, 2014), systems and technology (Gallos, 2006, p. 130). To produce a sustainable competitive advantage, the acquirer must transfer from the acquired firm, assets and people with different and better skills and knowledge than it and its competitors already possess, and ensure the transfer of practices that allow differentiation from competitors (Thakur & Bansal, 2015). These forms of process holistically lead to integration.

It is the post-M&A integration (PMI) phase which involves the major changes in the merging organizations. The PMI process refers to a host of activities undertaken to combine two previously separate organizations into one after the merger agreement is completed. With the prevalence of the M&A phenomenon, companies around the globe are keenly seeking to develop integration capabilities as poor integration management is a hindrance in not only achieving the organization's financial and strategic goals, but also in surfacing psychological, cultural and people issues in the merged organization (Thakur & Bansal, 2015; Davy, Kinicki, Scheck, & Kilroy, 1989; Rees & Edwards, 2009).

Often, processes of M&As result in organizational downsizing and large-scale redundancies. These processes have a strong impact on those who were forced to leave as well as on the 'survivors' (i.e. the employees who do not lose their jobs and remain in the organization). For the survivors, restructuring often produces a high level of uncertainty and dissatisfaction, stress, and increased level of distrust (Bansal, 2015 in press). These impediments to integration need to be taken into account while M&A planning. Consequently, researchers (Thakur & Bansal, 2015; Barmeyer & Mayrhofer, 2008; Marks & Mirvis, 2001) have largely held the poorly managed diversity of cultures between the two organizations responsible for the emergence of the negative psychological outcomes amongst M&A survivors. The ignorance of the diversity of culture and HR aspects of the M&A lead to negative psychological outcomes. Thus, training is required in M&As specifically on issues such as managing cultural differences in the given merger, studying the effects of cultural differences on human resources, managing resistance to change, and, dealing with conflict during the post-merger integration. Moreover, employees going through structural and role changes during M&As need to understand their expected roles and thus, need to be prepared better. Therefore, while considering the importance of 'learning' in order to understand and perform new job functions, the current study also takes into account of the effectiveness awareness training and human capital development training. Furthermore, a more integrated learning model of growth suggests that each individual is essentially motivated to grow and thrive in some form and it is important to provide environmental enablers that can help him or her to grow, and training can be a best enabler for that (Spreitzer & Porath, 2012). Employees delegated with important responsibilities during the change process, and the ones who are allowed to participate in the decision-making process in crucial scenarios like M&As tend to feel more empowered and thus more enthusiastic to perform their duties. Psychological empowerment helps to create a positive outlook of the whole M&A process which further assists in developing the psychological outcomes of satisfaction and commitment. Thus, training is imperative to employees' appreciation of the phenomena of empowerment and thriving, leading to the building of their psychological outcomes of satisfaction and commitment. Also, providing training helps improve the effectiveness of knowledge integration and with the effective absorption and acquisition of knowledge, employees are more likely to be encouraged to use this knowledge further. Thus, the current research is focused on studying the post-M&A training perceptions of M&A survivors with the emphasis on their thriving and psychological empowerment phenomena. The objectives of this study are:

1. To investigate the impact of training initiatives on employees' psychological outcomes.
2. To investigate the impact of thriving and psychological empowerment on employees' psychological outcomes of satisfaction and commitment.

THEORETICAL FRAMEWORK AND REVIEW OF LITERATURE

The Costs of Poor Integration in M&A

The poor management of post-M&A integration phase may lead to adverse outcomes for the merged organizations, including: loss or waste of valuable resources; problems with organizational communication; breakdown of collaborative working relationships; loss of tacit knowledge; damage to organizational culture; damage to organizational image and brand equity; loss of key talent; loss of trust in the leadership of the organization; possible increase in conflicts and grievances; loss of market share and consumers; and may also result in the demise of the organization from the market (Chaudhuri & Tabrizi, 1998; Ghauri & Buckley, 2003). Dass (2008) in his study suggests that the impact of M&A is not only limited to the organizational level but also has implications for the individuals associated with the M&A deal. At the *individual level*, negative consequences of M&A can include, for example: damage to social networks and social support; increased anxiety and stress due to uncertainty, loss of control, loss of identity, personal shame and the notion of change itself; loss of employment, loss of trust, negative impact on benefits, possible adverse changes to the employment contract and possible transfer to a less favourable location (Cartwright & Cooper, 1992). In a related study, Huy (2002) found that affective processes suffer during times of organizational upheaval which can contribute to feelings of lack of control and reduced autonomy.

Flogging a Dead Horse? Creating a Positive Climate in Order to Arrest the Downward Spiral of Negativity

Timely action to address the employee concerns during M&As can assist in ensuring employees commitment and satisfaction during integration (Hassett, 2012). Watson Wyatt Worldwide Inc. (1999) survey indicated that cultural compatibility was consistently rated as the biggest barrier to successful integration, yet this area was least researched by planners during the due-diligence phase of information collecting for integration planning. Cartwright and Cooper (1993) introduce the term 'culture collision' to describe organizational problems that result from poor cultural integration of the acquiring and acquired firms. Sarala (2010) further underlined that very often a confrontation between different organizational cultures is created when two or more companies are merged together which may lead to acculturative stress and post-acquisition conflict. Slowinski et al. (2002) explored employee reactions using the well-cited model of Maslow's Hierarchy. It was noted that employees felt threatened by the changes which incited fear and a worried mindset driving them into a 'survival' mode at the bottom tier of the Maslow's triangle. Employees thus become overwhelmed with self-concern, and they focused on wanting to know how the merger or acquisition would impact on them. Researchers (Fish, 2007; Pritchett, Robinson, & Clarkson, 1997) refer to this phenomenon as 'organizational dissonance' or a 'shudder' that vibrated through a company when acquired. The dissonance manifested itself in ambiguity, weakening levels of trust and focus on self-preservation. The resulting impact is negative and appears in the form of high turnover rate among employees, lower morale and productivity, competitive deterioration, and reduced revenues and profits (Pritchett et al., 1997).

Most of the survivors, especially from the acquired company, embroil in uncertainty and ambiguity which may lead to lowering of commitment to, and satisfaction with, the organization (Thakur & Juneja, 2011). Synonymous with this, entropy and the merger syndrome result from poor communication and employee insecurity. Thus, it becomes imperative for managers to attempt to arrest the downward spiral of negative feelings and help, if possible, to foster positive ones. One such energizing feeling that has been proposed by the proponents of integrated learning is the concept of 'thriving' (Spreitzer & Porath, 2012). Thriving is the inner urge to grow and learn and this is linked to both 'cause' and 'effects' of the facilitation processes during integration. 'Thriving' is defined as 'the joint experience of vitality and learning' (Spreitzer, Sutcliffe, Dutton, Sonenshein, & Grant, 2005). While experiencing feelings of thriving, employees are not stagnating or languishing, but instead are growing and energized in their work. Thriving may be seen as having a number of elements including, firstly, a feeling of vitality at work and, secondly, a sense that one is learning or getting better at work. Spreitzer and Porath (2012) link Self-Determination Theory (SDT) and notions of thriving in order to build an integrative model of human growth. Self-determination also contributes to the concept of psychological empowerment which has also been described as boosting the motivation of employees (Gagne & Deci, 2005). Moreover, Spreitzer and Porath (2012) suggest that the feelings of self-determination, autonomy and competence serve as *nutrients* to thriving. In short, thriving embraces active, intentional engagement in the process of personal growth. Vitality and learning are markers of thriving, acting as an indication of the extent to which a person is thriving at any given point of time (Spreitzer et al., 2005, p. 538). Vitality indicates the sense that one is energized and has a zest for life, while learning signifies acquisition and application of knowledge and skills to build capability. The two encompass both the affective (vitality) and cognitive (learning) dimensions of the psychological experience of personal growth.

In addition, the effectiveness of integration enablers helps building employees' psychological empowerment in the newly merged organization. Though empowerment has become immensely popular in contemporary management thinking, its roots which can be traced in previous management commentaries including well-grounded body of research on alienation (Blauner, 1964; Seeman, 1959), participative management (Lawler, 1994), and job enrichment (Hackman & Oldman, 1980). While earlier work conceptualized empowerment as a set of management practices focused on delegating decision-making authority (Mainiero, 1986), recent research provides the conceptual base for a more psychological definition of empowerment in the workplace (Bansal & Thakur, 2013). Building on the work of Conger and Kanungo (1988a), Thomas and Velthouse (1990) define psychological empowerment as intrinsic motivation manifested in four cognitions that reflect an individual's orientation to his or her work role: meaning, competence, self-determination, and impact. Within this context, empowerment has been analysed as both a relational and a motivational construct.

Role of Training during M&As

Waldman and Javidan (2009) suggested that during M&As a firm can enhance its position through learning (Haspeslagh & Jemison, 1991) and access to new or improved resources. The learning can be generalized, in the form of cross-pollination resulting in a diverse set of skills, competencies, and resources or it can be specialized, focusing on the new markets that have been accessed through the acquisition (Morosini, Shane, & Singh, 1998). This helps in increased efficiency (Walter & Barney, 1990), enhanced corporate learning (Ghoshal, 1987), and monopolistic market power (Trautwein, 1990; Waldman & Javidan, 2009). It was also pointed out that whatever the intended degree of integration: preservation, absorption, reverse takeover, best of both or transformation, human and cultural issues play a crucial role in the integration success (Bansal, 2015; Marks & Mirvis, 2001). For example, whether the company intends remaining independent, or intends linking together certain parts of the business such as IT and procurement, or aims for a complete merger, intangibles such as insecurity, distrust, resistance, change, and stress have to be addressed (Devine, 2002). Thus, training becomes important to induce such learning in the merged organizations. Weber and Tarba (2010) hail training and development as pivotal in M&A success as managers and employees require training in order to meet the needs of new positions created and also to be able to replace those who leave as a result of the high turnover that follows mergers. The training must extend to the technologies being employed and to the systems and work processes being introduced. Apart from developing job-related competencies, training plays a crucial role in preparing the employees towards the change in the organization and helping them adapt better (Thakur & Bansal, 2015). Thus, M&A researchers (Barmeyer & Mayrhofer, 2008; Landis & Bhagat, 1996) have proposed three types of training methods crucial during merger and acquisition, that is emotional, cognitive and behavioural. In conjunction, during PMI, managers need to understand the various stages of integration and types of resistance during the transition and help employees work through their reactions as quickly as possible so that the whole team can become capable of learning through collaborating. Appropriate training along the stages can help to accelerate the process of integration. To develop integration capability, employees from both companies who are expected to be involved in the merger must learn about the other company in all its regards, for example, assets, people, structure, culture, HR practices, processes. Equally, it is important to understand what roles in transferring and coordinating specific resources across the two companies will be required, the roles of various staff, and, what the 'deliverables' will be throughout the integration process. In addition, focusing on the management of cultures between the two merging organizations is crucial for the successful integration. Training is required not only to manage these cultural differences but also to manage the employees resistant. *Cross-cultural training* is also important as it is associated with increased awareness and understanding about the change situation. Devine (2002) suggests that the starting point for each company is to understand its own culture before analysing the culture of another company and studying the possibility of conflict or amalgamation. In this way, mergers may be viewed as a corporate marriage where two identities need to study each other well before attempting to integrate.

Training also helps to improve the effectiveness of knowledge integration and absorbs or acquires knowledge by reliance on manuals, databases, processes, and routines that encourage repeated use of this knowledge (Weber & Tarba, 2010). Thus, *awareness training* initiatives are associated with providing knowledge and information to the employees and managers regarding various aspects of merger process. The idea behind providing this type of training is that the affected groups of employees have to be conscious of the way the management and cultural systems function by using orientation grids developed by the research and creation of intercultural management just as the relationship with authority, time and information. Awareness training provides knowledge and information. In addition to this, Marks (1997) points out that the human resource professionals should take an active role in educating senior executives about HR issues which can interfere with the success of the merger and with meeting key business objectives.

Another very important aspect of training related to change situation is *human capital development training*. This is based on the concept of competencies building in order to meet the requirements of the change situation. Competency provides a basis for integrating key HR activities such as selection and assessment, performance management, training, development and reward management, thus developing a coherent approach to the management of people in organizations (Lucia & Lepsinger, 1999; Thakur & Bansal, 2015).

Shook and Roth (2011) in their research on M&As suggest that the limited number of training and development interventions contributes to the employee stress level. Nevertheless, problems can arise and, in another regard, research points towards a 'we versus they' attitude of employees during M&As and also antagonism, condescending attitudes, distrust, tension, and hostility (Astrachan, 1990; Blake & Mouton, 1986; Levinson, 1970). Marks and Mirvis (1986, p. 41) explicate the 'merger syndrome', whereby employees of the acquired firm 'mourn a corporate death', and deal with worst-case rumours, various stress reactions, and constricted communication. Moreover, M&As can severely affect career plans of employees by forcing layoffs, relocation, and the loss of individual influence (Walsh, 1989). Appelbaum, Gandell, Yortis, Proper, and Jobin (2000) point at the advantages of customized training to avoid these negative feelings to inculcate new skill sets in the new system with its new demands (Pritchett et al., 1997). They also suggest that employees must be provided with a supportive working environment so that they will not feel threatened or insecure. Shook and Roth (2011) indicate that, overall, employee fear and stress levels escalate during downsizing which is one of the outcomes of M&As. The lack or limited number of training and development interventions contribute to the employee stress level. In spite of all these potential risks, in the majority of the firms, there is, however, little planning to manage the changes that affect employees, and the employees have a tremendous impact on the successful implementation of major organizational changes (Shook & Roth, 2011).

During M&As, the resistance of employees' ebbs and flow along the stages of shock, denial, blame, testing, experimenting, discovering, learning and finally integration (Devine, 2002; Kubler-Rosse, 1969). If customized training is given along these stages it can facilitate the achievement of synergy of technologies, processes, people, and culture. Devine (2002) suggests that organizations go into a loop of learning during an M&A, starting from the reacting stage, moving to the improvising, fire-fighting, adjusting, feedback, analysis, and finally learning stage in the new scenario. Having attained a moderate level of integration, the new organization evolves a new vision and purpose for itself and engages in post-integration planning and controlling. Customized training for survivors is also recommended to avoid 'Survivor sickness' (Marks & Mirvis, 1998). Searle and Keynes (2004) emphasize the role of training in alleviating feelings of distrust and ambiguity. They found that introduction of new systems, such as an in-depth training for supervision, new shop floor training analysis and appraisals systems gave new clarity and signal to the organization. Open communication therefore hopefully leads to transformation of feelings of apprehension to excitement and acceptance. The above argument leads to the development of Hypotheses 1 and 2:

Hypothesis 1. There is a significant positive relationship between employee perception of effectiveness of training initiatives and their level of satisfaction during M&As.

Hypothesis 2. There is a significant positive relationship between employee perception of effectiveness of training initiatives and their level of commitment during M&As.

Thriving

The Role of Training in Inducing Thriving and Psychological Empowerment
M&A-related training programs help employees to grow and learn, while thriving is a concept related with inner urge of grow and learn. Thriving can serve as a gauge for people to sense progress in their growth and development. This gauge helps people to understand the ways in which, what they are doing, and how they are doing it, and is increasing their short-term individual functioning and long-term resourcefulness to becoming more effective at work (Spreitzer & Porath, 2012). The Spreitzer model of growth suggests that the organizational enablers can motivate the individuals to grow and thrive. These enablers can be, for example, institutionalized practices, training, information, climate, feedback, and trust. In this study, we propose adherence to the longstanding idea which follows McGregor's (1960) well-known assumption of 'Y' that people generally want to 'thrive', and 'grow'. This too contributes to feeling of 'thriving' which foster positive feelings related to the change processes in the organization. The appropriate enablers are not only facilitative but can also trigger this inherent yearning to grow. The theoretical model advanced by Spreitzer et al. (2005) suggests that when people are thriving, they mindfully interrelate with others – that is, they look out for the needs of others with whom they work. Researches also point out that the feeling of thriving results in people going out of their ways to seek relationships (Spreitzer et al., 2005) and engage in affiliated and organizational citizenship behaviours (OCBs) which are healthier and generally lead to less fatigue (sic: burned out). Where thriving is not evidenced, loss of talent is a major risk for an organization. Apart from damage to the competitive position of a

business, the departure of the talented and valued employees can adversely affect the organization in other ways. Thakur and Juneja (2011) in their study report that role stress (involving role ambiguity, role isolation and role overload) contributes in lowering commitment and satisfaction during change in the organization. Thus, companies need to work on their human resources (HR) polices and their employee engagement policies in order to help not only to retain valued employees, but also to encourage them to contribute in a maximum manner (Bansal & Thakur, 2012). Thus, adapting majorly from the study of Spreitzer and Porath, current study proposes a framework for the study which is best suited in the context of M&As (Fig. 1). Various researchers point out that Positive Organizational Scholarship (POS) (Roberts et al., 2005), enthuse feelings of thriving and

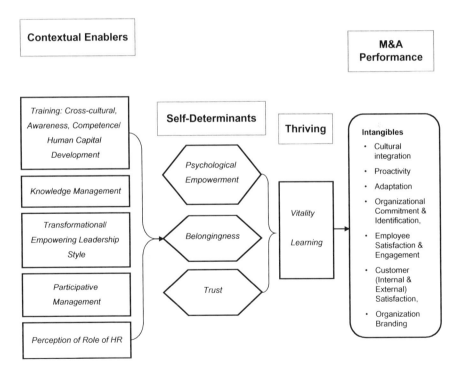

Fig. 1. Proposed Model of Enablers and Facilitators of M&A Performance. *Source*: Adapted from Spreitzer and Porath (2012).

psychological empowerment & contextual enablers increasing the satisfaction in the work setting (Spreitzer & Porath, 2012). Applying the above discussion to the context of M&As produces Hypotheses 3 and 4:

> **Hypothesis 3.** There is a significant positive relationship between employee feeling of thriving and their satisfaction during M&As.

> **Hypothesis 4.** There is a significant positive relationship between employee feeling of thriving and their commitment during M&As.

Psychological Empowerment as a Determinant of Thriving

In the context of M&As, it is suggested that organizations should make their employees feel empowered so that they experience 'thriving' which, in turn, would make them see the change in the organization as an opportunity to learn and grow. Training would facilitate the feelings of competence and self-determination which would thereby enhance the feeling of thriving. Quinn and Spreitzer (1997), for example, theorize how energy and positivity can be created in a conversation by enhancing one's feelings of autonomy, competence and relatedness.

The more that people are allowed to grow and learn — with the help of the appropriate enablers, such as extensive training, knowledge management, empowering leadership style, management of climate of trust and communication — the more likely they are to feel empowered, secure and happy. This, in turn, may energize them to indulge in proactive behaviours, acceptance of the new scenarios and propulsion towards self-growth and creative working. Thus, this has the potential to benefit the individual as well as the organization.

This leads the argument to Hypotheses 5–8:

> **Hypothesis 5.** There is a significant positive relationship between employee perception of training initiatives and their level of psychological empowerment during M&As.

> **Hypothesis 6.** There is a significant positive relationship between employee feeling of thriving and their level of psychological empowerment during M&As.

> **Hypothesis 7.** There is a significant positive relationship between employee level of psychological empowerment and their satisfaction during M&As.

Hypothesis 8. There is a significant positive relationship between employee level of psychological empowerment and their commitment during M&As.

RESEARCH METHODOLOGY

Research Design and Sampling

This study has adopted a mixed-method research design (qualitative and quantitative). We purposefully selected organizations where merger or acquisitions had taken place in the recent past and, in their efforts towards integration, those organizations were chosen which were conducting various training programs during post-M&A integration phase. This was done in order to study the relationship between perception of training and other variables such as psychological empowerment, thriving, commitment and satisfaction. Respondents were chosen randomly from the list of employees provided by the HR department. A majority of respondents' job roles were classified as engineers. Two hundred questionnaires were distributed of which 120 were returned, and finally 117 were included in the final analysis. Apart from the quantitative data, structured and open-ended interviews were also conducted, from which the qualitative data were obtained to assist the interpretation of the quantitative results.

Instrument

In the absence of an M&A integration instrument, an instrument has been developed with the help of adapted standardized questionnaires of different constructs. The Psychological Empowerment Scale (Spreitzer, 1995) was used to measure the dependent variable of psychological empowerment. This scale comprises 12 questions, three on each of the four dimensions of psychological empowerment: meaningfulness, competence, self-determination, and impact. It has reported the Cronbach alpha reliability as .87. To measure 'thriving' the questionnaire by Porath, Spreitzer, Gibson, and Garnett (2012) was used which consisted of two dimensions (10 items): learning and vitality. The reliability was found to be .83 (Cronbach Alpha). Commitment was measured using Meyer and Allen questionnaire, (2005) which had three dimensions: affective commitment, normative and continual. Satisfaction was measured using a single item 'are you satisfied with the merger (M&A)'. The perception of training initiatives questionnaire was constructed asking nine questions related to the dimensions of awareness training, cross-cultural training and human capital development training. The HR department conducted these three types of training programs as most of the people in the IT department were from a different cultural background with varying competencies. Most of them had an international exposure after having worked in international companies previously. Open-ended questions related to the employees feedback of empowering leadership style, communication, trust and perception of role of HR in the merger process were also included in the instrument to obtain deeper insights of the employees.

Analysis

The quantitative data were subjected to multivariate and regression analysis, while relational content analysis was performed on the qualitative data obtained from the responses of open-ended questions.

Qualitative data have inherent strengths and weaknesses. Though their objectivity and empirical status are often questioned, it is considered a rich aid to the survey data as it lends perspectives which an objective structured survey form may not lend (Onwuegbuzie, Johnson, & Collins, 2009; Pedrick, Babakus, & Richardson, 1993). Henwood and Nicholson (1995) suggest that although the methodological repertoire of psychology has generally included qualitative methods, these have tended to be seen as appropriate for the pilot phase of a project or as an adjunct to other research designs. Henwood and Pidgeon (1994) argue that the qualitative approaches with their emphasis on exploring the research participant's own situated experiences offset the critiques of much psychological research that the richness and significance of individual experience is neglected in favour of overarching reductionist explanations. Thus, both quantitative and qualitative data were analysed using descriptive statistics, inferential statistics and content analysis.

RESULTS OF THE STUDY

The purpose of this scientific investigation was to study the correlates of employee commitment and satisfaction within a merger or acquisition context. The study adopted an integrated model of learning and growth

(Spreitzer et al., 2005) and studied the relationship between satisfaction with mergers, training initiatives, psychological empowerment, thriving and perception of role of HR in the merger process. The empirical analysis of the data obtained supported the contention that the perception of training initiatives impacted on psychological empowerment and on thriving which in turn affected the employees' level of satisfaction and commitment. This study addresses the gap in research literature, related to the relationship between training initiatives, satisfaction with mergers and also the impact of psychological empowerment. Preciously, linkages between these variables have been studied separately, for example self-determination and thriving (Spreitzer et al., 2005), training and communication (Barmeyer & Mayrhofer, 2008; Weber & Tarba, 2010), psychological empowerment and commitment (Spreitzer, 1995), but a lacuna always existed regarding a model which would present linkages between all these variables and offer a framework incorporating these 'human' variables, HR interventions and merger performance. Interweaving the strands of inputs from all these studies, an attempt has been made to build a framework of relationships between these variables and satisfaction with mergers. This study combines all these factors (variables) in the scope of one design.

The relationship between the variables would be taken up one by one, while addressing the various hypotheses. The hypotheses are discussed and determined below:

Hypothesis 1. There is a significant positive relationship between employee perception of effectiveness of training initiatives and their level of satisfaction during M&As.

Hypothesis 2. There is a significant positive relationship between employee perception of effectiveness of training initiatives and their level of commitment during M&As.

Hypotheses 1 and 2 proposed relationships between the perception of effectiveness of training initiatives and employees' satisfaction and their level of commitment, respectively, with the newly merged organization. Pearson's correlations presented in Table 1 indicated the correlations of perception of different types of training initiatives institutionalized by the organization and employee level of satisfaction and commitment. Satisfaction was found to be significantly correlated with employees' favourable perception of training initiatives (Table 1: $r = .558$, $p < .01$). Significant correlation was found between employee satisfaction and their perception of effectiveness of awareness training ($r = .443$, $p < .01$),

Table 1. Results of Correlational Analysis: Correlation Coefficients between Employee Perception of Training Initiatives and Their Levels of Satisfaction and Commitment During M&As (H1 and H2) (*N* = 117).

		1	2	3	4	5	6	7	8	9
					Correlations					
Awareness training	Pearson correlation	1								
	Sig. (two-tailed)									
	N									
Human capital development training	Pearson correlation	.643**	1							
	Sig. (two-tailed)	.000								
	N	117	117							
Cross-cultural training	Pearson correlation	.650**	.581**	1						
	Sig. (two-tailed)	.000	.038							
	N	117	117	117						
Training Av.	Pearson correlation	.877**	.869**	.851**	1					
	Sig. (two-tailed)	.000	.000	.000						
	N	117	117	117	117					
Commitment: Affective	Pearson correlation	.095	.284**	.108	.194*	1				
	Sig. (two-tailed)	.309	.002	.245	.036					
	N	117	117	117	117	117				
Commitment: Normative	Pearson correlation	.426**	.622**	.565**	.625**	.399**	1			
	Sig. (two-tailed)	.000	.000	.000	.000	.000				
	N	117	117	117	117	117	117			
Commitment: Continual	Pearson correlation	.491**	.577**	.553**	.626**	.474**	.694**	1		
	Sig. (two-tailed)	.000	.000	.000	.000	.000	.000			
	N	117	117	117	117	117	117	117		
Commitment: Av.	Pearson correlation	.678**	.696**	.687**	.794**	.304**	.645**	.772**	1	
	Sig. (two-tailed)	.000	.000	.000	.000	.001	.000	.000		
	N	117	117	117	117	117	117	117	117	
Satisfaction with the merger	Pearson correlation	.443**	.533**	.467**	.558**	.336**	.641**	.737**	.877**	1
	Sig. (two-tailed)	.000	.000	.000	.000	.001	.000	.000	.000	
	N	117	117	117	117	117	117	117	117	117

**Correlation is significant at the .01 level (two-tailed).
*Correlation is significant at the .05 level (two-tailed).

human capital development training ($r = .533$, $p < .01$), and cross-cultural training ($r = .467$, $p < .01$). This discussion, thus accepts Hypothesis 1. However, highly significant positive correlation was obtained between employees level of commitment and their perception of overall effectiveness of training initiatives in the merged organization ($r = .794$, $p < .01$). Table 1 presented the significant positive correlation of employees perception of training effectiveness and their level of normative commitment ($r = .625$, $p < .01$) and continual commitment ($r = .626$, $p < .01$), while the correlations with affective commitment was not found to be significant ($r = .194$, $p < .01$). Thus, Hypothesis 2 is partially accepted.

Hypothesis 3. There is a significant positive relationship between employee feeling of thriving and their satisfaction during M&As.

Hypothesis 4. There is a significant positive relationship between employee feeling of thriving and their commitment during M&As.

The results of the study confirmed both of these hypotheses. Thriving and satisfaction (Table 2: $r = .476$, $p < .01$) were found to be significantly correlated with each other. This is in line with the works of Spreitzer et al. (2005) who provided preliminary evidence that thriving can occur at work during everyday moments and that it leads to satisfaction (Spreitzer & Porath, 2012). Since their inception, PSUs (Public Sector Utilities) have been functioning as the backbone of the Indian economy and leading the country along the road to development and self-sustenance. PSUs in India today are investing heavily in training of employees which serves as a major motivational factor.

Table 2 also presented significant relationship between thriving and commitment ($r = .585$, $p < .01$), which implies that employees in the merged organization would feel committed if they see themselves growing and learning. Thriving was also found to be significantly correlated with the dimensions of commitment, that is with affective commitment ($r = .242$, $p < .01$), normative commitment ($r = .475$, $p < .01$), and continual commitment ($r = .460$, $p < .01$).

Hypothesis 5. There is a significant positive relationship between employee perception of training initiatives and their level of psychological empowerment during M&As.

Though psychological empowerment was found to be less than average (Table 3: $M = 2.2$, SD $= .78473$), but interestingly the level of

Table 2. Results of Correlational Analysis: Correlation Coefficients between Thriving and Employee Levels of Satisfaction and Commitment during M&As (H3 and H4) ($N = 117$).

		Correlations					
		1	2	3	4	5	6
Thriving	Pearson correlation	1					
	Sig. (two-tailed)						
	N						
Satisfaction with the merger	Pearson correlation	.476**	1				
	Sig. (two-tailed)	.000					
	N	117	117				
Commitment: Affective	Pearson correlation	.242**	.336**	1			
	Sig. (two-tailed)	.009	.000				
	N	117	117	117			
Commitment: Normative	Pearson correlation	.475**	.641**	.399**	1		
	Sig. (two-tailed)	.000	.000	.000			
	N	117	117	117	117		
Commitment: Continual	Pearson correlation	.460**	.737**	.474**	.694**	1	
	Sig. (two-tailed)	.000	.000	.000	.000		
	N	117	117	117	117	117	
Commitment: Av.	Pearson correlation	.585**	.877**	.304**	.645**	.772**	1
	Sig. (two-tailed)	.000	.000	.001	.000	.000	
	N	117	117	117	117	117	117

**Correlation is significant at the .01 level (two-tailed).
*Correlation is significant at the .05 level (two-tailed).

Table 3. Descriptive Statistical Analysis of All the Variables.

			Descriptive Analysis		
	N	Minimum	Maximum	Mean	S.D.
Awareness Training	117	1.00	5.00	2.5923	.94633
Human Capital Development Training (HCD)	117	2.00	5.00	4.3077	.75955
Cross-cultural Training	117	1.00	4.00	2.4359	.84471
Perception of Training Effectiveness Av.	117	1.67	4.33	3.1120	.54749
Commitment – Affective	117	2.00	5.00	4.1538	.77254
Commitment – Normative	117	2.00	5.00	3.2051	1.07108
Commitment – Continual	117	2.00	5.00	3.6154	1.15106
Commitment Av.	117	1.67	4.67	3.2379	.71663
PEM (Psychological Empowerment – Meaningfulness)	117	1.00	4.00	2.1026	.84471
PEC (Psychological Empowerment – Competence)	117	1.00	4.00	2.2051	.88608
PED (Psychological Empowerment – Self-Determination)	117	1.00	4.00	2.5128	1.01383
PEI (Psychological Empowerment – Impact)	117	1.00	4.00	2.1538	1.00529
Psychological Empowerment Av.	117	1.00	4.00	2.2436	.78473
Satisfaction	117	2.00	5.00	3.5641	.95939
Thriving	117	2.00	5.00	4.3333	.83045
Valid *N* (list wise)	117				

employees feeling of thriving was found to be very high ($M = 4.3$, SD = .83045). Psychological empowerment has components of meaning, competence, self-determination and impact, often in a public sector employees bound in bureaucratic shackles, experience low levels of autonomy and impact.

Hypothesis 5 stated the relationship between the perception of training initiatives given to employees and psychological empowerment felt by the employees. The result findings confirm this hypothesis. The correlation between psychological empowerment and training was found to be significant ($r = .475$, $p < .01$). Though the mean of psychological empowerment ($M = 2.24$, SD = .78, $N = 117$) was average but its correlation with perception of training initiatives was significant. Similarly, psychological empowerment was found to be positively correlated with all the three types of training initiatives under study: awareness training: $r = .334$ ($p < .01$), human capital development training: $r = .409$ ($p < .01$) and cross-cultural training: $r = .489$ ($p < .01$). The results of the analysis thus accepted this hypothesis (Table 4).

Table 4. Results of Correlational Analysis: Correlation Coefficients between Employee Perception of Training Initiatives and Their Level of Psychological Empowerment during M&As (H5) (*N* = 117).

Correlations

		1	2	2	4	5
Awareness training	Pearson correlation	1				
	Sig. (two-tailed)					
	N					
Human capital development training	Pearson correlation	.643**	1			
	Sig. (two-tailed)	.000				
	N	117	117			
Cross-cultural training	Pearson correlation	.650**	.581**	1		
	Sig. (two-tailed)	.000	.038			
	N	117	117	117		
Training Av.	Pearson correlation	.877**	.869**	.851**	1	
	Sig. (two-tailed)	.000	.000	.000		
	N	117	117	117	117	
Psychological empowerment Av.	Pearson correlation	.334**	.409**	.489**	.475**	1
	Sig. (two-tailed)	.000	.000	.000	.000	
	N	117	117	117	117	117

**Correlation is significant at the .01 level (two-tailed).
*Correlation is significant at the .05 level (two-tailed).

Table 5. Results of Correlational Analysis: Correlation Coefficients between Thriving and Employee Level of Psychological Empowerment during M&As (H6) (*N* = 117).

		Correlations					
		1	7	8	9	10	11
Thriving	Pearson correlation	1					
	Sig. (two-tailed)						
	N						
PCM	Pearson correlation	.209*	1				
	Sig. (two-tailed)	.024					
	N	117	117				
PCD	Pearson correlation	.152	.801**	1			
	Sig. (two-tailed)	.101	.000				
	N	117	117	117			
PED	Pearson correlation	.471**	.512**	.371**	1		
	Sig. (two-tailed)	.000	.000	.000			
	N	117	117	117	117		
PEI	Pearson correlation	.155	.682**	.835**	.455**	1	
	Sig. (two-tailed)	.095	.000	.000	.000		
	N	117	117	117	117	117	
Psychological empowerment Av.	Pearson correlation	.301**	.879**	.885**	.711**	.886**	1
	Sig. (two-tailed)	.001	.000	.000	.000	.000	
	N	117	117	117	117	117	117

**Correlation is significant at the .01 level (two-tailed).
*Correlation is significant at the .05 level (two-tailed).

Hypothesis 6. There is a significant positive relationship between employee feeling of thriving and their level of psychological empowerment during M&As.

Hypothesis 6 was accepted as positive correlation between psychological empowerment and thriving (Table 5: $r = .301$, $p < .01$) was obtained. Out of the four dimensions of psychological empowerment, the strongest correlation of thriving was obtained with the dimension of self-determination ($r = .471$, $p < .01$). This can be explained by the fact that the key proponents of the integrated model of growth and learning (Spreitzer & Porath, 2012; Spreitzer et al., 2005) consider self-determination as integral to thriving. The model suggests that each individual has an inherent need to grow and flourish, so creating an environment conducive to the fulfilment of this yearning would enhance their satisfaction and motivation.

Hypothesis 7. There is a significant positive relationship between employee level of psychological empowerment and their satisfaction during M&As.

Hypothesis 8. There is a significant positive relationship between employee level of psychological empowerment and their commitment during M&As.

The analysis of the data revealed a very strong relationship of satisfaction (with merger) with the psychological empowerment ($r = .768$, $p < .01$) along with the four dimensions of psychological empowerment – meaningfulness ($r = .726$, $p < .01$), competence ($r = .604$, $p < .01$), self-determination ($r = .623$, $p < .01$) and impact ($r = .633$, $p < .01$) (Table 6). The highest correlation was with the dimension of meaningfulness ($r = .726$, $p < .01$) which has reflected very well in the relational analysis of the qualitative data.

Employees' psychological empowerment was found to be significantly correlated with the dimensions of commitment as well (Table 6). The correlational analysis revealed high correlation coefficient of psychological empowerment with normative commitment ($r = .602$, $p < .01$), and continual commitment ($r = .641$, $p < .01$), while a low correlation was obtained with affective commitment ($r = .386$, $p < .01$). These results represented that, though the employees may not feel emotionally attached with their new organization, they still continue their services in the newly merged organization as they see the cost of leaving their current organization is high.

Table 6. Results of Correlational Analysis: Correlation Coefficients between Employee Levels of Psychological Empowerment and Their Satisfaction and Commitment during M&As (H7 and H8) ($N = 117$).

		Correlations									
		1	2	3	4	5	6	7	8	9	10
PCM	Pearson correlation	1									
	Sig. (two-tailed)										
	N	117									
PCD	Pearson correlation	.801**	1								
	Sig. (two-tailed)	.000									
	N	117	117								
PED	Pearson correlation	.512**	.371**	1							
	Sig. (two-tailed)	.000	.000								
	N	117	117	117							
PEI	Pearson correlation	.682**	.835**	.455**	1						
	Sig. (two-tailed)	.000	.000	.000							
	N	117	117	117	117						
Psychological empowerment Av.	Pearson correlation	.879**	.885**	.711**	.886**	1					
	Sig. (two-tailed)	.000	.000	.000	.000						
	N	117	117	117	117	117					
Satisfaction with the merger	Pearson correlation	.726**	.623**	.604**	.633**	.768**	1				
	Sig. (two-tailed)	.000	.000	.000	.000	.000					
	N	117	117	117	117	117	117				
Commitment: Affective	Pearson correlation	.372**	.294**	.262**	.369**	.386**	.336**	1			
	Sig. (two-tailed)	.009	.000	.000	.000	.000	.000				
	N	117	117	117	117	117	117	117			
Commitment: Normative	Pearson correlation	.520**	.555**	.402**	.547**	.602**	.641**	.399**	1		
	Sig. (two-tailed)	.000	.000	.000	.000	.000	.000	.000			
	N	117	117	117	117	117	117	117	117		
Commitment: Continual	Pearson correlation	.520**	.509**	.525**	.588**	.641**	.737**	.474**	.694**	1	
	Sig. (two-tailed)	.000	.000	.000	.000	.000	.000	.000	.000		
	N	117	117	117	117	117	117	117	117	117	
Commitment: Av.	Pearson correlation	.603**	.552**	.653**	.591**	.718**	.877**	.304**	.645**	.772**	1
	Sig. (two-tailed)	.000	.000	.001	.000	.000	.000	.000	.000	.000	
	N	117	117	117	117	117	117	117	117	117	117

**Correlation is significant at the .01 level (two-tailed).
*Correlation is significant at the .05 level (two-tailed).

Results of Regression Analysis

Regression analysis showed human capital development training to be the only predictor of employees feeling of thriving. In this study, it was found that the employees were satisfied with the level of training and the level of self-determination was higher than other dimensions. Interestingly though thriving had a significant correlation with psychological empowerment (Table 5: $r = .301$, $p < .01$), yet psychological empowerment could not predict thriving. Only human capital development training emerged as predictor of thriving (Table 7: Step I, Adjusted $R^2 = .607$), creating 78% of variance in thriving as β value obtained was .781. Cross-cultural training had moderate scores but the qualitative data depicted that the employees were very dissatisfied with the effectiveness of cross-cultural training initiatives.

As has been found previously in the results of employees' perception survey, employees have been equivocal in response to many items with respect to their level of satisfaction in their newly merged organization. Here, in this relationship, these were not only the independent variables which were creating variance to the employees' level of satisfaction, but also the variables which were thought and proposed to mediate this relationship. However, this research does not attempt to establish this mediating relationship. Therefore, it was considered important to understand not only the degree but also the nature of relationship between satisfaction and independent variables along with other variables. The specific variable sought to be the explanatory variables are – perception of effectiveness of training initiatives, employees' psychological empowerment, and their feeling of thriving in the merged organization. Multiple regression analysis was conducted to determine which factors contributed to the variance in employees' level of satisfaction during M&As.

Four variables were found to be the significant predictors of employees' satisfaction, these are – meaningfulness, human capital development training, impact, and thriving (Table 8: Step IV, Adjusted $R^2 = .676$, $F = 61.577$, $p < .000$). The beta weights represented that the highest variance was created by the meaningfulness dimension of psychological empowerment. The analysis also finds support from the correlational analysis, which also shown high significant correlation coefficient between dependent variable and explanatory variables.

When run for employees' level of commitment, regression analysis has presented five significant predictors of commitment, these are – perception of effectiveness of training, meaningfulness, self-determination, impact and

Table 7. Results of Stepwise Regression Analysis: Beta Coefficient, Zero-Order and Partial Correlations of Training Methods and Employees' Psychological Empowerment Variables Entered into the Multiple Regressions on Employees' Feeling of Thriving.

Independent Variables	'r' Between Independent and Dependent Variable	R^2	Adjusted R^2	Standardized Coefficients (Beta)	't'	F	Sig.
1 (Constant)					7.434	180.397	.000
Human capital development training	.781[a]	.611	.607	.781	13.434		.000

Notes: [a]predictors: (Constant) Human Capital Development Training.

Table 8. Results of Stepwise Regression Analysis: Beta Coefficient, Zero-Order and Partial Correlations of Training Methods, Employees' Psychological Empowerment, and Thriving Variables Entered into the Multiple Regressions on Employees' Satisfaction.

	Independent Variables	'r' Between Independent and Dependent Variable	R^2	Adjusted R^2	Standardized Coefficients (Beta)	't'	F	Sig.
1	(Constant)					11.097	128.026	.000
	PE-Meaningfulness	.726[a]	.527	.523	.726	11.315		.000
2	(Constant)					2.354	106.033	.020
	PE-Meaningfulness	.726[a]	.650	.644	.628	10.926		.000
	HCD Training	.806[b]			.365	6.348		.000
3	(Constant)					2.247	78.445	.027
	PE-Meaningfulness	.726[a]	.676	.667	.483	6.533		.000
	HCD Training	.806[b]			.350	6.274		.000
	PE-Impact	.822[c]			.218	2.964		.004
4	(Constant)					.755	61.577	.452
	PE-Meaningfulness	.726[a]	.687	.676	.476	6.510		.000
	HCD Training	.806[b]			.213	2.460		.015
	PE-Impact	.822[c]			.230	3.160		.002
	Thriving	.829[d]			.175	2.058		.042

Notes: [a]predictors: (Constant) PE-Meaningfulness; [b]predictors: (Constant) PE-Meaningfulness, HCD Training; [c]predictors: (Constant) PE-Meaningfulness, HCD Training, PE-Impact; [d]predictors: (Constant) PE-Meaningfulness, HCD Training, PE-Impact, Thriving.

competence (Table 9: Step V, Adjusted $R^2 = .797$, $F = 92.254$, $p < .000$). Perception of training effectiveness has created highest variance in employ- ees level of commitment, that is 79% ($\beta = .794$). Interestingly, perception of training initiatives had a stronger relationship with commitment than with satisfaction. An important thing to be noted is that the highest mean amongst the three dimensions of commitment was of continual commit- ment. So though most of the employees were committed more for 'cogni- tive', 'practical' reasons than 'affective' yet in such a bureaucratic scenario, playing on their needs of thriving and psychological empowerment via opportunities of training and growth increases the satisfaction. Thus, we reiterate on the point that learning opportunities can serve as the biggest motivator (and predictor of commitment) during an M&A.

DISCUSSION AND CONCLUSION

The aim of this cross-sectional study was to investigate the relationship between the variables under study. Though, M&As in their scope can have number of variables to be assumed to be playing crucial role in predicting employees' satisfaction and commitment during M&As, but this study focuses on the model presented by Spreitzer & Porath, where the role of training, and its subsequent impact on psychological empowerment and then thriving was studied to predict employees' level of satisfaction and commitment.

Since the employees saw new opportunities of growth in the merger, the initiatives in the form of different types of training have also been appre- ciated by the employees as one of the employees reported: '*the only thing which brings me to the office was the opportunities of training and the expo- sure*'. Thus, these new growth opportunities would contribute the feelings of vitality and learning and thereby enhance thriving and commitment. In a typical downward spiral of negative feelings and entropy during an M&A, HR initiatives like human capital development training can moti- vate people to look forward to the merger as windows of opportunity for growth and employability.

Narratives and qualitative analysis are some of the best ways of under- standing cross-cultural management as it presents cultural vignettes which make assimilation and understanding of the cultural issues easier. History is replete with cases of cultural *faux pas* which have resulted industrial unrest and even strikes and losses. One of the MNC giants operating in India, which was known for its exemplary HR policies, witnessed an ugly

Table 9. Results of Stepwise Regression Analysis: Beta Coefficient, Zero-Order and Partial Correlations of Training Methods, Employees' Psychological Empowerment, and Thriving Variables Entered into the Multiple Regressions on Employees' Commitment.

	Independent Variables	'r' Between Independent and Dependent Variable	R^2	Adjusted R^2	Standardized Coefficients (Beta)	't'	F	Sig.
1	(Constant)					1.796	196.139	.075
	Training	.794[a]	.630	.627	.794	14.005		.000
2	(Constant)					.956	176.046	.341
	Training	.794[a]	.755	.751	.666	13.523		.000
	PE-Meaningfulness	.869[b]			.376	7.634		.000
3	(Constant)					1.330	133.098	.186
	Training	.794[a]	.779	.774	.591	11.433		.000
	PE-Meaningfulness	.869[b]			.300	5.802		.000
	PE-Determination	.883[c]			.198	3.507		.001
4	(Constant)					1.410	109.566	.161
	Training	.794[a]	.796	.789	.575	11.477		.000
	PE-Meaningfulness	.869[b]			.191	3.117		.002
	PE-Determination	.883[c]			.179	3.266		.001
	PE-Impact	.892[d]			.182	3.062		.003
5	(Constant)					1.368	92.254	.174
	Training	.794[a]	.806	.797	.605	11.915		.000
	PE-Meaningfulness	.869[b]			.302	3.946		.000
	PE-Determination	.883[c]			.135	2.366		.020
	PE-Impact	.892[d]			.310	3.878		.000
	PE-Competence	.898[e]			-.232	-2.341		.021

Notes: [a]predictors: (Constant) Training; [b]predictors: (Constant) Training, PE-Meaningfulness [c]predictors: (Constant) Training, PE-Meaningfulness, PE-Determination; [d]predictors: (Constant) Training, PE-Meaningfulness, PE-Determination, PE-Impact; [e]predictors: (Constant) Training, PE-Meaningfulness, PE-Determination, PE-Impact, PE- Competence.

episode of industrial unrest due to the 'offensive' behaviour of an expatriate from Japan. What may be a slight or a joke in one culture may be offensive in the other. In the current study, this can be understood from the issues arose in the organizations understudy.

As has been discussed, the smaller of the merged organizations was primarily made up of young engineers from the IT sector with international exposure, while the larger organization was a typical monolithic bureaucratic government sector organization progressing reasonably well in performance terms. The employees of the smaller (younger) IT organization felt that it was like going 'back to school' as they were issued a list of 'do's and don'ts' − for example having coffee in the winter sun in the parking lot with friends was 'disallowed'! The members of the larger organization felt that the other organization members were 'immature' and needed to be 'trained' into the 'senior management's values and credo'. When asked if this was dissatisfying, the younger IT organization employees reported that thought it was irritating but they reported that did not really pay too much attention to it because the learning exposure was good but the cultural issues were nevertheless irritating. The young IT engineers considered it objectionable to have separate canteens introduced for the senior and junior employees. One of the young engineers remarked: '*It is a reflection of their mindsets*'. The employees felt that if the HR department was aiming at a synergy they needed to ensure justice before anything else. One of the employees from the smaller of the two organizations remarked that they did not like the fact that their general manager had to make an appointment with the other group's general manager to meet him. The respondents animatedly enacted how she had to greet him 'first' which smelt of subservience. 'Why should she be the first one to greet − always?' − asked an engineer. The quantitative analysis of the data also showed that 76% of engineers felt that there were grave cultural issues which needed to be addressed, while 66.4% remarked that the senior management was not ready to change.

When asked about the various training initiatives, 92% rated the human capital development training as the best but the other two as not very effective, while 62% felt that trainers also need to train the senior management on cultural issues. A remarkable 97% of the young engineers (from the smaller of the two merged entities) felt that the HR department did not have a significant contribution. One of the employees remarked that: '*HR department does not have the guts to point out the mistakes of the senior management. They cannot dare to make the senior management attend cultural training classes and rate them correctly'. 'Why should we be giving cultural training while they are the ones who need it the most and are even not being asked to attend it?'* asked one of the engineers. Human capital development training initiatives were not credited to the HR department but to the 'need of the hour', as one of the employee stated: *'They need to develop us to maximize efficiency – and they don't care more because they know that we will not leave the government job'* said one of the employees.

The results revealed a significant positive relationship between employees' perception of training initiatives and their psychological empowerment. The results find support in works of Spreitzer et al. (2005), and Spreitzer and Porath (2012), who suggested that sharing of information (example via training) increases their abilities to quickly uncover problems as they arise, and to integrate and coordinate actions. This would also fuel learning new behaviours and make a person feel empowered and proactive. Wood and Bandura (1989) found the reverse that when people doubted their capabilities they would slacken their task focus and specially in challenging situations. Providing training during a challenging period as a major change in the organization (as in an M&A) would spike the confidence levels of employees and make them feel more enthusiastic about the change. Both the quantitative as well as the qualitative literature supported this proposition. As pointed earlier in the discussion human capital development training emerged as a predictor of thriving explaining 78.1% of the variance in thriving, thus, employees who reported being 'happy' with the training initiatives were also the ones who felt sure and confident about the future and themselves. This is also where, Hypothesis 5, which states that there will be a significant relationship between perception of training initiatives and level of psychological empowerment of employees, identifies an explanation. Employees feel invigorated and see a significant 'value proposition' in the opportunities which the trainings bring along. Research has pointed out that role ambiguity, role isolation and role inadequacy contribute to lowering of satisfaction and psychological empowerment during M&A. Marks and Mirvis (1998) hail transformation as the ideal state of integration where both the organizations synergize and move forward towards growing into a new organization.

The participants in this study included mostly the highly educated engineers from top-ranked engineering institutions. This study provides lessons for all organizations when merging with smaller IT or technically orientated and styled companies. As one of the Engineers stated: *'We run their show; they better treat us as equals, if not better than them'*. This was in line with the view of Carmel and Eisenberg (2006) who, while discussing national identities pointed out that Indian software engineers see themselves as contributing to the economic boom – not only do they see themselves as simply 'writing code' but also engaged in the more major mission of serving the nation in a significant way. Thus, companies cannot disregard their contribution, especially public sector organizations, which are steeped in high power-distance and centralized decision-making. Research has shown that often the best talent gets poached by competitors during M&As. Reasons of apprehended equity make them get into post-acquisition stress (Marks & Mirvis, 1998) and organizations need to anticipate this and attend to it before they are attracted to competitor's.

Furthermore, the theoretical model advanced by Spreitzer et al. (2005) suggests that when people thrive, they mindfully interrelate with others and may also engage in OCBs. This study also suggests that organization should attempt at creating feelings of thriving, such that resistance to change is lowered and even if people are dissatisfied with certain aspects of the merger, their commitment levels towards the organizations are high. The results supported the contention of Weber and Tarba (2010) who stated that the training for a specific situation such as mergers is perceived by managers and employees as a good development and career opportunity that helps them both on the job and in future hiring and retention. Inputs from qualitative interviews also corroborated this fact as reflected in their comments as: *'the good part about this merger is that we got to learn new skills and competencies'*, *'I was not very happy in the beginning but now I feel good about it as we have been given training on many new technologies'*.

Though quantitative and qualitative analyses both indicate significant relationships between training and satisfaction and commitment but at the same time qualitative data present the resentments of the employees regarding the cross-cultural conflict. Thus, the results of this study demonstrate that though quantitative data may point towards a particular direction, the qualitative data can help unearth undercurrents.

IMPLICATIONS OF THE STUDY

This study has important implications for organizations intending to or undergoing through the process of mergers or acquisitions. M&As are very common in the contemporary business scenario, especially in the era of globalization. Thus, this study broadens the scope of HR as a provider of learning to the employees through employing different training initiatives. This research also has implications for researchers who still have not thought of studying psychological empowerment and feeling of thriving into the context of M&As. Moreover, this study provides significant evidence which may let the Indian researchers to focus on the HR aspects of M&As also.

LIMITATIONS OF THE STUDY

The variables measuring employee perceptions and their feelings and attitudes possesses implicit difficulties. The current study employs self-reporting questionnaires which may be affected by a factor of social desirability. The social desirability factor needs to be taken into account when interpreting the results of these self-reports as what people report about what they have done, cannot be relied upon as a categorical accurate account of what they actually did or what they would have done. Moreover, the self-reported data often are affected by common method bias. Another limitation of the study was the scarcity of the literature available of thriving and psychological empowerment from the change context. Furthermore, the possible limitation is the ambiguity in the literature over the appropriate time period of collecting data of perceptions and attitudes in situations like M&As. Schweiger and Denisi (1991) also stated that 'no clear consensus exists regarding the appropriate time to assess employee attitudes following a merger'. However, it is safe to state that the merger survivors' attitudes and perceptions of organizational training initiatives and attitudes of commitment, satisfaction and their feelings of thriving and empowerment evolve, develop and change over time. The data in this case were collected approximately two years following every M&A transaction. This provided adequate time for merger survivors to develop or not to develop their perceptions and attitudes in the organization. And, the final limitation is that the current study could not present the interplay between the variables in the form of a structural and measurement model, and thus this study sets the directions for the future research.

REFERENCES

Appelbaum, S. H., Gandell, J., Yortis, H., Proper, S., & Jobin, F. (2000). Anatomy of a merger: Behavior of organizational factors and processes throughout the pre- during- post-stages (part 1). *Management Decision, 38*(9), 649–662.

Astrachan, J. H. (1990). *Mergers, acquisitions, and employee anxiety: A study of separation anxiety in a corporate context.* New York, NY: Praeger.

Bansal, A. (2015). Understanding the integration mechanisms practiced during organizational change: Evidence from five M&A transactions. *Journal of Organizational Change Management, 28*(6), 929–947.

Bansal, A. (2016). Employee trust dynamics during organizational change: A context of mergers and acquisitions. *Asia-Pacific Journal of Business Administration, 8*, 55–69.

Bansal, A., & Thakur, M. (2013). The impact of perception of organizational transfer climate factors and trainees' characteristics on training transfer: The context of mergers and acquisitions. *Journal of International Business and Economics, 1*(1), 51.

Bansal, A., & Thakur, M. S. (2012, October 4–5). Shifting the spotlight on the H-factor (Human Factor) during M&A: A study of correlates and predictors of successful mergers. Paper presented at the 5th Euromed international conference, Montreux, Switzerland.

Barmeyer, C., & Mayrhofer, U. (2008). The contribution of intercultural management to the success of international mergers and acquisitions: An analysis of the EADS group. *International Business Review, 17*, 28–38.

Blake, R. R., & Mouton, J. S. (1986). How to achieve integration on the human side of the merger. *Organizational Dynamics, 13*(3), 41–56.

Blauner, R. (1964). *Alienation and freedom: The factory worker and his industry.* Chicago, IL: UCP.

Carmel, E., & Eisenberg, J. (2006). Narratives that software nations tell themselves: An exploration and taxonomy. *Communications of the Association for Information Systems, 17*(1), 39.

Cartwright, S., & Cooper, C. L. (1992). *Mergers and acquisitions: The human factor* (pp. 4–6). Oxford: Butterworth-Heinemann.

Cartwright, S., & Cooper, C. L. (1993). The psychological impact of merger and acquisition on the individual: A study of building society managers. *Human Relations, 46*(3), 327–347.

Chaudhuri, S., & Tabrizi, B. (1998). Capturing the real value in high-tech acquisitions. *Harvard Business Review, 77*(5), 123–130.

Conger, J. A., & Kanungo, R. N. (1988a). The empowerment process: Integrating theory and practice. *Academy of Management Review, 13*(3), 471–482.

Dass, T. K. (2008). *Human resource processes and the role of the human resources function during mergers and acquisitions in the electricity industry.* Doctoral dissertation, University of Cincinnati.

Davy, J. A., Kinicki, A., Scheck, C., & Kilroy, J. (1989). Acquisitions make employees worry: Companies ease the pain through effective communication. *Personnel Administrator, 34*, 84–90.

Dean, F. E. (2007). *A study of entropy in post-merger and post-acquisition integration.* A dissertation presented in University of Phoenix.

Devine, M. (2002). *Successful mergers: Getting the people issues right.* London: The Economist.

Ellis, K. M., & Lamont, B. T. (2004). "Ideal" acquisition integration approaches in related acquisitions of equals: A test of long-held beliefs. *Advances in Mergers and Acquisitions, 3,* 81–102.

Fish, D. E. (2007). *A study of entropy in post-merger and post-acquisition integration.* University of Phoenix, Arizona.

Gagne, M., & Deci, E. L. (2005). Self-Determination Theory and work motivation. *Journal of Organizational Behavior, 26,* 331–362.

Gallos, J. V. (2006). The OD core: Understanding and managing planned change, part 2. In J. V. Gallos (Ed.), Organizational development: A Jossey-Bass reader (pp. 129–131). San Francisco, CA: Jossey-Bass.

Ghauri, P. N., & Buckley, P. J. (2003). International mergers and acquisitions: Past, present and future. *Advances in Mergers and Acquisitions, 2*(1), 207–229.

Ghoshal, S. (1987). Global strategy: An organizing framework. *Strategic Management Journal, 8*(5), 425–440.

Hackman, J. R., & Oldman, G. R. (1980). *Work redesign.* Reading, MA: Addison-Wesley.

Haspeslagh, P. C., & Jemison, D. B. (1991). *Managing acquisitions: Creating value through corporate renewal.* New York, NY: Free Press.

Hassett, M. (2012). Organisational commitment in acquisitions. *Advances in Mergers and Acquisitions, 10,* 19.

Henwood, K., & Pidgeon, N. (1994). Beyond the qualitative paradigm: A framework for introducing diversity within qualitative psychology. *Journal of Community & Applied Social Psychology, 4*(4), 225–238.

Henwood, K. L., & Nicholson, P. (1995). *Qualitative approaches in psychology.* Reading, MA: Addison-Wesley.

Huy, Q. N. (2002). Emotional balancing of organizational continuity and radical change: The contribution of middle managers. *Administrative Science Quarterly, 47*(1), 31–69.

Kubler-Rosse, E. (1969). *On death and dying.* New York, NY: Macmillan.

Landis, D. E., & Bhagat, R. S. (1996). *Handbook of intercultural training.* New York, NY: Macmillan.

Lawler, E. (1994). Total quality management and employee involvement: Are they compatible? *Academy of Management Executive, 8*(1), 68–76.

Levinson, H. (1970). A psychologist diagnoses merger failures. *Harvard Business Review, 48*(2), 139.

Lucia, A. D., & Lepsinger, R. (1999). *Art & science of competency models.* San Francisco, CA: Jossey-Bass.

Mainiero, L. A. (1986). Coping with powerlessness: The relationship of gender and job dependency to empowerment-strategy usage. *Administrative Science Quarterly,* 633–653.

Marks, M. L. (1997). Let's make a deal, *HR Magazine,* 42.

Marks, M. L., & Mirvis, P. H. (1986). The merger syndrome: When companies combine, a clash of cultures can turn potentially good business alliances into financial disasters. *Psychology Today, 20*(10), 36.

Marks, M. L., & Mirvis, P. H. (1998). *Joining forces: Making one plus one equal three in mergers, acquisitions, and alliances.* San Francisco, CA: Jossey-Bass.

Marks, M. L., & Mirvis, P. H. (2001). Making mergers and acquisitions work: Strategic and psychological preparation. *Academy of Management Executive, 15*(2), 80–92.

McGregor, D. (1960). Theory X and theory Y. *Organization Theory*, 358–374.

Meyer, J. P., & Allen, N. J. (2004). *TCM employee commitment survey academic users guide 2004*. London: The University of Western Ontario, Department of Psychology.

Mirc, N. (2014). Human impacts on the performance of mergers and acquisitions. In S. Finkelstein & C. Cooper (Eds.). *Advances in mergers and acquisitions* (Advances in Mergers and Acquisitions, Vol. 12, pp. 1–31). Bingley, UK: Emerald Group Publishing Limited.

Mitleton-Kelly, E. (2005). Co-evolutionary integration – The co-creation of a new organisatational form following a merger or acquisition. *Barth, T., Casti, JL, Mitleton-Kelly, E., Sanders, IT*, pp. 39–66.

Morosini, P., Shane, S., & Singh, H. (1998). National cultural distance and cross-border acquisition performance. *Journal of International Business Studies*, 29, 137–158.

Onwuegbuzie, J., Johnson, A., & Collins, K. (2009). Call for mixed analysis: A philosophical framework for combining qualitative and quantitative. *International Journal of Multiple Research Approaches*, 7(3), 114–139.

Pedrick, D., Babakus, E., & Richardson, A. (1993). The value of qualitative data in quality improvement efforts. *The Journal of Services Marketing*, 7(3), 26.

Porath, C., Spreitzer, G., Gibson, C., & Garnett, F. G. (2012). Thriving at work: Toward its measurement, construct validation, and theoretical refinement. *Journal of Organizational Behavior*, 33(2), 250–275.

Pritchett, P., Robinson, D., & Clarkson, R. (1997). *After the merger: The authoritative guide for integration success*. New York, NY: McGraw-Hill.

Quinn, R., & Spreitzer, G. (1997). The road to empowerment: Seven questions every leader should consider. *Organizational Dynamics*, 26(2), 37–49.

Rees, C., & Edwards, T. (2009). Management strategy and HR in international mergers: Choice, constraint and pragmatism. *Human Resource Management Journal*, 19(1), 24–39.

Roberts, L. M., Spreitzer, G., Dutton, J., Quinn, R., Heaphy, E., & Barker, B. (2005). How to play to your strengths. *Harvard Business Review*, 83(1), 75–80.

Rottig, D., Reus, T. H., & Tarba, S. Y. (2014). The impact of culture on mergers and acquisitions: A third of a century of research. In S. Finkelstein & C. Cooper (Eds.), *Advances in mergers and acquisitions* (Advances in Mergers and Acquisitions, Vol. 12, pp. 135–172). Bingley, UK: Emerald Group Publishing Limited.

Sarala, R. M. (2010). The impact of cultural differences and acculturation factors on post-acquisition conflict. *Scandinavian Journal of Management*, 26(1), 38–56.

Schweiger, D. M., & Denisi, A. S. (1991). Communication with employees following a merger: A longitudinal field experiment. *Academy of Management Journal*, 34(1), 110–135.

Searle, R. H., & Ball, K. S. (2004). The development of trust and distrust in a merger. *Journal of Managerial Psychology*, 19(7), 708–721.

Seeman, M. (1959). On the meaning of alienation. *American Sociological Review*, 24, 783–791.

Shook, L., & Roth, G. (2011). Downsizings, mergers, and acquisitions: Perspectives of human resource development practitioners. *Journal of European Industrial Training*, 35(2), 135–153.

Slowinski, G., Rafii, Z. E., Tao, J. C., Gollob, L., Sagal, M. W., & Krishnamurthy, K. (2002). After the acquisition: Managing paranoid people in schizophrenic organizations. *Research-Technology Management*, 45(3), 21–32.

Spreitzer, G., Sutcliffe, K., Dutton, J., Sonenshein, S., & Grant, A. M. (2005). A socially embedded model of thriving at work. *Organization Science, 16*(5), 537–549.

Spreitzer, G. M. (1995). Psychological empowerment in the workplace: Dimensions, measurement, and validation. *Academy of Management Journal, 38*(5), 1442–1465.

Spreitzer, M., & Porath, C. (2012). Self-determination as nutriment for thriving: Building an integrative model of human growth at work. In M. Gagne (Ed.), *Oxford handbook of work engagement, motivation, and self-determination theory*. New York, NY: Oxford University Press.

Thakur, M., & Bansal, A. (2015). A framework of HR enablers for successful M&A integrat. In A. Risberg, D. R. King, & O. Meglio (Eds.), *The Routledge companion to mergers and acquisitions* (pp. 40–56). London: Routledge Publications, Taylor & Francis Group.

Thakur, M. S., & Juneja, R. (2008). Understanding the dynamics between role stress, commitment and satisfaction. A comparative empirical investigation of employees of an acquired and of an acquiring organization in India. *International Journal of Knowledge, Culture and Change Management, 7*(10).

Thomas, K. W., & Velthouse, B. A. (1990). Cognitive elements of empowerment: An "interpretive" model of intrinsic task motivation. *Academy of Management Review, 15*(4), 666–681.

Trautwein, F. (1990). Merger motives and merger prescriptions. *Strategic Management Journal, 11*(4), 283–295.

Waldman, D. A., & Javidan, M. (2009). Alternative forms of charismatic leadership in the integration of mergers and acquisitions. *The Leadership Quarterly, 20*(2), 130–142.

Walsh, J. P. (1989). Doing a deal: Merger and acquisition negotiations and their impact upon target company top management turnover. *Strategic Management Journal, 10*(4), 307–322.

Walter, G. A., & Barney, J. B. (1990). Research notes and communications management objectives in mergers and acquisitions. *Strategic Management Journal, 11*(1), 79–86.

Watson Wyatt Worldwide Inc. (1999). *Human capital index: Human capital as a lead indicator of shareholder value*. Arlington, Virginia.

Weber, Y., Rachman-Moore, D., & Tarba, S. Y. (2012). HR practices during post-merger conflict and merger performance. *International Journal of Cross Cultural Management, 12*(1), 73–99.

Weber, Y., & Tarba, S. Y. (2010). Human resource practices and performance of mergers and acquisitions in Israel. *Human Resource Management Review, 20*(3), 203–211.

Wood, R., & Bandura, A. (1989). Social cognitive theory of organizational management. *Academy of Management Review, 14*(3), 361–384.

ON THE ROLE OF THE POLITICAL REGIME IN THE CHOICE BETWEEN INTERNATIONAL ACQUISITIONS AND JOINT VENTURES WHEN ENTERING AN EMERGING MARKET: EVIDENCE FROM RUSSIA

Olivier Bertrand, Marie-Ann Betschinger,
Nina Bertschy and Roman Shidlauskas

ABSTRACT

We focus on the determinants of the choice between international joint ventures and acquisitions when entering emerging countries. We empirically explore if subregional variation in the political regime matters for the entry mode decision of foreign investors. Based on an analysis of 151 foreign entries into Russia for the period 2002–2008, our results indicate that the entry mode choice is linked to regional variation in

Advances in Mergers and Acquisitions, Volume 15, 37–52
ISSN: 1479-361X/doi:10.1108/S1479-361X20160000015003

the level of democracy. Foreign entries in more democratic regions are
more likely to take the form of joint ventures, and vice versa.

Keywords: Foreign entry mode; international acquisition;
international joint venture; political regimes; emerging
country; Russia

During the past decade, emerging markets have become one of the most
attractive locations for firm expansion. However, institutional voids have
led to the emergence of business patterns which are different from those in
developed countries (e.g., Khanna & Palepu, 1997, 2000). Market exchange
predominantly takes place in networks and is not based on arm's length
rule-based transactions (e.g., Peng, 2003). Therefore, foreigners often need
local partners to successfully run their business in these host markets. As
resources and capabilities lie within local firms, foreign entrants mainly
have two options: They can either start a joint venture (JV) with a local
firm or acquire control of an existing company (Hennart, 2009). A majority
international acquisition uses assets of a local firm and combines them with
the foreign investor's resources. It provides control of the operations. An
international JV provides an alternative route for accessing selected
resources of a local partner without the responsibilities arising from taking
over an existing organization. It minimizes risks, but gives only shared
control over the resources and profits (e.g., Anand & Delios, 2002; Meyer,
Estrin, Bhaumik, & Peng, 2009).

Within emerging countries, subnational regions can be quite heterogeneous, leading to various subnational markets that foreign investors need
to consider in their entry mode choice. For instance, Chan, Makino, and
Isobe (2010) find that subnational regional differences are significant in
explaining foreign affiliate performance. Also, they observe the relevance of
subnational regions to be stronger in emerging countries (specifically,
China) than in developed countries (specifically, United States). Regional
heterogeneity in emerging countries stems not only from economic differences between regions, but also from variation in their political systems
(Snyder, 2001).

Especially, subnational variation in the level of democracy is frequent
(Gibson, 2005; Libman, 2012). While, at the country level, politics in

general and the level of democracy in particular have been shown to influence foreign investors in their international business activities (Jensen, 2003; Li & Resnick, 2003), the impact of regional variation in democracy within a country on the foreign entry mode choice has, to our knowledge, not been analyzed. In general, there is very little research on the impact of regional variation in democracy on economic outcomes. One exception is Libman (2012) that analyses the role of democracy for regional economic growth in Russia and identifies a nonlinear relationship between the two.

In this chapter, we also focus on Russia. In Russia, media anecdotes suggest that local political structures are important for international business decisions: "Development in the Russian regions always starts with meeting local authorities, because companies are dependent at every stage on regional governments, said Krysht of Tkachik, director of regional expansion of Leroy Merlin Russia" (Bazenkova, 2015). Based on an econometric analysis of 151 foreign entries into Russia for the period 2002–2008, we investigate if regional variation within Russia of the level of democracy affects the entry mode strategy of foreign investors. We confirm that the regional political system matters. When a region is more democratic, JVs become more likely, and vice versa.

This study therefore adds to several literatures. Most directly, we contribute to the literature on international mergers and acquisitions (M&As) and foreign entries into emerging economies (Lebedev, Peng, Xie, & Stevens, 2014). We consider international M&As as a possible (investment) entry mode into an emerging market and contrast it with the alternative JV. While the relevance of the institutional environment for the choice between international JVs and acquisitions has been investigated (Meyer et al., 2009), we still know very little on the importance of the political system for this choice. Environments with stronger market institutions have been argued to increase the likelihood of an acquisition (as opposed to a JV) as a foreign entry mode. This chapter focuses on the level of democracy at the regional level in an emerging economy featuring a generally weak institutional environment for foreign investments.

Moreover, we analyze the implications of within-country variation in political institutions by examining the specific role of democracy at the regional level. The relevance of within-country dispersion is an underinvestigated field of study in strategy and international business (McCann & Mudambi, 2005). For market mode research, to our knowledge only Meyer and Nguyen (2005) highlight the role of the variation in subnational institutions for the choice between a JV or wholly owned greenfield investment, focusing on access to scarce resources for foreign investors.

In the following, we present a short overview of the existing literature, present our empirical setup, and then discuss our results before we conclude.

LITERATURE REVIEW AND THEORY DEVELOPMENT

Acquisition Versus JV

The mode of entry into a foreign market is one of the most important decisions a firm has to make during its internationalization process. Not surprisingly it has been a key area in international business research (Brouthers & Hennart, 2007; Zhao, Luo, & Suh, 2004). Brouthers and Hennart (2007) and Datta, Herrmann, and Rasheed (2002) provide comprehensive reviews of the literature. In this research, we follow, for instance, Kogut and Singh (1988), Singh and Kogut (1989), Hennart and Reddy (1997), and Datta, Musteen, and Herrmann (2009) in analyzing the choice between a JV and acquisition entry, "represent[ing] two of the most widely used investment-based modes of entry" (Datta et al., 2009, p. 930).

Both entry modes involve a local partner that helps a foreigner overcome the liability of foreignness and mitigate risks through the availability of local knowledge, networks, and other local resources. But they differ in a number of aspects that may have implications regarding their exposure to the local political system. First, ownership and control are different for the two modes. More control, as provided by the acquisition mode, permits the parent firm to implement global strategies, facilitating the integration and the coordination of business activities across countries (Peng, 2003). But majority ownership is a difficult burden when the local firm cannot be monitored well or the foreign owner cannot retain excellent local managers, for instance, those connected to the local political system. Local managers might follow their private interests at the detriment of the foreign owner.

Second, acquisitions are riskier than JVs in the presence of institutional differences between the home and host country (Folta, 1998; Meyer et al., 2009). In such environments, the risk of overpaying for the target is larger (e.g., Hennart & Reddy, 1997) since it is more difficult for the foreign firm to carry out due diligence and capture the true value of the target. Moreover, in an emerging economy, business practices are often less transparent than in a developed economy. JVs then provide a means to reduce these risks. They include option value since they give the opportunity to gain new information on the market and local partner before deciding to invest more (Brouthers, Brouthers, & Werner, 2008).

Third, Datta et al. (2009) highlight the fact that there are different time-horizons prevailing when deciding on one or the other mode of entry. JVs are more short-term investments than acquisitions since the latter require rather long-term commitments. Furthermore, JVs are often entered with a finite goal in mind. In the Russian context, this characteristic is of high relevance because the Russian local firm could expect benefits from the JV in a much shorter period than Western partners do, being more short-term oriented (Carr, 2006). This conflict of interests is reduced in the case of an acquisition.

Lastly, there might be more political barriers to majority acquisitions than to JVs, in particular in regulated industries.

Political Regimes and Entry Modes

The political regime, either at the national or subnational regional level, is likely to shape the business environment firms face. In this chapter, we focus on the degree of democracy at the regional level and link it to the foreign entry mode.

The influence of the degree of democracy on business decisions is unclear. Autocratic regimes are usually considered as offering less stability and safety to investors than democracies because autocrats face lower insti-tutional constraints. Autocrats cannot commit to property rights protection (Jensen, 2003; Olson, 1993). Once the investment is sunk, there is always a high risk that autocrats can reverse their previous position because there is a lower number of checks and balances or veto players that could impede them from action and because audience costs are lower than in a democ-racy: if democratically elected rulers do not hold what they promise, elec-toral costs can be large (Jensen, 2003). However, the leeway autocrats have, may also provide firms with political opportunities that could not exist in a political context where political decisions are constrained (Garcia-Canal & Guilen, 2008; O'Donnell, 1978).

These contrasting effects translate into an ambiguous role of the political regime for the foreign entry mode choice. On the one hand, the higher level of uncertainty that is inherent to autocracies could increase the risk of doing acquisitions in contexts where acquisition-making itself is already a risky process. In less developed markets, due diligence of firms is difficult as such markets are characterized by a high level of informational asymmetry

(Meyer et al., 2009). Since JVs could form a way to learn more about the true value of the partner's business in its region, JVs could mitigate the uncertainty created by an autocratic and instable regime. There would be the option to later on acquire the firm.

On the other hand, there could be a higher probability of observing acquisitions in more autocratically governed regions because of the political opportunities provided by an autocratic regime. Foreign investors are able to negotiate directly with policy decision-makers and to obtain preferential treatment when political decisions are discretionary (i.e., not constrained) (Garcia-Canal & Guilen, 2008; Li & Resnick, 2003). In our context, acquirers could acquire a local target firm in a more favorable regulatory context. For instance, deal restructuring, which often includes layoffs or reduction in wages, could be rendered easier in an autocracy than in a democracy. Better deals could be struck with autocrats because there is lower pressure from local stakeholders (Jensen, 2003). With a lower involvement of the local constituency (such as labor unions) in the political or economic governance in a region, regional politicians are more likely to protect foreign firms from local pressures (Li & Resnick, 2003). In the opposite, democratic leaders face more constraints and cannot influence to the same degree the business environment firms have to cope with. This line of argumentation could suggest that foreign firms would be more likely to acquire in more autocratic regimes due to the political opportunities given by autocrats. However, in an autocratic regime, a JV could be a way to access and involve the local political and economic networks (cronies) of the local autocrat. Acquisitions are known to lead to a higher than normal turnover of top managers (Krug & Hegarty, 1997; Walsh, 1988, 1989), in particular, if the acquirer is a foreigner (Krug & Hegarty, 1997) or the incumbent managers, consider the cultural differences between the acquirer and target to be significant (Lubatkin, Schweiger, & Weber, 1999). This turnover implies that the embeddedness of the local firm in personalized exchanges and networks easily disappears. Hence, the lower ability to build close relationships with cronies of the local autocrat could cancel out the advantages provided by the preferential treatment of the autocrat and shielding from local pressures in a control acquisition. When the interests of the foreign firm and a crony collide with each other, it is likely that the autocrat will support the local firm.

As we see, depending on the relative size of these various effects, foreign investors may opt for international acquisitions or JVs. The extent to which the level of democracy influences the entry mode choice at the regional level can only be resolved empirically.

EMPIRICAL SETUP

Sample

We obtain the information on international JVs and acquisitions from the Zephyr database which is provided by the Bureau Van Dijk. We include all those deals that were announced or completed between 2002 and 2008. International JVs are deals where a foreign and local company start a new venture, each party usually owning about 50% in the new firm. We restrict our analysis to majority international acquisitions, hence those acquisitions where more than 50% were acquired.[1] Also, financial investment or company's reorganization deals were excluded.[2] Moreover, we eliminated deals where the acquirer was located in an offshore financial center (e.g., Cyprus, Bahamas, or Virgin Islands).

We then merge the information with Russian firm level data on target firms or JV partners using the Ruslana database (Bureau Van Dijk). After deleting records with missing data on firm characteristics, we end up with a final sample of 151 entries into Russia for the period 2002−2008. Out of 151 deals, 63 (88) entries took the form of international JVs (international acquisitions). These entries are spread out across the country: The deals took place in 37 (out of the over 80) Russian federal regions.

Estimation Methodology and Model

Following the existing literature (e.g., Datta et al., 2009; Hennart & Reddy, 1997), the dependent variable is a binary variable which takes on the value 1 for an acquisition and 0 for a JV. We, accordingly, employ a binary logistic regression analysis. We adjust the standard errors for heteroscedasticity.

Independent Variables

For measuring the role of the subregional political regime for the entry mode choice, we use the regional level of democracy as provided by the Carnegie Center Moscow (Libman, 2012). The level of democracy in a region is assigned by experts, who rate the Russian regions along 10 dimensions, such as freedom of elections, media independence, political pluralism, openness, or the role of civil society. Each dimension can obtain a maximum of five points which corresponds to the highest democratic value.

We transformed the total score (maximum of 50) into a measure ranging between 0 and 1, with 0 relating to a full autocracy and 1 to a full democracy. Due to data restrictions, this is a time-invariant measure which is based on the average for the years 2000–2004 and which we apply over the whole estimation period. In our sample of 37 regions, the level of democracy ranges between 0.46 and 0.9; the average value is 0.69, with a standard deviation of 0.12.

Control Variables

Given our small data sample, we have to take a parsimonious base specification of control variables. We test the sensitivity of the results by adding other explanatory variables in robustness checks.

At the target firm level (i.e., at the level of either the acquired firm or the JV partner), we include measures for asset digestibility and profitability. Hennart and Reddy (1997) highlight the digestibility of assets of the local firm as a major determinant of the entry choice. An international JV is more likely if the assets of the local firm are less digestible. We proxy asset digestibility with the number of employees of the local firm (natural logarithm transformed). Local firm profitability is measured using the return on assets. All firm level variables are calculated for the year prior to the year when the deal was completed.

At the industry level, we account for the technology intensity of the target industry. Local firms in more technology intensive industries are more difficult to value, thereby discouraging acquisitions (Kogut & Singh, 1988; Singh & Kogut, 1989). Due to missing information at the firm level on, for instance, research and development intensity, we include an industry indicator variable that takes on the value 1 if an industry is classified as High Tech from the US Bureau of Labor Statistics; otherwise, it is 0. Due to the relevance of the natural resource industry in Russia and the fact that this industry faces restrictions in terms of the ability of foreigners to carry out acquisitions, we also add a dummy variable to identify whether an industry is resource based or not. We add (but do not report) further industry dummies in all specifications (based on the two-digit NAICS 2007 classification). They are supposed to account for industry unobservable specificities, such as industry-specific restrictions to establish JVs or acquisitions.

RESULTS AND DISCUSSION

Table 1 provides the descriptive statistics and correlation matrix. There is no indication of multicollinearity. Table 2 presents the outcome of our empirical regressions. In Model 1, we only include our control variables. They follow the predictions, providing reliability to our overall model and data. With respect to features of the local (Russian) firm, firm size strongly matters: With increasing size local firms become less easily digestible and encourage foreign entries through JVs. More profitable firms are more likely to become acquisition targets. They could have a better organization, making it easier to integrate them, or have competitive advantages that foreigners would like to internalize. High Tech Industry and Natural Resource Industry entries are more likely to experience JVs.

In Model 2 in Table 2, we add our main variable of interest, the regional level of democracy (variable Regional Democracy). The level of democracy has a negative and statistically significant impact across all specifications. Foreigners tend to enter with JVs in regions which are more democratic. International acquisitions are more likely in more autocratically run regions. Hence, it seems that in more autocratically run regions, regional governments can provide foreigners with better acquisition deals. While, in general, international JVs are considered a safer option to enter an insecure overseas market (Meyer et al., 2009), JV partners can also pose a contractual risk to a foreigner. Strong owners are more likely to wish to extract private rents from the joint company and may try to leverage direct contacts to an (autocratic) regional governor, not to improve the performance of the JV to the benefit of both the foreign and local owner, but to get rid of the foreign partner ex-post.

In robustness checks, we add further variables to account for possible omitted variable bias and check the sensitivity of these main results. First, in Model 3 in Table 2, we add a measure of deal relatedness (Balakrishnan & Koza, 1991, 1993). If the industries of the foreigner and the local target are aligned, information asymmetries should be lower and could lead to a higher likelihood of acquisitions (Balakrishnan & Koza, 1991; Reuer & Koza, 2000). If the foreign and local firms are in the same four-digit industry (based on the NAICS 2007 industry classification), the variable Relatedness is assigned a value of 1 (and 0 otherwise). We find that the variable Relatedness exerts a significant and positive impact: Acquisitions are more likely if the foreign and local firms are active in the same industry.

Table 1. Descriptive Statistics.

	Mean	S.D.	(1)	(2)	(3)	(4)	(5)	(6)	(7)	(8)	(9)	(10)	(11)	(12)	(13)
(1) Number of employees (Log)	5.69	2.19	1												
(2) Return on assets	0.10	0.30	0.05	1											
(3) State controlled	0.07	0.25	0.13	0.19	1										
(4) Firm age (Log)	2.34	1.08	0.41	0.09	-0.01	1									
(5) Relatedness	0.39	0.49	0.00	-0.06	-0.03	0.10	1								
(6) High Tech Industry	0.27	0.45	0.04	0.06	0.04	-0.17	-0.15	1							
(7) Natural resource industry	0.30	0.46	0.07	0.09	0.22	0.14	0.19	-0.25	1						
(8) Regional democracy	0.69	0.12	0.14	0.14	-0.16	0.21	0.05	0.04	-0.04	1					
(9) Regional GDP per capita	7.95	0.65	-0.17	0.15	0.20	-0.12	-0.11	0.08	0.05	-0.10	1				
(10) Regional trade intensity	0.53	0.26	-0.12	-0.04	-0.08	-0.05	-0.13	0.03	-0.10	0.07	0.37	1			
(11) Moscow dummy	0.27	0.45	-0.17	-0.04	0.10	-0.16	-0.01	0.01	-0.02	-0.26	0.60	0.14	1		
(12) Foreign partner: Developed country	0.87	0.34	0.07	0.13	0.01	-0.01	-0.01	0.13	-0.10	0.13	0.03	-0.02	-0.07	1	
(13) Cultural distance	3.29	1.57	0.02	0.15	0.06	0.03	0.04	-0.13	0.07	0.09	0.12	0.09	0.02	0.45	1

Table 2. The Effect of the Level of Regional Democracy on the Entry Mode Decision.

	(1)	(2)	(3)	(4)	(5)	(6)	(7)	(8)
Number of employees (Log)	-0.230**	-0.283**	-0.278**	-0.265**	-0.291***	-0.329***	-0.307**	-0.268**
	(0.0932)	(0.110)	(0.116)	(0.132)	(0.103)	(0.103)	(0.127)	(0.118)
Return on assets	1.314	3.562***	3.622***	3.576***	4.041***	3.880***	3.652***	3.429***
	(0.825)	(1.061)	(1.134)	(1.063)	(1.144)	(1.115)	(1.133)	(1.028)
High Tech Industry	-2.007***	-3.053***	-3.148***	-2.971***	-3.519***	-3.119***	-2.809***	-3.558***
	(0.665)	(0.653)	(0.685)	(0.651)	(0.821)	(0.682)	(0.642)	(0.823)
Natural resource industry	-1.516**	-2.475***	-2.701***	-2.344***	-2.891***	-2.566***	-2.631***	-2.841***
	(0.652)	(0.828)	(0.834)	(0.833)	(0.893)	(0.903)	(0.835)	(0.885)
Regional democracy		-4.531**	-4.630**	-5.221**	-4.994**	-5.740**	-4.342**	-4.706**
		(2.057)	(2.022)	(2.146)	(2.110)	(2.262)	(1.973)	(2.147)
Relatedness			1.108**					
			(0.557)					
State controlled				-1.612*				
				(0.972)				
Firm age (Log)				0.0399				
				(0.230)				
Regional GDP per capita					-0.133			
					(0.397)			
Regional trade intensity					2.467**			
					(1.209)			
Moscow dummy						-1.060*		
						(0.570)		
Foreign partner: developed country							-1.335	
							(1.055)	

Table 2. (*Continued*)

	(1)	(2)	(3)	(4)	(5)	(6)	(7)	(8)
Cultural distance							0.317	
							(0.209)	
Constant	3.937***	7.991***	7.846***	8.369***	8.582**	9.593***	7.754***	5.445**
	(1.136)	(1.913)	(1.935)	(1.966)	(3.821)	(2.212)	(2.041)	(2.455)
Observations	151	132	132	132	132	132	132	132
Pseudo-R-squared	0.26	0.33	0.35	0.34	0.36	0.35	0.35	0.43
Chi-square	44.15	49.82	44.77	49.65	41.64	57.13	49.51	61.22

Robust standard errors are reported in parentheses.
Industry dummies are included in all regressions.
Year dummies are included in Model 8.
*** $p < 0.01$, ** $p < 0.05$, * $p < 0.1$.

In a second estimation (Model 4 in Table 2), we control for other target firm characteristics, namely, firm age and state ownership. The age of the local firm is captured by the number of years the company operated in Russia (natural logarithm transformed). We create an indicator variable that takes on the value 1 when more than 50% of the equity of the local firm is held by federal and regional state bodies or state-controlled firms (Source: Ruslana). As expected, we find that state-controlled firms are less likely to be acquired: Large-scale privatizations where a foreigner can acquire a majority stake in the privatized Russian firm are less frequent.

In Models 5 and 6 in Table 2, we add other characteristics of the Russian regions that could drive the entry mode choice (Source: Gosstat, Russian Federation Federal State Statistics). In Model 5, we include the regional gross domestic product per capita (variable Regional GDP per Capita), natural logarithm transformed. GDP per capita has been widely used as a measure for market development in cross-country research (Datta et al., 2009). We also add the variable Regional Trade Intensity, measured as the sum of exports and imports divided by the gross regional product. It is a proxy for the openness toward foreigners in a region, in general. We observe that more open regions are more likely to see acquisitions. In Model 6, we add an indicator variable which takes on the value 1 if the local firm is located in Moscow city or Moscow region. Almost 30% of the deals in our sample are based in or around Moscow.

In Model 7 in Table 2, we turn to the relevance of home country characteristics for the entry mode choice. We take into account the cultural distance between the country where the foreign firm is incorporated and Russia. It is measured using the Kogut and Singh (1988) index and the Hofstede data (Hofstede, Hofstede, & Minkov, 2010). Moreover, the model includes a variable that indicates if the foreign entrant is based in a developed country. Both variables are insignificant. Finally, to control for general time trends we add year dummies in Model 8 in Table 2.

Across all these sensitivity checks, the regional level of democracy continues to exercise a significant and negative impact. Entries in more democratic regions are more likely to be JVs.

CONCLUSION

This study analyzes the decision to enter an emerging country via an international JV or acquisition. We focus on the role of the level of subregional democracy in this context. Using a sample of 151 entries into Russia for the period 2002–2008, we find that regional politics matters: Ceteris paribus, acquisitions are more likely in more autocratic regional regimes, while JVs are the preferred mode of entry in more democratic regimes.

Data constraints have limited our investigation, pointing to avenues for future research. In future research, it would be interesting to go down to the micro-level and analyze in more detail how the deals are implemented. It could also be interesting to look at acquirer characteristics and examine whether (and if so how) they moderate the effect of the political regime. Also, it could be valuable to study the performance of foreign entry modes; for instance, do JVs in more democratically run regions turn out to be more profitable? In general, to enhance the robustness of our results, it would be desirable to have a larger sample of entries and analyze other emerging countries in this regard. Future research should try to overcome these limits.

NOTES

1. We only included those deals where the initial stake of the acquirer did not exceed 5%; otherwise, the deal would have no longer been classified as a market entry.
2. We excluded deals with acquirers in NAICS 2007 codes 523 – "Securities, Commodity Contracts, and Other Financial Investments and Related Activities" and 525 – "Funds, Trusts, and Other Financial Vehicles" NAICS 2007.

ACKNOWLEDGMENT

We are grateful for support by the School of Business Administration, National Research University Higher School of Economics, Moscow.

REFERENCES

Anand, J., & Delios, A. (2002). Absolute and relative resources as determinants of international acquisitions. *Strategic Management Journal*, 23(2), 119–134.
Balakrishnan, S., & Koza, M. P. (1991). *Organization costs and a theory of joint ventures.* Unpublished manuscript, University of Minnesota.

Balakrishnan, S., & Koza, M. P. (1993). Information asymmetry, adverse selection and joint-ventures: Theory and evidence. *Journal of Economic Behavior and Organization*, *20*, 99–117.

Bazenkova, A. (2015). Why Foreign Investment in Russia's regions is falling. *The Moscow Times*, April 27. Retrieved from http://www.themoscowtimes.com/business/article/why-foreign-investment-in-russia-s-regions-is-falling/519873.html. Accessed on August 21, 2015.

Brouthers, K. D., Brouthers, L. E., & Werner, S. (2008). Real options, international entry mode choice and performance. *Journal of Management Studies*, *45*, 936–960.

Brouthers, K. D., & Hennart, J. (2007). Boundaries of the firm: Insights from international entry mode research. *Journal of Management*, *33*, 395–425.

Carr, C. (2006). Russian strategic investment decision practices compared to those of Great Britain, Germany, the United States, and Japan. *International Studies of Management and Organization*, *36*(4), 82–110.

Chan, C. M., Makino, S., & Isobe, T. (2010). Does sub-national region matter? Foreign affiliate performance in the United States and China. *Strategic Management Journal*, *31*(11), 1226–1243.

Datta, D. K., Herrmann, P., & Rasheed, A. (2002). Choice of foreign market entry modes: Critical review and future directions. *Advances in International Management*, *14*, 85–153.

Datta, D. K., Musteen, P., & Herrmann, P. (2009). Board characteristics, managerial incentives, and the choice between foreign acquisitions and international joint ventures. *Journal of Management*, *35*, 928–953.

Folta, T. B. (1998). Governance and uncertainty: The tradeoff between administrative control and commitment. *Strategic Management Journal*, *19*(11), 1007–1028.

Garcia-Canal, E., & Guilen, M. F. (2008). Risk and the strategy of foreign location choice in regulated industries. *Strategic Management Journal*, *29*(10), 1097–1115.

Gibson, E. L. (2005). Boundary control: Subnational authoritarianism in democratic countries. *World Politics*, *58*(1), 101–132.

Hennart, J. F. (2009). Down with MNE-centric theories: Market entry and expansion as the bundling of MNE and local assets. *Journal of International Business Studies*, *40*(9), 1432–1454.

Hennart, J. F., & Reddy, S. (1997). The choice between mergers/acquisitions and joint ventures: The case of Japanese investors in the United States. *Strategic Management Journal*, *18*, 1–12.

Hofstede, G., Hofstede, G. J., & Minkov, M. (2010). *Cultures and organizations: Software of the mind* (3rd ed.). New York, NY: McGraw Hill Professional.

Jensen, N. M. (2003). Democratic governance and multinational corporations: Political regimes and inflows of foreign direct investment. *International Organization*, *57*(3), 587–616.

Khanna, T., & Palepu, K. (1997). Why focused strategies may be wrong for emerging markets. *Harvard Business Review*, *75*(4), 41–51.

Khanna, T., & Palepu, K. (2000). The future of business groups in emerging markets: Long-run evidence from Chile. *The Academy of Management Journal*, *43*(3), 268–285.

Kogut, B., & Singh, H. (1988). The effect of national culture on the choice of entry mode. *Journal of International Business Studies*, *19*, 411–432.

Krug, J. A., & Hegarty, W. H. (1997). Postacquisition turnover among U.S. top management teams: An analysis of the effects of foreign vs. domestic acquisitions of U.S. targets. *Strategic Management Journal, 18*(8), 667–675.

Lebedev, S., Peng, M. W., Xie, E., & Stevens, C. E. (2014). Mergers and acquisitions in and out of emerging economies. *Journal of World Business, 50,* 651–662.

Li, Q., & Resnick, A. (2003). Reversal of fortunes: Democratic institutions and foreign direct investment inflows to developing countries. *International Organization, 57,* 175–211.

Libman, A. (2012). Democracy, size of bureaucracy, and economic growth: Evidence from Russian regions. *Empirical Economics, 43*(3), 1321–1352.

Lubatkin, M., Schweiger, D., & Weber, Y. (1999). Top management turnover in related M&A's: An additional test of the theory of relative standing. *Journal of Management, 25,* 55–73.

McCann, P., & Mudambi, R. (2005). Analytical differences in the economics of geography: The case of the multinational firm. *Environment and Planning, 37*(10), 1857–1876.

Meyer, K. E., Estrin, S., Bhaumik, S. K., & Peng, M. W. (2009). Institutions, resources, and entry strategies in emerging economies. *Strategic Management Journal, 30,* 61–80.

Meyer, K. E., & Nguyen, H. V. (2005). Foreign investment strategies and sub-national institutions in emerging markets: Evidence from Vietnam. *Journal of Management Studies, 42*(1), 63–93.

O'Donnell, G. (1978). Reflections on the patterns of change in the bureaucratic-authoritarian state. *Latin American Research Review, 13*(1), 3–38.

Olson, M. (1993). Dictatorship, democracy, and development. *American Political Science Review, 87*(3), 567–576.

Peng, M. W. (2003). Institutional transitions and strategic choices. *Academy of Management Review, 28*(2), 275–296.

Reuer, J. J., & Koza, M. P. (2000). Asymmetric information and joint venture performance: Theory and evidence for domestic and international joint ventures. *Strategic Management Journal, 21,* 81–88.

Singh, H., & Kogut, B. (1989). *Industry and competitive effects on the choice of entry mode.* Academy of management proceedings (pp. 116–120).

Snyder, R. (2001). Scaling down: The subnational comparative method. *Studies in Comparative International Development, 36,* 93–110.

Walsh, J. P. (1988). Top management turnover following mergers and acquisitions. *Strategic Management Journal, 9*(2), 173–183.

Walsh, J. P. (1989). Doing a deal: Merger and acquisition negotiations and their impact upon target company top management turnover. *Strategic Management Journal, 10*(4), 307–322.

Zhao, H., Luo, Y., & Suh, T. (2004). Transaction cost determinants and ownership-based entry mode choice: A metaanalytical review. *Journal of International Business Studies, 35,* 524–544.

CULTURAL DUE DILIGENCE IN MERGERS AND ACQUISITIONS

Daniel R. Denison and Ia Ko

ABSTRACT

Due diligence refers to a comprehensive process of investigating and evaluating business opportunities in mergers and acquisitions. While early-stage due diligence usually encompasses financial and strategic assessment, one of the most important things in due diligence is looking at organizational culture at an early stage. This chapter takes stock of the existing research and practice in the area of cultural due diligence and evaluates the strengths and limitations. Based on the review of literature, we developed a framework for cultural due diligence to address the limitations of existing approaches. The framework illustrates a process to screen the M&A targets, gain insight into the target firm's culture, and identify integration challenges. The process starts with more unobtrusive, indirect, and informal assessments of the target firm's culture and moves onto more obtrusive, direct, and formal assessments.

Keywords: Cultural due diligence; due diligence; mergers and acquisitions; due diligence framework; organizational culture; corporate culture

Advances in Mergers and Acquisitions, Volume 15, 53–72
ISSN: 1479-361X/doi:10.1108/S1479-361X20160000015004

Despite becoming a nearly essential strategy for firms trying to grow and improve their ability to compete, many mergers and acquisitions still end in failure (Cartwright & Schoenberg, 2006; Lubatkin, 1983). Estimates of the failure rate range between 20% and 70% depending on how success is defined (Appelbaum, Gandell, Yortis, Proper, & Jobin, 2000; Marks, 1988; Weber, 1996). One of the most common themes used to explain the high failure rate is the compatibility of the cultures of the organizations and the way that these dynamics are managed (Appelbaum et al., 2000; Mirvis & Marks, 1992). When organizations join forces, they not only combine buildings, technologies, and market share, they also combine people, structures, and cultures. The way in which the cultural integration process is managed appears to make a big difference.

Culture is often defined as "the way we do things around here" (Fralics & Bolster, 1997; Peters & Waterman, 1982). Organizational culture refers to the norms, values, and underlying assumptions that influence an organization's management system as well as the set of management practices and behaviors that exemplify the underlying mindset (Denison, 1990). Since early 1990s, "culture clash" has been a mainstay of the M&A literature (e.g., Mirvis & Marks, 1992). Nearly all companies now recognize this as a critical success factor in the integration phase. In the past decade, culture has also appeared as a focus area during the combination phase, and a large and growing body of academic publications have focused on post-merger, integration phase that follows (Calipha, Tarba, & Brock, 2010). But progress has still been very slow in research on the pre-combination phase, when companies are trying to understand the cultures of potential acquisition targets and anticipate the challenges of the integration process (Jones, 2008).

Due diligence refers to a comprehensive process of investigating and evaluating business opportunities in mergers and acquisitions (Angwin, 2001). It typically occurs before major decisions are made or immediately after an M&A deal is announced. Due diligence almost always includes the review and analysis of "hard data" about the business — products, financial assets, business models, and technology — with a primary focus on legal and financial issues (Stachowicz-Stanusch, 2009). When done correctly, due diligence helps organizations uncover key issues that can impede negotiations or integration (Angwin, 2001).

Cultural due diligence has begun to receive more attention from both researchers and practitioners. This typically involves a process of gathering and analyzing key cultural elements during the due diligence phase. There are usually two main objectives of cultural due diligence. The first is to inform the deal team so they can make decisions around the deal. Is the culture gap so formidable that it might be a "deal-breaker?" The second, and perhaps more important purpose is to highlight the culture gaps and to clarify the integration challenges posed by the cultural differences so that the merged firm can be better prepared for those challenges. While many executives may acknowledge the importance of cultural due diligence, actually doing it continues to be a challenge. For example, in a survey of 190 CEOs and CFOs involved in M&A's worldwide in the late 1990s, only 46% had examined organizational culture and dynamics of change as opposed to 90% who had examined the "hard assets" of the company in question (Jones, 2008). Jones's article points to the lack of well-tested practice as one of main reasons why culture is overlooked; executives see the importance but are not clear how to do it.

This chapter takes stock of the existing research and practice in the area of cultural due diligence and evaluates the strengths and limitations. Next, we offer a set of due diligence strategies that are designed to overcome the limitations of existing approaches. We then integrate those into an overall framework of the cultural due diligence process.

MANAGING CULTURE THROUGHOUT THE M&A PROCESS

Culture reflects various lessons that an organization has learned through their history and encompasses the many habits and routines that have developed over time (Denison, Hooijberg, Lane, & Lief, 2012). While many elements of organizational culture are unclear or invisible to organizational members, dramatic events such as mergers and acquisitions (M&As) make culture – either one's own or others' – salient (Weber, Belkin, & Tarba, 2011).

Many authors point to organizational culture and intangible assets as key drivers of post-M&A performance (e.g., Buono, Bowditch, & Lewis, 1985; Datta, 1991; Hassan, 2010; Teerikangas & Very, 2006). Organizational culture emerged as an important success factor in a study of 146 organizations involved in mergers (Munteanu & Grosu, 2011) and also from a laboratory study (Weber & Camerer, 2003). Existing research shows that the failure to manage cultural differences has a negative impact on M&A success (Stachowicz-Stanusch, 2009). Managing culture during or post-integration is important and that has been the focus of the current literature and practice. However, research evidence has been slow to accumulate to show that the lack of cultural due diligence early in the process and the failure to understand differences between organizational cultures and strategy fit has adverse effects on post-M&A performance (Horwitz et al., 2002).

This growing attention to culture as an important determinant of performance in M&A is supported by an extensive literature on how various aspects of corporate culture influence patterns of profitability, growth, and other performance measures over time. Sackmann (2010) has provided the best review of this literature, summarizing over 50 studies of culture and performance published over the past decade. The authors of this chapter have contributed to this literature by developing a model and method for assessing the impact that organizational culture has on measures of firm performance and effectiveness (Denison, Nieminen, & Kotrba, 2014).

Given the impact of organizational culture on performance, it is important to understand how to manage cultural dynamics at each stage of the M&A process. In their review of the M&A literature, Calipha et al. (2010) report a number of approaches that define from two (Boland, 1970) to seven stages (Kazemek & Grauman, 1989) of M&A. A more common view of the M&A process includes three phases. For example, Marks and Mirvis' (2011) framework starts with the first stage, the *pre-combination stage*. In this stage, the acquiring organization defines and chooses a target acquisition. When the negotiations are complete, the deal is then referred to shareholders and regulators for legal approval. The second stage is called the *combination stage*, during which the organization determines their integration plan and begins the transition process. The final stage is the *post-combination stage* in which full implementation of the integration process occurs and people begin to settle into the new combined organization.

While the research literature and industry practices for managing culture in the combination and post-combination stages have evolved over the past few decades (e.g., Cartwright & Schoenberg, 2006), looking at cultural dynamics in any systematic way at the early stage of the M&A process is rare. Understanding the cultures of both the acquiring organization and the target firm at the starting point of the due diligence process can help inform the deal, highlight the integration challenges, and prepare for a smooth transition and successful integration.

CULTURAL DUE DILIGENCE: A REVIEW OF RESEARCH

Our review of the literature identified 68 studies of due diligence focused on cultural or human capital factors over the past decade. This discussion summarizes the primary studies from that literature. Many of these studies have stressed the importance of cultural due diligence (Hassan, 2010; Horwitz et al., 2002; Munteanu & Grosu, 2011; Weber & Camerer, 2003). They argue that due diligence must include non-traditional strategic, cultural, and human capital characteristics of the target organization (Galpin, Maellaro, & Whittington, 2011). Several authors have proposed various approaches and frameworks to cultural due diligence (e.g., Bouchikhi & Kimberly, 2012; Harding & Rouse, 2007; Tieman & Hartman, 2013; Weber & Tarba, 2012a, 2012b). They suggest a data-driven approach, which often involves archival data analysis, in-depth interviews with stakeholders, and a large-scale survey.

Appelbaum et al. (2000) assert that CEOs and HR departments of both firms need to collaborate before announcing the deal and closing legal issues in the pre-merger phase and develop plans to manage culture in the post-merger phase. They argue that the most important cultural due diligence activity is to decide which model of organizational culture will be executed; use of one or other culture, creating the best of both world culture, or creating a completely new culture.

Harding and Rouse (2007) proposed a framework and a process for *human due diligence*. Their framework is designed to help "cultural acquirers" understand the culture and people of the other firm. The process begins with understanding the target organization's structure as a key manifestation of culture. Next, organizations examine internal dynamics, review hard data, map decision-making process, and document assets and capabilities of the target organization. Based on the information gathered, organizations then conduct a culture audit, an employee survey that addresses their perceptions of culture. Finally, Harding and Rouse recommend holding a joint workshop involving managers from both companies to help them understand cultures of both organizations and address issues related with culture. They state the best time to start the human due diligence is right after the M&A announcement.

Stachowicz-Stanusch (2009) illustrates a cultural due diligence process using the HP-Compaq merger as a case example. Stachowicz-Stanusch points out that HP and Compaq had different management style and employee attitudes, given different roots and history. Immediately after the merger was announced, the companies began a comparable analysis of their organizational cultures. Interviews and focus group with executives, managers, and employees were conducted to gather data on similarities and differences of the two cultures. The cultural due diligence findings were organized on the following 10 competing dimensions: precedence versus inquiry, internal versus external focus, systematic versus spontaneous, precision versus speed, reflection versus iteration, winner versus issue focused, competition versus cooperation, dominance versus value, threat versus opportunity, and reaction versus initiation. From there, they created new organizational core values and business objectives. Then, they designed a two-day program dedicated to accelerate the process of livening up the new core values.

Galpin et al. (2011) uses a comprehensive M&A process flow model (Galpin & Herndon, 2007) to provide a guideline to OD professionals who the authors argue could add more value throughout the M&A process. Galpin et al. highlight that the importance of conducting strategic self-analysis (examining internal high-performing organizational culture and key talents) and assessing organizational structure as the first step of due diligence. As to more detailed due diligence, they maintain that the acquiring company should explore every possible facet of the target company and state culture assessment and talent evaluations are two important activities for identifying potential deal-breakers. To facilitate culture analysis, they created a cultural comparison matrix that allows companies to compare cultures on 12 cultural levers (i.e., strategy, values, organization structure, staffing and selection, etc.).

Weber et al. (2011) argue that cultural differences can influence negotiation process and decisions. They propose a framework that addresses culture in the negotiation state. While the authors are mainly concerned with broader culture in the context of cross-cultural M&As, their ideas seem to apply to organizational cultures. They state that understanding the other party's culture can reduce uncertainty during the negotiation phase, address the issue of fit (or lack thereof) early on, and improve the negotiation outcomes. Also, they highlight the importance of uncovering how work and groups are organized in the other organization and how they make decisions, as these two are highly impacted by organizational culture.

Building upon their prior work, Weber and Tarba (2012a, 2012b) provide a framework for addressing culture from planning to negotiation to integration stages of M&A. For the planning stage, they argue that organizations should focus on identifying cultural differences for screening for

M&A. They recommend organizations compare cultures by asking a small number of raters (e.g., executives, employees.) to rank the target organization on the following seven key cultural dimensions: innovation, risk taking, lateral interdependence/cooperation, top management contact, autonomy and decision-making, performance orientation, and reward orientation. All the collected information is cross-checked for reliability and examined against other content to ensure validity. Weber and Tarba state that this comparison allows organizations to identify how strong the cultural differences are and where the differences exist (e.g., function). They also suggest that organizations evaluate cultural differences using primary and secondary sources of information provided by companies and financial reports, when such information is available.

Bouchikhi and Kimberly (2012) recommend firms conduct an *identity audit* in the pre-merger phase. The identity audit starts with an examination of archival data, followed by a series of in-depth interviews with key stakeholders, and then completed with a large-scale survey. According to Bouchikhi and Kimberly, either too strong or too weak consensus among the target's stakeholders around an identity should raise a red flag as it could hinder the realization of synergies. Also, they state the identity audit results should inform the decision to merge. While this framework is interesting and makes sense, its practical application is unknown; the lack of empirical support makes it difficult to understand how an organization might do an identity audit before the M&A decision is made.

In addition, Panda (2013) proposes a six-step cultural due diligence process that allows organizations to compare each other on 10 dimensions of culture. Panda suggests that organizations start the process with identifying outcomes of the cultural due diligence initiatives and forming the due diligence team. Then, organizations can list out the cultural indicators and start their "dip stick" (or "quick and dirty") diligence. For more detailed diligence, Panda state organizations can collect different types of culture data through observation, interview, survey, etc. and analyze the culture data. Table 1 provides a brief summary of these studies.

Overall, these authors provide interesting approaches and frameworks on how an organization might do cultural due diligence. They suggest that organizations (1) do cultural diligence early in the pre-combination stage, (2) gather data from multiple sources, and (3) compare cultures on specific dimensions to identify similarities, differences, and potential issues. They also commonly stress the importance of understanding organizational

Table 1. Selected Examples of Cultural Due Diligence Frameworks and Approaches.

Source	Bouchard and Pellet (2002)	Harding and Rouse (2007)	Stachowicz-stanusch (2009)	Galpin et al. (2011)	Weber and Tarba (2012a, 2012b)	Bouchikhi and Kimberly (2012)	Panda (2013)
Culture dimensions assessed	– Customer satisfaction – Employee satisfaction – Formal procedures – Governing principles – Informal practices – Key business drivers – Leadership and management – Organizational characteristics – Perceptions and expectations	– Communication – Organization structure – Rules and policies – Staffing and selection – Strategy – Training – Values	– Competition vs. cooperation – Dominance vs. value – Internal vs. external focus – Precedence vs. inquiry – Precision vs. speed – Reaction vs. initiation – Reflection vs. iteration – Systematic vs. spontaneous – Threat vs. opportunity – Winner vs. issue focused	– Ceremonies and events – Decision-making – Goals and measures – Innovation – Physical environment – Rewards and recognition – Risk taking	– Autonomy and decision-making – Lateral interdependence, cooperation – Leadership – Performance orientation – Reward orientation – Top management contact	– Business drivers – Cultural artifacts – Direction and results – Infrastructure – Organizational values – Practices	– Credibility, respect, fairness, price, and camaraderie – Employees' perception – Uncomfortable questions
Steps		1. Define the new structure 2. Assess culture: archive, survey, interview, survey, joint workshop 3. Identify key talents; develop retention plans 4. Manage employee perceptions: Past survey data, front-line interviews	1. Gather data from executives, managers, and employees 2. Data analysis 3. Identify cultural similarities and differences 4. Design, develop, and administer a dedicated workshop to speed up the integration	1. Formulate 2. Locate 3. Investigate 4. Negotiate 5. Integrate 6. Motivate 7. Evaluate *Due diligence occurs in the first three stages.	1. Gather feedback from raters	1. Examine archival data 2. Conduct in-depth interviews with key stakeholders 3. Conduct large-scale employee survey	1. Determine outcomes of the cultural due diligence 2. Form the due diligence team 3. List out the cultural indicators 4. Dip stick diligence 5. Detailed diligence 6. Analyze culture data and debrief
Data sources	– Finance & HR – Past survey – Culture survey – Interview		– Focus group – Interview	– Culture assessment – Talent evaluation	– Rater's subjective ratings – Primary and secondary	– Archives – Employee survey – Interview	– Survey – Interview – Observation

structure and decision-making process as two important elements impacted by organizational culture. However, the lack of empirical evidence suggests limited practicality or challenges of implementing cultural due diligence (and perhaps a great opportunity and a niche). This points to a need for a better method for assessing and managing cultural differences in the due diligence phase.

A FRAMEWORK FOR CULTURE DUE DILIGENCE

Based on the review of literature, we developed a framework for cultural due diligence to address the limitations of existing approaches. The framework illustrates a process to screen the M&A targets, gain insight into the target firm's culture, and identify integration challenges. The process starts with more unobtrusive, indirect, and informal assessments of the target firm's culture and moves onto more obtrusive, direct, and formal assessments. Before we describe each step, we first explain the overall process of culture due diligence and clarify those aspects of culture organizations to focus on throughout the due diligence effort. Fig. 1 illustrates the four main stages of culture due diligence.

Understand Your Own Culture First

The cultural due diligence process starts with understanding one's own organizational culture. This entails assessing their own cultures to define strengths they are trying to build and weaknesses they are trying to overcome through M&A. While measuring organizational culture can seem challenging when culture is viewed as abstract, idiosyncratic, and residing at a very deep or perhaps subconscious level (e.g., Rousseau, 1990), several models of organizational culture have emerged as useful for comparative

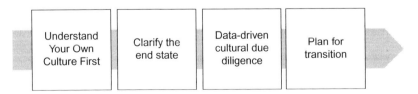

Fig. 1. Culture Due Diligence Process.

research (e.g., Cooke & Lafferty, 1989; Denison & Mishra, 1995; Quinn & Rohrbaugh, 1981). This chapter adopts the Denison Organizational Culture Model (Fig. 2) for its linkage to organizational effectiveness (Denison et al., 2012). The Denison model was developed based on a line of research examining the cultural characteristics of high-performing organizations (Denison, 1984, 1990; Denison, Haaland, & Goelzer, 2003; Denison & Mishra, 1995; Fey & Denison, 2003). These studies revealed four essential culture traits of high-performing organizations including mission, consistency, involvement, and adaptability. Mission refers to an organization's purpose and direction, and reflects a focus external to the organization and on stability. Consistency refers to shared values, and efficient systems and processes; it reflects an internal and stable focus. Involvement concerns the personal engagement of individuals within the organization and reflects a focus on the internal dynamics of the organization and on flexibility. Finally, adaptability refers to the ability to understand what the customer wants, to learn, and to change in response to

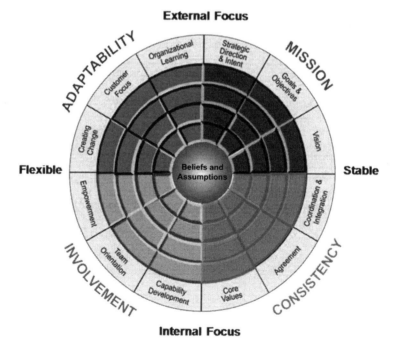

Fig. 2.   Denison Organizational Culture Model.

demand; the focus of adaptability is external and flexible. Using the Denison model helps clarify the key aspects of organizational culture to measure, serves as a useful framework to compare the similarities and differences between the firms, and facilitates integrating data from different sources and synthesizing the findings. Also, keeping this framework throughout the M&A process helps firms manage organizational culture beyond the due diligence stage.

The Denison Organizational Culture Survey was developed based on the Denison model (Denison & Neale, 1996). A recent review identified the Denison Organizational Culture Survey as the most well-researched effectiveness culture measure (Denison et al., 2012). The results from this diagnostic process reveal the level of clarity and alignment around its culture and allows firms to identify the ideal culture for their target acquisition. The existing literature supports that the survey method is useful for assessing observable and measurable aspects of culture and making comparisons between organizations using the same set of culture concepts (Ashkanasy, Broadfoot, & Falkus, 2000; Cooke & Rousseau, 1988). Also, when benchmarking is available — as is the case for the Denison survey — firms can gain insight into their strengths and weaknesses compared to other firms (Denison et al., 2012). In addition, surveys allow the firm to collect culture data relatively easily as surveys are not as resource intensive as other methods such as ethnography, and to replicate the process at later time — in post-combination phase (Ashkanasy et al., 2000).

Clarify the Cultural Dynamics

How much change will there be in the acquirer's and the acquired firm's culture? When organizations merge, there are often different levels of expectations around the degree of change in the post-merger organization. Thus, organizations going through an M&A need "a high-level vision of this endstate before agreeing to a deal" (Marks & Mirvis, 2011, p. 866). Marks and Mirvis (2010, 1992) developed a framework that describes five different end states depending on the degree of change in the acquired company as well as the acquiring company (Fig. 3).

First is *preservation* in which both companies preserve their own cultures and continue their businesses as usual. Second is *absorption*; the acquired company is absorbed by a parent company, and its culture also becomes assimilated into the acquirer's. Third, in *reverse merger* cases, the acquired company becomes cultural acquirer and the buyer adopts the target firm's

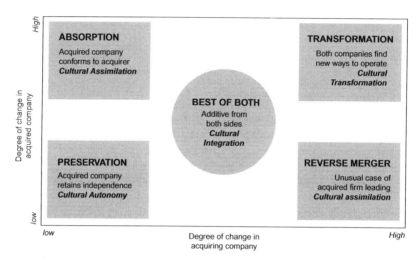

Fig. 3. Cultural Dynamics of M&A. *Source*: Adapted from Marks & Mirvis (1992).

culture. Next is *transformation*; this is when both companies go through major changes after combination and adopt new ways of doing things. The last is *best of both* − in which synergy occurs by leveraging strengths from each legacy company, although this often results in the substantial changes in both firms (e.g., layoffs).

Defining the end-state helps clarify each firm's expectations and prepare for the transition and integration stages. Also, it should be noted that there will always be differences when two organizations join forces. It is not simply about not having cultural differences. While research shows that the cultural differences at the top of the organization are associated with lower effectiveness and financial performance of the finalized merger (Weber, 1996), it is the level of integration that the firms try to achieve (Slangen, 2006). The higher the cultural differences and the higher levels of integration, the lower the firm performance. Also, cultural differences, when managed well, could enhance post-merger performance (Marks & Mirvis, 2011).

Conduct Data-Driven Cultural Due Diligence

Doing a cultural due diligence might seem like navigating through a "data desert" because of the limited access to data needed to fully understand the target firm's culture. What is highly desirable to collect might not be legally possible to gather. For instance, in the negotiation phase or before the deal is final, it is not easy, or sometimes unlawful, to interview the leaders and employees of the target organization. Thus, it is critical to start with unobtrusive measures and maximize the use of existing data. The proposed framework describes a data-driven due diligence process starting with social media data analysis (see Fig. 4).

Social Media Data Analysis

The use of social media data in M&A is relatively new. A recent survey reports that about 56% of people use social media for target identification and 30% for due diligence (Deloitte, 2013). But the focus seems to be largely on customer voice. Our focus is on employee voice and assessing the target firms' culture. Employees voluntarily make comments about their employers on various social media such as Glassdoor.com and Indeed.com. These websites often have a combination of a set of questions for which people can rate their endorsement for the organization's culture, leadership,

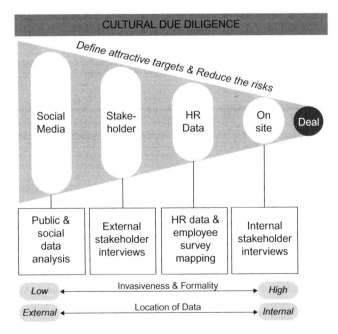

Fig. 4. Cultural Due Diligence Framework.

and management as well as with open-ended question(s) for which people can share their perception of the organization based on their experience as an employee. Before the target is determined, social data analysis can serve as an unobtrusive method to narrow potential targets and identify the target. After the target is determined, mining the social media data and analyzing the data can highlight issues related to organizational culture. It can also help analyzing the competitive landscape by comparing the target firm's data against its competitors. In analyzing the qualitatively data, we categorize the themes using the Denison Model and create an estimate of culture profile. Fig. 5 shows an example of recent acquisition case in which social media data analysis was used as in due diligence.

External Stakeholder Interviews
Semi-structured interviews can help gain insight into the target's current culture. Potential interviewees include former executives, customers,

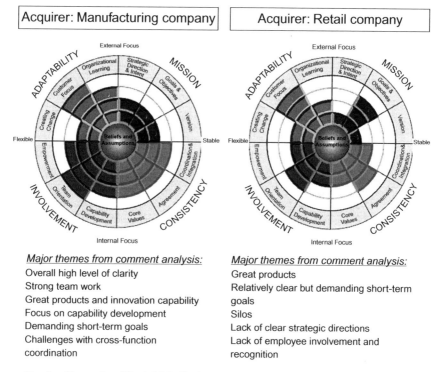

Acquirer: Manufacturing company	Acquirer: Retail company

Major themes from comment analysis:
Overall high level of clarity
Strong team work
Great products and innovation capability
Focus on capability development
Demanding short-term goals
Challenges with cross-function
coordination

Major themes from comment analysis:
Great products
Relatively clear but demanding short-term
goals
Silos
Lack of clear strategic directions
Lack of employee involvement and
recognition

Fig. 5.   Example of Social Media Analysis for Assessing Target Firm Culture.

vendors, channel partners, and former employees. These early-stage interviews should focus on identifying key strengths and issues from each stakeholder's perspective. While conducting an interview is more obtrusive than doing a social media analysis, it does not require direct interaction with current employees.

HR Data and Document Review
Once the target is identified and the deal team is formed, it is often possible to gain access to the target firm's internal archival data related to its HR and management practices. Common HR data and documents include tenure data, hiring and staffing data, performance appraisal templates and processes, compensation structure, and various training programs. One important data that can potentially provide rich information is existing employee survey data and results. A recent article reports that about 96% of organizations Fortune 500 companies administers some type of employee surveys. Reviewing the most recent survey results from both firms and conducting additional analysis can help identify the areas of convergence and divergence between the two. Here, two analytical techniques can be useful. One is mapping. While it is unlikely that the two companies have used exactly the same survey, employee surveys usually cover similar topic areas including teamwork, leadership, and employee involvement. Thus, the survey items and constructs can be conceptually mapped into an organizational culture model – such as the Denison model. When there is a high level of convergence between the surveys, the survey data can also be mapped to benchmarked culture survey tools – such as the Denison culture survey – to obtain a more accurate comparison between the two firms on the same topic areas. The other is content analysis. Employee surveys often include open-ended comments. Analyzing the comments using the culture model as a framework for content coding can add additional layer of insight into the target's culture.

Internal Stakeholder Interviews
When nearing the deal, it is important to conduct interviews with the target firm's leadership team, sample of middle managers, and sample of front-line employees. These internal stakeholder interviews can strengthen the process to assess the target firm culture. If this does not happen during the due diligence, we still recommend that conducting structured interviews with top leadership at the early stage of the transition period – after the deal is announced – will help organizations gather the leader's insights on the firm's cultural strategy, or lack thereof. At this state, the inter view

questions should focus on the strategic problems the firm is trying to solve through the M&A as well as organizational culture in terms of its mission, consistency, involvement, and adaptability. The following show a few example questions:

1. What are the things that are valued most in your organization? What gets people in trouble, recognized and rewarded?
2. What makes for good or effective leadership in your organization?
3. What is your long-term vision? Do the people in your organization understand that?
4. Are you a process-driven, standardized organization or do you think things are more free form and flexible?
5. What is the level of cross-level and cross-functional coordination required in your organization? How well do you do that?
6. How well have you managed large-scale change?

Use a Framework to Integrate and Synthesize Findings
The final step in the cultural due diligence work is integration and synthesis of findings. Collecting data in the data desert is a big challenges in due diligence. But making sense out of all the data from different sources is yet another challenge. Aforementioned, the key is to use a culture model as a guiding framework throughout the data collection, analysis, and synthesis. Using the Denison Model as a framework, we suggest the due diligence team clarify (a) what they have learned about the target firm's mission, adaptability, involvement, and consistency, (b) what integration challenges they need to highlight and inform the deal team; and (c) what initial recommendations they might have on handling those integration challenges.

Planning for Transition and Integration: Keeping Culture on the Table

The focus of this chapter is on cultural due diligence. However, culture should always stay on the table throughout the M&A process. After the due diligence and deal is signed, companies should quickly move onto planning for a transition. An important part of transition is communication and the transition team alignment. Communicating the deal and change clearly to the employees will help prevent what Marks and Mirvis describe as "merger syndrome" − a phenomenon characterized by increased centralization and decreased top-down communication (Marks & Mirvis, 1985). When communicating the change, the message around implications of change being done to the employees need to be clear. As Levinson (1976) stated, "all change is a loss experience." There will be emotional reactions stemming from experiencing loss of how they were doing things, whether they were bad or good habits. Even when adapting to new culture and learning new good habits, anxiety associated with learning and evaluation can have a real impact on performance.

CONCLUSION

Many leaders and organizations seem to "get" the importance of culture in mergers and acquisitions. Our review of literature also revealed that organizations and leaders are aware of the importance of and the need for cultural due diligence. However, a methodology on "how" to do the cultural due diligence is not as clear as the importance of such effort. One challenge in this is the difficulty of defining and measuring culture. Another challenge is assessing culture of an organization to which you have limited access. To address these challenges, we have developed a cultural due diligence framework based on our review of literature and industry practices. The most important thing in due diligence is looking at organizational culture at an early stage. While early-stage due diligence usually encompasses financial and strategic assessment, our proposed framework allows for an unobtrusive culture assessment for target identification and assessment by utilizing social and public data. We hope our framework serves as a useful guide for conducting cultural due diligence and helps organizations manage culture throughout the M&A process – from due diligence to transition and to integration.

REFERENCES

Angwin, D. (2001). Mergers and acquisitions across European borders: national perspectives on preacquisition due diligence and the use of professional advisors. *Journal of World Business, 36*(1), 32–57.

Appelbaum, S. H., Gandell, J., Yortis, H., Proper, S., & Jobin, F. (2000). Anatomy of a merger: Behavior of organizational factors and processes throughout the pre-during-post-stages (part 1). *Management Decision, 38*(9), 649–662.

Ashkanasy, N., Broadfoot, L., & Falkus, S. (2000). Questionnaire measures of organizational culture. In A. N. Ashkanasy, C. Wilderom, & M. Peterson (Eds.), *The handbook of organizational culture and climate* (2nd ed., pp. 131–162). Thousand Oaks, CA: Sage.

Boland, R. J. (1970). Merger planning: How much weight do personnel factors carry? *Personnel, 47*, 8–13.

Bouchard, P. J., & Pellet, L. (2002). *Getting you shift together. Making sense of organization culture change.* CCI Press.

Bouchikhi, H., & Kimberly, J. R. (2012). Making mergers work. *MIT Sloan Management Review, 54*(1), 63–70.

Buono, A. F., Bowditch, J. L., & Lewis, J. W. (1985). When cultures collide: The anatomy of a merger. *Human Relations, 38*(5), 477–500.

Calipha, R., Tarba, S., & Brock, D. (2010). Mergers and acquisitions: A review of phases, motives, and success factors. *Advances in Mergers and Acquisitions, 10*, 1–24.

Cartwright, S., & Schoenberg, R. (2006). Thirty years of mergers and acquisitions research: Recent advances and future opportunities. *British Journal of Management, 17*, s1–s5.

Cooke, R. A., & Lafferty, J. C. (1989). *Organizational culture inventory.* Plymouth, MI: Human Synergistics.

Cooke, R., & Rousseau, D. (1988). Behavioral norms and expectations: A quantitative approach to the assessment of organizational culture. *Group and Organizational Studies, 13*, 245–273.

Datta, D. K. (1991). Organisational fit and acquisition performance: Effects of post-acquisition integration. *Strategic Management Journal, 12*, 281–297.

Deloitte. (2013, October 17). *Let's make a deal: Analytics and social media in M&A.* Retrieved from http://deloitte.wsj.com/cio/2013/10/17/lets-make-a-deal-analytics-and-social-media-in-ma/#. Accessed on July 1, 2014.

Denison, D., Hooijberg, R., Lane, N., & Lief, C. (2012). *Leading culture change in global organizations: Aligning culture and strategy* (Vol. 394). New York, NY: Wiley.

Denison, D., Nieminen, L., & Kotrba, L. (2014). Diagnosing organizational cultures: A conceptual and empirical review of culture effectiveness surveys. *European Journal of Work and Organizational Psychology, 23*(1), 145–161. doi:10.1080/1359432X.2012.713173

Denison, D. R. (1984). Bringing corporate culture to the bottom line. *Organizational Dynamics, 13*, 4–22.

Denison, D. R. (1990). *Corporate culture and organizational effectiveness.* New York, NY: Wiley.

Denison, D. R., Haaland, S., & Goelzer, P. (2003). Corporate culture and organizational effectiveness: Is Asia different from the rest of the world? *Organizational Dynamics, 33*(1), 98–109.

Denison, D. R., & Mishra, A. (1995). Toward a theory of organizational culture and effectiveness. *Organizational Science, 6*, 204–223.

Denison, D. R., & Neale, W. S. (1996). *Denison organizational culture survey.* Ann Arbor, MI: Aviat.

Fey, C. F., & Denison, D. R. (2003). Organizational culture and effectiveness: Can American theory be applied in Russia? *Organizational Science, 14*, 686–706.

Fralics, R. D., & Bolster, C. J. (1997). Preventing culture shock. *Modern Healthcare, 11*, 50.

Galpin, B. T., Maellaro, R., & Whittington, J. L. (2011). Evidence from the field: OD tools and methods that positively impact M&As. *OD Practitioner, 44*, 13–18.

Galpin, T., & Herndon, M. (2007). *The complete guide to mergers and acquisitions: process tools to support M&A integration at every level.* New York, NY: Wiley.

Harding, D., & Rouse, T. (2007). Human due diligence. *Harvard Business Review, 85*(4), 124–142.

Hassan, R. (2010). Merger and acquisition: The organization well being and impact to the employees of the acquired organization. *Business Management Quarterly Review,* *1*(1), 31–40.

Horwitz, F. M., Andersen, K., Bezuidenhout, A., Cohen, S., Kirsten, F., Mosoeunyane, K., ... van Heerden, A. (2002). Due diligence neglected: managing human resources and organizational culture in mergers and acquisitions. *South African Journal of Business Management, 33,* 1–10.

Jones, G. (2008). Enhancing due diligence – Examination of the organisational culture of a merger and acquisition target. *Journal of Business & Economics Research, 6*(1), 11–16.

Kazemek, E. A., & Grauman, D. M. (1989). Awareness of phases helps achieve successful mergers. *Healthcare Financial Management, 43,* 82.

Levinson, H. (1976). *Psychological man.* Cambridge, MA: The Levinson Institute.

Lubatkin, M. (1983). Mergers and the performance of the acquiring firm. *Academy of Management Review, 8*(2), 218–225.

Marks, M. L. (1988). The merger syndrome: The human side of corporate combinations. *Journal of Buyouts and Acquisitions, 1,* 18–23.

Marks, M. L., & Mirvis, P. H. (1985). Merger syndrome: Stress and uncertainty. *Mergers and Acquisitions, 20*(2), 50–55.

Marks, M. L., & Mirvis, P. H. (1992). Rebuilding after the merger: Dealing with "survivor sickness". *Organizational Dynamics, 21*(2), 18–32.

Marks, M. L., & Mirvis, P. H. (2010). *Joining forces: Making one plus one equal three in mergers, acquisitions, and alliances* (2nd ed.). San Francisco, CA: Jossey-Bass.

Marks, M. L., & Mirvis, P. H. (2011). A framework for the human resources role in managing culture in mergers and acquisitions. *Human Resource Management, 50*(6), 859–877.

Mirvis, P., & Marks, M. (1992). The human side of merger planning: Assessing and analyzing "fit". *Human Resource Planning, 15*(3), 69–92.

Munteanu, S., & Grosu, M. (2011). A practical perspective on human capital post merger integration in central and eastern Europe. *Review of International Comparative Management, 12*(3), 586–601.

Panda, A. (2013). Do you know who you are dealing with? Cultural due diligence: What, why and how. *Vikalpa, 38*(2), 1–20.

Peters, T. J., & Waterman, R. H. (1982). *In search of excellence: Lessons from America's best-run companies.* New York, NY: Harper & Row.

Quinn, R., & Rohrbaugh, J. (1981). A competing values approach to organizational effectiveness. *Public Productivity Review, 5,* 122–140.

Rousseau, D. M. (1990). Assessing organizational culture: The case for multiple methods. In B. Schneider (Ed.), *Organizational culture and climate* (pp. 153–192). San Francisco, CA: Jossey-Bass.

Sackmann, S. A. (2010). Culture and performance. In N. Ashkanasy, C. Wilderon, & M. Peterson (Eds.), *Handbook of organizational culture and climate* (pp. 188–224). Thousand Oaks, CA: Sage.

Slangen, A. H. L. (2006). National cultural distance and initial foreign acquisition performance: the moderating effect of integration. *Journal of World Business, 41,* 161–170.

Stachowicz-stanusch, A. (2009). Culture due diligence based on HP/Compaq merger case study. *Journal of Intercultural Management, 1,* 64–81.

Teerikangas, S., & Very, P. (2006). The culture-performance relationship in M&A: From yes/no to how. *British Journal of Management, 17,* s31–s48.

Tieman, D., & Hartman, J. (2013). Data analytical due diligence is driving M&A deals. *Financial Executive, April*, 32–35.

Weber, R., & Camerer, C. (2003). Cultural conflict and merger failure: An experimental approach. *Management Science, 49*(4), 400–415.

Weber, Y. (1996). Corporate culture fit and performance in mergers and acquisitions. *Human Relations, 49*(9), 1181–1202.

Weber, Y., Belkin, T., & Tarba, S. (2011). Negotiation, cultural differences, and planning in mergers and acquisitions. *Journal of Transnational Management, 16*(2), 107–115.

Weber, Y., & Tarba, S. Y. (2012a). Mergers and acquisitions process: the use of corporate culture analysis. *Cross Cultural Management: An International Journal, 19*(3), 288–303. doi:10.1108/13527601211247053

Weber, Y., & Tarba, S. Y. (2012b). Cross-cultural analysis at mergers and acquisitions stages. *OD Practitioner, 44*(3), 37–44.

TRANSITIONAL GOVERNANCE TRAJECTORIES: ORGANIZATION, PLACE, AND SPACE

Isabel Estrada, Florian Noseleit and Killian McCarthy

ABSTRACT

Alliances often turn into acquisitions (i.e., one alliance partner is acquired by the other). In these transitional governance trajectories, geography-related factors can play a crucial role. Factors like location and distance can notably influence the decision to acquire the alliance partner, as well as the performance implications of such a transition. However, existing studies on transitional governance tend to underemphasize the geographic dimension of the phenomenon. In this chapter, we take a first step toward connecting the field of transitional governance and the discipline of economic geography, which does emphasize location and distance as critical determinants of economic activities. We discuss how economic geography can inform the field of transitional governance and propose some promising avenues for future studies linking organization, place, and space in transitional governance trajectories.

Keywords: Organizational boundaries; alliances; acquisitions; governance decisions; real options; geography

Advances in Mergers and Acquisitions, Volume 15, 73–93
ISSN: 1479-361X/doi:10.1108/S1479-361X20160000015005

INTRODUCTION

Few issues have attracted more attention in the strategy literature than the topic of firm's governance decisions and their implications for organizational boundaries. In particular, there is rich evidence on the use of alliances and acquisitions as tools for expanding the organizational boundaries of the firm. In contrast to the traditional premise, which suggests that alliances and acquisitions are two alternative modes to organize a transaction (e.g., Hennart & Reddy, 1997), scholars have begun to emphasize the links between them as transitional governance (TG) trajectories. The notion of TG implies that alliances confer upon firms the possibility for a subsequent acquisition, in such a way that what starts as an alliance often turns into an acquisition (Kogut, 1991; Reuer & Tong, 2005).

Scholars in this TG tradition, building on several theories within the realm of strategy such as real options theory (e.g., Kogut, 1991) and transaction cost economics (e.g., Vanhaverbeke, Duysters, & Noorderhaven, 2002), have generated solid theoretical foundations on the rationale and strategic implications of TG trajectories. For example, existing studies reveal the conditions under which firms are more likely to (i) initiate TG trajectories, (ii) turn alliances into acquisitions, and (iii) create value through these strategies. Overall, this collection of literature has provided rich insights into the organization aspects of TG trajectories. However, existing studies on TG, and the traditional strategy literature as a whole, "have exhibited a relatively underdeveloped view of geographic space (and place)" in which the phenomenon is embedded (Beugelsdijk, McCann, & Mudambi, 2010, p. 486). To the extent that firms increasingly use alliances and acquisitions to access novel resources in disperse settings (Rosenkopf & Almeida, 2003), distance and location are often crucial determinants of the decision to ally with and/or acquire specific partners but also of the performance of such interfirm transactions. The lack of attention to distance and locational issues in existing TG literature is therefore problematic because it limits our conceptual understanding of TG trajectories.

In contrast, these issues have been extensively discussed in economic geography. In this discipline, place and space are, in fact, at the center of the conversation to explain economic activities across the world (Agnew, 2011; Beugelsdijk et al., 2010). Some of these ideas about the role of place and space have started crystalizing in specific streams of the strategy literature (cf. Beugelsdijk & Mudambi, 2013); yet, the TG field still remains quite independent from these insights. Recently, several scholars have emphasized the advantages of adopting an interdisciplinary approach that builds on both economic geography and the strategy literature to better understand the global economy (Beugelsdijk et al., 2010; Boschma et al., 2014). We adhere to this view and argue that incorporating insights from economic geography into the TG conversation can help to explain the locational and spatial environment of TG trajectories, enriching our understanding of the phenomenon. In this chapter, we aim to establish the analytical connections between the two fields and propose a research agenda that connects *organization*, *place*, and *space* (Beugelsdijk et al., 2010) in TG trajectories.

In the following pages, we first review the extant literature on TG. Subsequently, we introduce the basic premises of economic geography and discuss how they can inform the field of TG. The chapter concludes by highlighting promising avenues for future research.

OVERVIEW OF EXTANT TRANSITIONAL GOVERNANCE LITERATURE

Alliances and Acquisitions: From Independent to Interdependent Governance Choices

In analyzing the choice between alliances and acquisitions, scholars have traditionally built on transaction cost economics (Williamson, 1991). This theory assumes that the firm's choice of alliances over acquisitions is a matter of maximizing efficiency and minimizing transactions costs (Hennart & Reddy, 1997). In this way, alliances and acquisitions have been traditionally viewed as alternative, independent governance modes that offer distinctive advantages.[1]

In contrast to this traditional view that alliances and acquisitions are discrete choices made at a certain point in time, TG scholars posit a more dynamic perspective, in which the interdependences between the two governance forms become apparent. In particular, the TG literature emerges to acknowledge that, in practice, many interfirm transactions are initiated as alliances and, over time, turn into acquisitions (Kogut, 1991; Yang, Lin, & Peng, 2011). Fig. 1 illustrates the existence of this phenomenon, reporting as an example the number of alliance-to-acquisition transitions involving US firms in the period 1990−2010. The underlying data were obtained using Thomson SDC Platinum database. We first identified the total set of alliances and acquisitions. Based on the CUSIP codes of the firms involved,

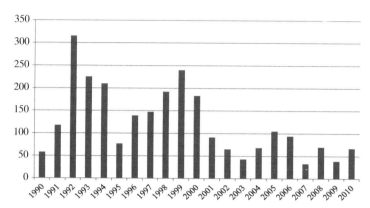

Fig. 1. Alliance-to-Acquisition Transitions Involving US Firms, per Year (1990–2010). *Source*: Own elaboration based on data from Thomson SDC Platinum database.

we subsequently identified the number of alliance-to-acquisition transitions. In particular, we identified 2,578 alliances that turned into acquisitions between 1990 and 2010, involving firms from all 50 US states and partners from 67 unique countries. These numbers suggest that, in the focal period, 3.6% of all alliances involving US firms transitioned to acquisitions and that, on average, 169 alliances transitioned to acquisitions per year.

TG: Theoretical Foundations

The core premise in the TG literature is that firm's governance decisions often describe a transitional trajectory (rather than a discrete choice), such that a transaction can be initially organized as an alliance and subsequently evolve into an acquisition. Below, we review the two main theoretical frameworks providing foundations to this premise: Real options theory and transactions costs economics.

Real options theory is the dominant framework in the TG field (Folta, 1998; Kogut, 1991; Reuer & Tong, 2005). Drawing on the analogy between financial and real options, real options scholars focus on explaining firm's sequential investments under uncertainty (e.g., Bowman & Hurry, 1993; see Li, James, Madhavan, & Mahoney, 2007, for a review of this literature). A real option is "a right – without an obligation – to invest in resources (e.g., labor, money, time) toward a course of action at a future point in time" (McCarter, Mahoney, & Northcraft, 2011, p. 624). A critical assumption in this theory is that future strategic opportunities are determined by prior investment commitments (Bowman & Hurry, 1993; Tong & Reuer, 2007). Real options allow firms to position themselves to expand in the future, if convenient, while requiring a relatively limited commitment of resources (Kogut, 1991). Under conditions of uncertainty, the right conferred by real options to make future choices and postpone full commitment is thus very valuable. As noted by Li et al. (2007, p. 35), real options offer managers flexibility "to act upon new information such that the upside economic potential is retained while the downside loses are contained" (see also Trigeorgis, 1996, p. 122).

In the TG setting, alliances are investment platforms that provide firms with the option to expand sequentially (Kogut, 1991). In particular, forming an alliance provides the option to acquire the partner sometime in the future (Reuer & Tong, 2005). Under this view, pre-acquisition alliances represent valuable mechanisms to maintain flexibility and deal with uncertainty. As noted by McCarter et al. (2011), in the context of TG, such uncertainty manifests itself on two different levels: environmental and relational uncertainty. Environmental uncertainty, the exogenous component of uncertainty, is rooted in the firm's lack of complete information about the business environment — for example, industry and market conditions, technological standards, etc. (Folta, 1998; Folta & Miller, 2002). Relational (or social) uncertainty arises because the firm has incomplete information about the intentions and/or capabilities of a potential target, and is therefore endogenous to the relationship (McCarter et al., 2011). Pre-acquisition alliances can help in dealing with both types of uncertainty. They can mitigate environmental uncertainty by allowing the firm to delay the acquisition decision until critical information (e.g., value of a certain technology) becomes available (Bowman & Hurry, 1993). Furthermore, alliances provide rich information about the partners that is normally not available for outsiders (Reuer & Lahiri, 2014). Alliances also enable partners to develop mutual trust and commitment (Doz, 1996). In this regard, pre-acquisition alliances also mitigate relational uncertainty:[2] engaging first in an alliance (instead of outright acquisition) is a "testing the waters" strategy to get to know the partner (McCarter et al., 2011). Overall, the real options rationale for TG trajectories implies that alliances provide the option (but not the obligation) to acquire the target in the future, while helping to mitigate the uncertainty surrounding the acquisition decision.

A second important theoretical framework in the TG literature is transaction cost economics (Williamson, 1991). Close to the real option insights above discussed, transaction cost theory emphasizes that prior alliances might alleviate ex ante and ex post costs of subsequent acquisitions (Folta, 1998; Hagedoorn & Sadowski, 1999). Transaction cost theory stresses the existence of information asymmetries between acquiring firms and targets, which result into serious risk of adverse selection (Vanhaverbeke et al., 2002). Acquirers should incur important costs to gather detailed information about the target in the pre-acquisition phase (due diligence). By forming an alliance, the firm can gain fine-grained information about the target (Reuer & Lahiri, 2014). In this regard, pre-acquisition alliances are effective *due diligence* mechanisms that can mitigate the risk and costs of adverse selection (Vanhaverbeke et al., 2002). Furthermore, alliances help partners to learn how to collaborate with one another (Doz, 1996). In this way, pre-acquisition alliances can reduce post-acquisition integration costs (Zollo & Singh, 2004). Alliances also mitigate such ex post costs by generating partner-specific absorptive capacity, which allows the acquirer to overcome "indigestibility" problems (Zaheer, Hernandez, & Banerjee, 2010). In sum, transaction cost theory proposes that TG trajectories exist because engaging first in an alliance with a potential target can minimize the transaction costs of a subsequent acquisition.

Empirical Evidence on TG Trajectories

Drawing on these theoretical insights, scholars have empirically examined several aspects of the TG phenomenon. Table 1 presents an overview of empirical studies.

Following Folta (1998) and Faems and Madhok (2009), two key decisions can be distinguished in TG trajectories: (i) the initiation decision (i.e., the firm decides whether to start the TG trajectory by forming an alliance) and (ii) the exercise decision (i.e., the firm decides whether to exercise the option to acquire the partner). Building on the real options rationale (e.g., Kogut, 1991), the transactions cost rationale (e.g., Hagedoorn & Sadowski, 1999), or a combination of both (e.g., Folta, 1998), the majority of studies have focused on one of these two decisions. Scholars focusing on the initiation decision (e.g., Estrada, de la Fuente & Martín-Cruz, 2010; Folta, 1998; Vanhaverbeke et al., 2002) provide evidence on the specific conditions under which firms are likely to engage in TG trajectories. For instance, Folta (1998) examines R&D transactions in the biotechnology industry and finds, among other, that firms prefer equity alliances over acquisitions when exogenous technological uncertainty is high at the industry level.

Table 1. Overview of Empirical Studies on Transitional Governance.

Study	Theoretical Framework	Research Purpose	Sample	Dependent Variable	Key Findings
Kogut (1991)	ROT	To investigate whether joint ventures (JVs) are created as real options to expand in response to future technological and market developments	92 manufacturing JVs, located in the United States and involving at least one American partner, 1975–1983	Acquisition of the JV by one of the partners	The likelihood of acquisition of the JV increases with (i) increased valuation of the JV (e.g., unexpected growth in the product market) and (ii) industry concentration
Folta (1998)	ROT TCT	To examine motives for initiating equity-based R&D collaborations versus outright acquisitions	402 R&D transactions (minority investments, JV, acquisitions) involving a US target in the Biotechnology industry, 1978–1992	Minority investment versus JV versus acquisition	Equity collaborations are preferred over acquisitions (i) when partners have dissimilar primary business operations and (ii) in technical subfields with greater value, higher technological uncertainty and fewer rivals. U.S. transactions are more likely to be organized as acquisitions.
Hagedoorn and Sadowski (1999)	TCT	To examine determinants of the transition from technology alliances to acquisitions	6,425 strategic technology alliances involving 2,848 firms, 1970–1993	Alliance transformed into acquisition versus alliance nontransformed into acquisition	The number alliances than turn into acquisitions in high-tech sectors is relatively smaller than in other sectors. Alliances that turn into acquisitions tend to involve alliance partners of different sizes (i.e., large firms acquire their smaller partners).

Table 1. (*Continued*)

Study	Theoretical Framework	Research Purpose	Sample	Dependent Variable	Key Findings
Folta and Miller (2002)	ROT TCT	To examine factors influencing the decision to acquire additional equity in partner firms	285 minority equity collaborations, in which established non-biotechnology firms take equity stakes in US biotechnology firms, 1978–1999	Acquisition of a majority stake (>50%) of the biotechnology partner Acquisition of additional stakes (up to 50%) of the biotechnology partner	The likelihood of partner buyout increases: (i) with increased partner valuation, (ii) when low uncertainty is combined with high valuation, and (iii) when buyout options are more proprietary. The likelihood of partner buyout decreases: (i) in the presence of an explicit buyout option and (ii) under high uncertainty. However, under high uncertainty, the less proprietary the buyout option, the higher the likelihood of partner buyout.
Vanhaverbeke et al. (2002)	TCT	To examine factors influencing the choice between strategic technology alliances and acquisitions	145 alliances (118 partner firms) and 140 acquisitions (52 acquirers, 120 acquired) established in the Application Specific Integrated Circuits Industry, 1985–1994	Alliance versus acquisition Non-equity alliance versus equity alliance versus acquisition	Acquisition likelihood increases: (i) with the number of previous alliances between two firms and (ii) industry maturity. Acquisition likelihood decreases in the presence of smaller network distance between dyad partners and in inter-triad situations. Minority investments are preferred over JVs when: (i) partner firms are dissimilar and (ii) the value of the technology is high.

Study	Theory	Objective	Sample	Dependent variable	Findings
Porrini (2004)	OLT	To investigate whether a previous alliance between an acquirer and a target affects post-acquisition performance	437 acquisitions in manufacturing by public American acquirers acquiring public American targets, 1988–1997	Return on Assets	Pre-acquisition alliances between acquirers and targets have a positive impact on acquisition performance. Target-specific learning effects are stronger in R&D, technology transfer, manufacturing and marketing alliances than in licensing alliances. Target-specific learning effects are particularly salient in technology transfer and manufacturing alliances.
Reuer and Tong (2005)	ROT TCT	To investigate determinants of firms' use of explicit call options to acquire equity in their international joint ventures (IJVs)	2,594 IJV transactions (based outside US and involving at least one US firm), 1995–2002	Call option (indicating whether the US partner firm in the IJV held an explicit option to acquire equity in the venture)	Explicit call options are contractual safeguards that are used (i) more often in IJVs that are related to the core business areas of the firm and (ii) less often in IJVs created in host countries that have more strict intellectual protection regimes and higher risk of political turmoil.
Zaheer et al. (2010)	TCT OLT	To examine whether prior alliances with potential targets yield superior stock returns upon acquisition	408 acquisitions by US public firms in high-tech industries, 1990–1998	Acquisition performance (acquirer's stock price reaction to the acquisition announcement)	Broadly speaking, acquisitions with prior alliances do not perform better than acquisitions without prior alliances. However, cross-border acquisitions with prior alliances perform better domestic acquisitions. Acquisitions with stronger prior alliances perform better than acquisitions with weaker prior alliances.

Table 1. (Continued)

Study	Theoretical Framework	Research Purpose	Sample	Dependent Variable	Key Findings
Estrada et al. (2010)	ROT	To examine under which conditions firms form technological joint ventures (TJVs)	A panel of 4,050 Spanish industrial manufacturing firms, 1998–2005 (29,376 observations 565 technological JVs)	TJV formation	A firm's propensity to form TJVs is positively related to (i) its absorptive capacity and (ii) the degree of exogenous technological uncertainty, and negatively related to (i) the risk of pre-emption by rivals and (ii) the existence of opportunity costs.
Yang et al. (2011)	Behavioral learning Network theory	To examine determinants of the acquisition of alliance partners	Alliances US Computer Industry, 1986–1996	Acquisition of alliance partner	Exploration alliances are more likely to turn into acquisitions than exploitation alliances, particularly in the presence of (i) high degree of joint brokerage of alliance partners and (ii) high level of relative centrality between alliance partners.

Note: ROT: real options theory; TCT: transaction cost theory; OLT: organizational learning theory.

Examining the exercise decision, other studies (e.g., Folta & Miller, 2002; Kogut, 1991) propose factors explaining the firms' propensity to acquire equity stakes in partner firms. Analyzing minority equity collaboration in biotechnology, Folta and Miller (2002), for instance, conclude that the likelihood of partner buyouts usually decreases with the degree of exogenous uncertainty. Environmental uncertainty therefore arises as a major determinant of the initiation and exercise decisions.

An additional line of research concerns performance issues in TG settings (e.g., Porrini, 2004; Zaheer et al., 2010). These studies show that acquiring options embedded in TG trajectories (Reuer & Tong, 2005) and exercising them (e.g., Porrini, 2004; Zaheer et al., 2010) can, under specific circumstances, create value. For instance, Zaheer et al. (2010), focusing on acquisitions by US firms in high-tech industries, report that acquisitions with prior alliances perform better than outright acquisitions when the target is international.

INCORPORATING INSIGHTS FROM
ECONOMIC GEOGRAPHY

TG across Place and Space

Overall, the existing literature on TG has provided relevant evidence on the conditions under which firms (i) initiate TG trajectories, (ii) move from alliances to acquisitions, and (iii) create value through these strategies. To the extent that this field of research has mainly developed within the realm of the strategy literature, TG scholars have tended to adopt an organizational perspective (Beugelsdijk et al., 2010). In this way, existing studies on TG have elaborated, for instance, the organization-level implications of allying with potential targets and of acquiring alliance partners. At the same time, however, TG scholars have tended to overlook the spatial and locational dimensions of the phenomenon.

This underdeveloped view of place and space issues is surprising given that, in practice, firms increasingly engage in alliances and acquisitions to access knowledge and technology from other countries or, at least, in distant locations (Reuer & Lahiri, 2014; Rosenkopf & Almeida, 2003). To illustrate these arguments, Fig. 2 presents a global map of the same alliance-to-acquisition transitions described above (i.e., acquisitions of alliance partners by US firms in the period 1990−2010 based on SDC

Platinum database). It is interesting to see that, of the 2,578 alliances that turned into acquisition, 66% were domestic. The average distance between these domestic partners is 2,307 kilometers (1,433 miles), which is approximately equivalent to the distance between Boston and Miami. The remaining 34% of alliances include international partners from 67 different countries. In these 876 cases, the average distance between partners is 8,865 kilometers (5,508 miles), which is approximately equal to the distance between London and San Francisco.

Overall, Fig. 2 shows that firms often have to deal with both space and place issues such as geographic distance and national borders when pursuing TG strategies. Therefore, we argue that TG scholars should also pay attention to place and space, issues that have been extensively developed in economic geography. In the following section, we introduce the basics premises of this discipline and suggest some ways in which it can complement our understanding of TG trajectories.

How Can Economic Geography Inform TG?

Economic geography deals not only with the location and distribution of economic activities across the world but is also concerned with the spatial organization of these activities. Without aiming to provide a deep reflection on the long-lasting discussion on the definition of place (cf. Agnew, 2011), the concept of place is central to our discussion of *a geography of TG*. We use a conceptualization in which place is the location where things, in our case the transition from an alliance to an acquisition, happen. Next, TG commonly implies that two actors that are usually located at different places are involved. Hence, spatial relations matter in the form of geographic and other forms of proximity between actors, which is the second key concept relevant to our discussion.

In our view, a geography of TG can mainly contribute to two important, currently understudied, perspectives. First, it highlights that place matters. Similar to perspectives that view the firm as a bundle of resources (Penrose, 1959), a place also provides a bundle of resources and opportunities for the firm (Gluckler, 2007). Like in the resource-based view of the firm with its strong emphasis to rare and therefore valuable, non-substitutable and difficult to imitate resources (Barney, 1991), the heterogeneity of space is full of localized resource profiles that provide (often unique) access to social capital, human capital, and institutional resources as well as tangible inputs. However, while it is common to highlight the heterogeneity in resources

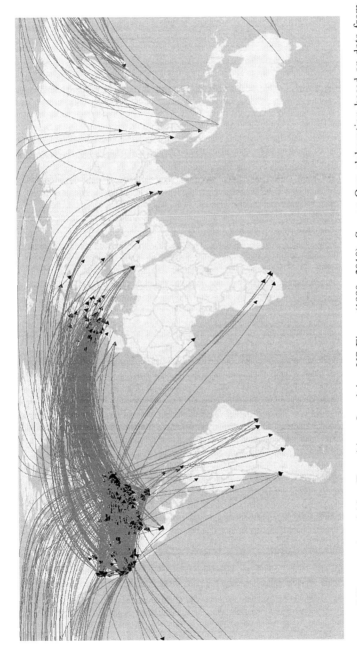

Fig. 2. Alliance-to-Acquisition Transitions Involving US Firms (1990–2010). *Source*: Own elaboration based on data from Thomson SDC Platinum database. *Notes*: The map has been performed using ArcGIS. The line between two points joins the two firms that participated in a strategic alliance. The arrow points in the direction of the target, suggesting the direction of the transition from an alliance to an acquisition.

and opportunities that different places offer, different places are also linked to varying degrees of uncertainty – for example, regarding the development of economic conditions. This is especially relevant for TG but the uncertainty of locations has not received much attention yet.

The second perspective provided by economic geography is that proximity regarding spatial relations influences economic processes and, of special relevance in this context, governance structure and changes thereof (cf. Boschma & Frenken, 2010). Heterogeneity in geographical proximity can imply differences in uncertainty since more distant partners, markets, and local conditions are less known. Such uncertainty can make TG trajectories more interesting options than outright acquisitions. At the same time, proximity can also facilitate the transfer of information and knowledge (Boschma, 2005) that can cause substantial heterogeneity in updating information. Therefore, distance is likely to play a role at various points in time throughout the TG trajectory. Below, we elaborate how place and space might influence the initiation and exercise decisions in the TG process.

Initiation Decision

TG trajectories are likely to be more interesting to firms relative to outright acquisition when (i) the primary location of business operations of the involved partners is geographically far away from each other, (ii) uncertainty in the local market of the potential target is high, and (iii) the location of the potential target offers relatively fewer alternatives of outright acquisition candidates. In all three situations, uncertainty is relatively high and therefore the willingness to initiate TG trajectories instead of engaging in outright acquisition is expected to be high as well (Estrada et al., 2010; Folta, 1998). However, the factors underlying such uncertainty are different. The second and third options highlight that different locations offer different opportunities and associated uncertainties (Gluckler, 2007). In contrast, in the first situation, uncertainty mainly originates from low availability of information commonly associated to large geographic distance (Reuer & Lahiri, 2014). In addition to enhanced uncertainty, both economic geographers and management scholars acknowledge the enhanced novelty value of more distant knowledge sources (cf. Boschma, 2005; Rosenkopf & Almeida, 2003). In this respect, more distant firms may be a particularly interesting choice. This combination of higher novelty value of more distant opportunities with greater uncertainty of these distant places makes TG trajectories a particularly valuable strategy compared to outright acquisition.

Exercise Decision

Unlike the initiation decision, the transition itself — that is, going from an alliance to an acquisition—might be less likely when the primary location of business operations of the involved partners is geographically far away from each other. Obtaining additional critical information — which is needed to decide whether to exercise the option or abandon it (Bowman & Hurry, 1993) — is more difficult when physical distance is large and the information to be transmitted is subject to noise, which reduces the value of the information. Literature in economic geography has extensively emphasized the beneficial role of geographical proximity for knowledge transfer in space. Most empirical contributions focus on the geography of innovation activities and spatial knowledge spillovers (e.g., Acs, Audretsch, & Feldman, 1992; Adams & Jaffe, 2002; Feldman, 1994; Jaffe, 1989). Similarly, management scholars highlight that geographical proximity facilitates interorganizational understanding and implies less uncertainty (Knoben & Oerlemans, 2006). Economic geographers commonly assume that tacit knowledge (Polanyi, 1966) is particularly difficult to transfer across larger geographical distances. Therefore, the likelihood of transition from an alliance to an acquisition would be more strongly influenced by geographical proximity if the knowledge required to make the exercise decision is tacit. When geographic distance is large, it might be more difficult to collect information about a potential target than about local markets and economic conditions, because the former is usually less codifiable and difficult to transfer across space (Reuer & Lahiri, 2014). Therefore, the type of information that needs to be transferred to reduce uncertainty can strongly influence how geographic proximity impacts the exercise decision. For example, uncertainty about local markets may be more easily mitigated even when distance is large, compared to uncertainty about the target itself.[3]

CONCLUSION AND RESEARCH AGENDA

As a final reflection, we present some ideas for future research incorporating insights from economic geography to further develop the field of TG.

Geography-Related Uncertainty

Existing studies on TG have traditionally focused on technological uncertainty — normally measured at the industry level (e.g., Estrada et al.,

2010; Folta, 1998) — as the main exogenous type of uncertainty relevant to TG decisions. Economic geography, however, suggests the importance of *geography-related uncertainty*. Heterogeneity in uncertainty associated to different locations and spatial relations may impact the initiation and exercise decisions. In order to expand our understanding of the phenomenon, future studies should account for both types of exogenous uncertainty in the TG setting. Furthermore, some TG scholars stress the social side of uncertainty in TG, acknowledging that part of the uncertainty is relational or endogenous to the interfirm transaction (McCarter et al., 2011). Therefore, future TG studies should explore the interconnections between the three types of uncertainty (i.e., technological, geography-related, and relational) and their implications for TG decisions and performance. For example, it could be explored how geography-related uncertainty shapes relational uncertainty, or whether a crowding out effect exists when decision-makers face high uncertainty at different levels.

Geographic Distance versus Border Crossing

Economic geography highlights that place and space represent interconnected but different concepts, which can have different implications on firm's economic activity (Agnew, 2011; Beugelsdijk & Mudambi, 2013). Place and space issues have not received much explicit attention in TG settings and, in any case, the distinction between them remains blurry. Economic geographers, however, suggest that studies on MNEs should examine both within-country and between-country distance, because "border and distance effects are not the same" (Beugelsdijk & Mudambi, 2013, p. 416). In a similar vein, Boschma (2005) makes a distinction between geographic proximity and other four types of proximity between economic actors (e.g., institutional, organizational, cognitive, and social proximity). According to this view, geographic or physical distance triggers operational problems (e.g., face-to-face interaction is difficult), whereas border crossing reduces institutional proximity (e.g., cultural norms are different). Extending these insights into our setting, we suggest that future studies should make an explicit distinction between geographic distance and border issues in TG settings, and account for their distinct effects, both theoretically and methodologically. For instance, a promising line for future research is to examine performance differences between acquisitions preceded by alliances affected by geographic distance in domestic and cross-border contexts.

The Multilocation Nature of TG Actors

Building on the premises of economic geography that place and space matter in global economic activities, scholars have started emphasizing the multilocation nature of MNEs (cf. Beugelsdijk & Mudambi, 2013). Economic geography suggests that, due to differences in location, different units within MNEs are likely to face different opportunities and challenges. In order to explain MNE strategic behavior, therefore, the identification of these locational differences matter. Given the importance of MNEs as global economic actors, TG scholars should also acknowledge that TG trajectories often involve decision-making in multilocation entities. For example, given the locational differences between headquarters and subsidiaries, it could be relevant to make a distinction between them and identify the role of each in the TG trajectory. The extant TG literature assumes that the parents firms are the major actors in the initiation and exercise decision; we argue that this is only one piece of the puzzle. For the sake of illustration, Fig. 3 shows different types of alliance-to-acquisition transitions, focusing on US acquirers and North American targets (e.g., including Canada and Mexico): (i) transitions in which a parent firm acquired another parent firm, (ii) transitions in which a parent firm acquired a subsidiary firm (or vice versa), and (iii) transitions in which one subsidiary acquired another subsidiary. Overall, Fig. 3 shows that, in practice, both headquarters and subsidiaries are involved in TG decisions. In order to explain TG decisions and performance, therefore, it could be relevant to account for their locational differences (and for other aspects reflecting the multi-locational nature of TG actors).

CONCLUSION

In this chapter, we have taken a first step toward connecting the field of TG, which has traditionally focused on organization aspects, and the discipline of economic geography, which stresses place and space as key determinants of the global economy. Space and place can play a crucial role in the TG process, influencing both the initiation and exercise decisions and their performance implications. Therefore, we hope that our work motivates TG scholars to incorporate insights from economic geography and explicitly connect *organization*, *place* and *space* in TG settings.

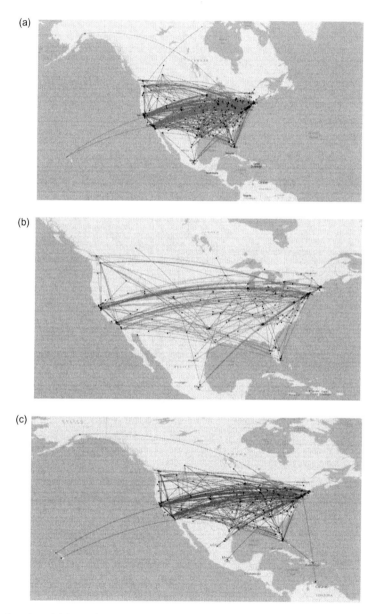

Fig. 3. Acquisitions by US Firms of Alliance Partners in North America (1990–2010). (a) Parent-to-Parent Transitions. (b) Parent-to-Subsidiary/Subsidiary-to-Parent Transitions. (c) Subsidiary-to-Subsidiary Transitions. *Source*: Own elaboration based on data from Thomson SDC Platinum database. *Note*: The maps have been performed using ArcGIS.

NOTES

1. While acquisitions offer the advantages of hierarchical control (Folta, 1998), alliances are more attractive than acquisitions in two main scenarios (cf. Vanhaverbeke et al., 2002). First, in order to evaluate a potential target, the acquirer often has to rely on proprietary information provided by the target itself, which can behave opportunistically, due to information asymmetries, and offer inaccurate information. In the presence of such adverse selection risk, alliances are preferred to acquisitions, since alliances entail lower degree of commitment. Furthermore, due to assets specificity, a common problem in acquisitions is that of 'indigestibility' (Hennart & Reddy, 1997): acquisitions entail buying undesired resources that the target possess and that are inexorably linked to the desired resources that motivated the transaction in the first place. In these circumstances, acquisitions become less attractive than alliances, which may be designed to focus only to the desired resources.

2. For a critical assessment of this and other assumptions of the TG literature, see Faems and Madhok (2009).

3. Geography is likely to matter also once the exercise decision has been made and the partner is acquired − an aspect that is not discussed in more detail here. For example, the success of the post-acquisition integration process is likely to be dependent on space. Some studies suggest that a proximate partner can be more easily integrated (e.g., Knoben & Oerlemans, 2006; Larsson & Finkelstein, 1999). Similarly, firms are likely to make assumptions about the potential integration costs and difficulties to obtain information before the initiation and exercise decision. These expectations (influenced by geography) are likely to influence firm behavior as well.

ACKNOWLEDGMENT

The authors thank Klaske Hollema for her assistance with the literature review.

REFERENCES

Acs, Z. J., Audretsch, D. B., & Feldman, M. P. (1992). Real effects of academic research: Comment. *The American Economic Review, 82*(1), 363–367.

Adams, J. D., & Jaffe, A. B. (2002). Bounding the effects of R&D: An investigation using matched firm and establishment data. *Rand Journal of Economics, 27*, 700–721.

Agnew, J. (2011). Space and place. In J. Agnew & D. Livingstone (Eds.), *The Sage handbook of geographical knowledge* (pp. 316–331). London: Sage.

Barney, J. (1991). Firm resources and sustained competitive advantage. *Journal of Management, 17*(1), 99–120.

Beugelsdijk, S., McCann, P., & Mudambi, R. (2010). Introduction: Place, space and organization – Economic geography and the multinational enterprise. *Journal of Economic Geography, 10*(4), 485–493.

Beugelsdijk, S., & Mudambi, R. (2013). MNEs as border-crossing multi-location enterprises: The role of discontinuities in geographic space. *Journal of International Business Studies, 44*(5), 413–426.

Boschma, R. (2005). Proximity and innovation: A critical assessment. *Regional Studies, 39*(1), 61–74.

Boschma, R. A., & Frenken, K. (2010). The spatial evolution of innovation networks. A proximity perspective. In R. A. Boschma & R. Martin (Eds.), *Handbook on evolutionary economic geography* (pp. 120–135). Cheltenham: Edward Elgar.

Boschma, R., Makino, S., Qian, G., Ma, X., Li, L., & Mudambi, R. (2014). Zoom in, Zoom out, and Beyond: Locational boundaries in international business. Call for Papers, Special Issue. *Journal of International Business Studies.*

Bowman, E. H., & Hurry, D. (1993). Strategy through the option lens: An integrated view of resource investments and the incremental-choice process. *Academy of management review, 18*(4), 760–782.

Doz, Y. L. (1996). The evolution of cooperation in strategic alliances: Initial conditions or learning processes? *Strategic Management Journal, 17*(S1), 55–83.

Estrada, I., de la Fuente, G., & Martín-Cruz, N. (2010). Technological joint venture formation under the real options approach. *Research Policy, 39*(9), 1185–1197.

Faems, D., & Madhok, A. (2009). Transitional governance: A critical review of implicit process assumptions. In S. Finkelstein & C. Cooper (Ed.), *Advances in mergers and acquisitions* (pp. 61–78). New York, NY: JAI Press.

Feldman, M. P. (1994). *The geography of innovation.* Boston, MA: Kluwer Academic Publishers.

Folta, T. B. (1998). Governance and uncertainty: The tradeoff between administrative control and commitment. *Strategic Management Journal, 19*(11), 1007–1028.

Folta, T. B., & Miller, K. D. (2002). Real options in equity partnerships. *Strategic Management Journal, 23*(1), 77–88.

Gluckler, J. (2007). Economic geography and the evolution of networks. *Journal of Economic Geography, 7*, 619–634.

Hagedoorn, J., & Sadowski, B. (1999). The transition from strategic technology alliances to mergers and acquisitions: An exploratory study. *Journal of Management Studies, 36*(1), 87–107.

Hennart, J. F., & Reddy, S. (1997). The choice between mergers/acquisitions and joint ventures: The case of Japanese investors in the United States. *Strategic Management Journal, 18*(1), 1–12.

Jaffe, A. B. (1989). Real effects of academic research. *The American Economic Review,* 957–970.

Knoben, J., & Oerlemans, L. A. (2006). Proximity and inter-organizational collaboration: A literature review. *International Journal of Management Reviews, 8*(2), 71–89.

Kogut, B. (1991). Joint ventures and the option to expand and acquire. *Management Science, 37*(1), 19–33.

Larsson, R., & Finkelstein, S. (1999). Integrating strategic, organizational, and human resource perspectives on mergers and acquisitions: A case survey of synergy realization. *Organization Science, 10*(1), 1–26.

Li, Y., James, B., Madhavan, R., & Mahoney, J. T. (2007). Real options: Taking stock and looking ahead. *Advances in Strategic Management, 24*(1), 31–66.

McCarter, M. W., Mahoney, J. T., & Northcraft, G. B. (2011). Testing the waters: Using collective real options to manage the social dilemma of strategic alliances. *Academy of Management Review, 36*(4), 621–640.

Penrose, E. T. (1959). *The theory of the growth of the firm.* Oxford: Blackwell.

Polanyi, M. (1966). The logic of tacit inference. *Philosophy, 41*(155), 1–18.

Porrini, P. (2004). Can a previous alliance between an acquirer and a target affect acquisition performance? *Journal of Management, 30*(4), 545–562.

Reuer, J. J., & Lahiri, N. (2014). Searching for alliance partners: Effects of geographic distance on the formation of R&D collaborations. *Organization Science, 25*(1), 283–298.

Reuer, J. J., & Tong, T. W. (2005). Real options in international joint ventures. *Journal of Management, 31*(3), 403–423.

Rosenkopf, L., & Almcida, P. (2003). Overcoming local search through alliances and mobility. *Management Science, 49*(6), 751–766.

Tong, T. W., & Reuer, J. J. (2007). Real options in strategic management. *Advances in Strategic Management, 24*(1), 3–28.

Trigeorgis, L. (1996). *Real options: Managerial flexibility and strategy in resource allocation.* Cambridge, MA: MIT press.

Vanhaverbeke, W., Duysters, G., & Noorderhaven, N. (2002). External technology sourcing through alliances or acquisitions: An analysis of the application-specific integrated circuits industry. *Organization Science, 13*(6), 714–733.

Williamson, O. E. (1991). Comparative economic organization: The analysis of discrete structural alternatives. *Administrative Science Quarterly, 36*, 269–296.

Yang, H., Lin, Z. J., & Peng, M. W. (2011). Behind acquisitions of alliance partners: Exploratory learning and network embeddedness. *Academy of Management Journal, 54*(5), 1069–1080.

Zaheer, A., Hernandez, E., & Banerjee, S. (2010). Prior alliances with targets and acquisition performance in knowledge-intensive industries. *Organization Science, 21*(5), 1072–1091.

Zollo, M., & Singh, H. (2004). Deliberate learning in corporate acquisitions: Post-acquisition strategies and integration capability in US bank mergers. *Strategic Management Journal, 25*(13), 1233–1256.

ARE MERGERS AND ACQUISITIONS SOCIALLY RESPONSIBLE? EVIDENCE FROM THE BANKING INDUSTRY

Olimpia Meglio

ABSTRACT

Acquisitions have generally been portrayed as a means to improving shareholders' wealth. To date, the debate regarding how to measure acquisition performance has generally discarded the idea that performance should reflect the interests of stakeholders other than shareholders. In this chapter, I advance the importance of enlarging the domain of acquisition performance to include stakeholders other than shareholders. Drawing on literature streams related to corporate social performance and stakeholder theory and providing empirical data from an Italian merger in the banking industry, I demonstrate how the failure to consider neglected − but relevant − stakes put at risk by acquisitions, such as those of employees and consumers, produces measures of acquisition performance that do not do justice to the multiplicity of outcomes that these deals generally cause.

Keywords: Mergers and acquisitions; M&As; acquisition performance measurement; multidimensionality of acquisition performance; corporate social performance; acquisition stakeholders

Advances in Mergers and Acquisitions, Volume 15, 95–113
ISSN: 1479-361X/doi:10.1108/S1479-361X20160000015006

INTRODUCTION

Mergers and acquisitions (heretofore also acquisitions or M&As) have generally been portrayed as an effective strategy for value creation (Haspeslagh & Jemison, 1991). In the academic and practitioner discourse about M&As, acquisition performance and value creation are often intertwined. Shareholder value is observed in the majority of the empirical articles that measure acquisition performance and is generally operationalized as the market's reaction to the announcement of the deal (Capron, 1999). The widespread use of this measurement seems to indicate that acquisitions represent the field in which the acquiring and target companies' shareholders compete for the maximum return (Meglio, 2015).

While this portrait is still dominant, there is a growing awareness among scholars and practitioners that acquisitions are influenced by network of the merging companies' internal and external stakeholders. This perspective is central to the field of business and society and was recently advanced by Nordic management scholars advocating for the adoption of a stakeholders' lens in the analysis of acquisitions (Anderson, Havila, & Nilsson, 2013). In this work, I embrace this position and discuss how the consideration of stakes and stakeholders contributes to a better understanding of the mechanisms through which acquisitions produce the variety of financial and nonfinancial outcomes that they do. This investigation is also in line with the idea that financial performance measures too narrowly account for what companies produce. In other words, this chapter intends to apply the current discourse on corporate social responsibility and corporate social performance to the realm of mergers and acquisitions. Therefore, the goal of this chapter is to analyze ways in which the idea that companies are responsible toward their stakeholders can inform current measures of acquisition performance. I achieve this goal by grounding my analysis in the literatures of different research streams: acquisition performance, stakeholder analysis and corporate social performance. As an illustrative example, I also provide the analysis of a deal involving two Italian banks, focusing on the deal's effects on employees and business consumers with the aim of comparing the intended goals with the produced outcomes. The choice to focus on these stakeholders is in line with Cording, Harrison, Hoskisson, and Jonsen (2014) who recently outlined how the stakes of consumers and employees, although different, are intertwined and mutually influential.

This chapter intends to contribute to the research on both acquisition performance and corporate social performance. The chapter adds to acquisition research by viewing the multidimensionality of acquisition performance through the stakeholder's lens. To this end, the chapter outlines the importance of enlarging the domain of acquisition performance measurements. Also, the chapter contributes to corporate social performance research by addressing social issues in an acquisition context. From a managerial standpoint, this chapter first highlights that acquisition performance is the result of different and often conflicting stakes put at risk by the acquisition and second indicates that executives must achieve a balance among these pressures.

The remainder of this chapter is organized as follows: in the next section, I describe the current understanding of acquisition performance measurement and advocate for incorporating social issues in the acquisition performance measurement; next, I analyze acquisitions from a stakeholder perspective in an attempt to investigate the impact of acquisitions on both acquiring and target companies' stakeholders; and finally, I present and discuss evidence from an Italian merger involving two domestic banks. Implications for research and practice are illustrated in the concluding section.

FROM CORPORATE FINANCIAL PERFORMANCE TO CORPORATE SOCIAL PERFORMANCE IN M&AS

The conventional discourse on acquisitions is primarily concerned with understanding how they perform and what makes them succeed. This interest has produced a vast number of studies measuring acquisition performance (e.g., Capron, 1999; Cording, Christman, & King, 2008; Fowler & Schmidt, 1988) and meta-analyses that attempt to synthesize existing results (Datta, Pinches, & Narayan, 1992; King, Dalton, Daily, & Covin, 2004).

A review of the articles measuring acquisition performance reveals the multiplicity of meanings attached to the acquisition performance construct, which, in turn, leads to the multitude of measurement methods, variables and indicators found in the existing literature all labeled as acquisition performance (Meglio, 2009; Meglio & Risberg, 2011; Zollo & Meier, 2008). The majority of the 101 articles reviewed by Meglio and Risberg (2011) measure acquisition performance as financial performance: that is, as the market reaction to the announcement of the deal. Cumulative abnormal returns (CAR) is the most frequently used indicator for acquisition performance. Accounting-based performance indicators generally measure acquisition performance as growth and are less frequently used. Where I to identify the stakeholders behind these measures, following Meglio and Risberg (2011), I would conclude that the shareholders have primacy over all other stakeholders because shareholder value is a common measure of performance (e.g., Capron, 1999). Growth reflects the interest of the top management, whose pay is generally linked to this same indicator. Similar considerations apply to nonfinancial measures for acquisition performance, such as success or survival. These measures also reflect the interests of the top management, although indirectly. Survival may also reflect employees' interests because it implies their ability to retain their jobs.

The preceding considerations indicate that market or accounting measures for acquisition performance tend to privilege the perspectives and the interests of the shareholders and top management. However, acquisitions typically produce a multiplicity of outcomes over the entire network of internal or external stakeholders of the merging companies. If we focus exclusively on the stakes of shareholders or top management when measuring performance, we risk overlooking other stakes (such as those of consumers or employees) that are likely to affect the integration process and, therefore, acquisition outcomes. By way of example, an acquisition is frequently pursued with the aim of "acquiring" the target company's consumers. Consumer retention is essential to achieving this goal, but acquisitions can traumatize the relationship between the target company and its consumers who might continue or terminate their relationship with the new company after the deal. These alternatives are not neutral across acquisition outcomes. The lack of consideration for consumers' stakes could harm the integration process and eventually weaken performance. Identifying different stakes in acquisitions is therefore conducive to a better understanding of the mechanisms that produce acquisition outcomes.

Prior research into the discourse and framing techniques used by the media and executives helps us explain how mergers and acquisitions are perceived by various stakeholder groups (Risberg, Tienari, & Vaara, 2003; Vaara, Risberg, Søderberg, & Tienari, 2003; Vaara & Tienari, 2002) and identify how they might react to an acquisition. Newspapers often report expectations and behaviors of active stakeholders and their influences over different phases of an acquisition process (Ciambotti, Aureli, & Demartini, 2011). Media texts indicate some stakeholders (i.e., shareholders, employees and trade unions) and consumers play prominent roles. Shareholders and employees have generally received a great deal of attention regarding the effect of consumers' issues on performance, whereas scant research exists that prioritizes business-to-business consumers over end consumers (cf. Öberg, 2013).

With the exception of Nordic scholars, the academic literature generally treats employees and consumers as means to the pursuit of acquisition goals. Therefore, the consideration of these groups as stakeholders influenced by and influential to acquisition outcomes is a recent addition to existing literature (Anderson et al., 2013). Along with Nordic scholars, I argue for the consideration of the multiplicity of stakes in an acquisition to overcome the narrow view that acquisitions should only serve shareholder's interests – an interest that is satisfied by increasing shareholder value. Enlarging the domain of acquisition performance to consider multiple stakes represents a shift from corporate financial performance to corporate social performance that involves considering more than just financial outcomes throughout the stakeholder network (Borglund, 2013). These notions overcome the limitations suffered by current measures of acquisition performance and help illuminate the mechanisms that produce acquisition outcomes.

THEORETICAL BACKGROUND

Corporate Social Responsibility

The concept of corporate social responsibility (CSR) has steadily evolved since it was first introduced a century ago. According to Lee (2008), the first instance of a CSR attitude dates back to Henry Ford's conception of business as a service in 1917. In that era, the idea was received with suspicion, while today CSR has gained recognition and prominence in management practice, education and research. For example, CSR is a pillar of the European Commission's initiatives that aim to disseminate the idea as the responsibility of enterprises for their impacts on society. The Commission encourages enterprises to work in close collaboration with their stakeholders to integrate social, environmental, ethical, human rights and consumer concerns into their business operations and core strategy (European Commission, 2011). From this definition emerges the idea that companies are responsible toward their stakeholders for a range of outcomes beyond purely economic and financial results. CSR and stakeholders are therefore strictly intertwined.

Despite the popularity of CSR in the management discourse, it remains a contested concept (Okoye, 2009), especially due to the difficulties of identifying: (a) what corporate responsibility means, (b) to whom companies should be responsible, and (c) how this responsibility should be operationalized. In his reconstruction of its theoretical underpinnings, Lee (2008) observes that from 1970s onward, there has been a process of progressive rationalization that has moved the concept from the orientation of an ethical obligation to a managerial tool tightly coupled with financial returns. Baden and Harwood (2013) describe the debate about CSR as polarized around the positions of Friedman (1962), who conceived CSR as an unnecessary burden on shareholders that imposes unfair costs on companies, and Freeman (1984), who drew attention to companies' responsibilities toward all stakeholders. Wallich and McGowan (1970) offer an important contribution to the idea that companies are socially responsible, outlining that while it is agreeable that shareholders maximize the value of their shares, modern corporate equity holding patterns have evolved into diversified portfolios of shares to spread the risk. Owners of a diversified portfolio would want to achieve social optimization through joint profit maximization and social expenditures. This idea is consistent with the concept of corporate social performance, which first emerged at the end of the 1970s (Carroll, 1979).

Corporate Social Performance

According to Wood (2010), the intellectual roots of CSP (corporate social performance) scholarship are found in the general systems theory that gained consensus in the 1950s (Boulding, 1956). Seeing corporations as open systems embedded within a larger environment led scholars to question the meaning of such responsibility and its implications on the companies' lives. Carroll (1979) first attempted to offer a conceptual model for CSP, outlining the difficulties of measuring responsibility and introducing the concept of CSP because it was easier to operationalize. Carroll further identified four domains for CSR: economic, legal, ethical, and discretionary responsibilities. Carroll's model was the starting point for further refinements, such as Wood (1991) who revises Carroll's (1979) model to add dynamism. Wood's primary contribution is the identification of principles that guide managerial choices and processes of social responsiveness that produce outcomes and impact performance.

Wood's (1991) depiction of CSP "views the business organization ('corporate') as the locus of actions that have consequences for stakeholders and society as well as for itself ('social performance')... Corporate social performance ... is a set of descriptive categorizations of business activity, focusing on its impacts and outcomes for society, stakeholders and the firm. Types of outcomes are determined by linkages, both general and specific, defined by the structural principles of CSR" (Wood, 2010, p. 54). In her model, Wood (1991) identifies a relationship between processes and outcomes and conceives of social performance as encompassing financial performance. Financial performance, Wood postulates, is one dimension of an overall measure for performance, not a competing type of performance. This position contrasts the dichotomous view of CSP as something that a firm should do in addition to achieving its economic goals.

Because such opposing views exist, a huge number of empirical analyses have investigated the relationship between CSP and CFP (e.g., Cochran & Wood, 1985; Griffin & Mahon, 1997; Margolis & Walsh, 2001; Orlitsky, Schmidt, & Rynes, 2003; Scherer & Palazzo, 2007). The results of these studies, taken together, indicate that the relationship should be recognized as complex, ambiguous and nuanced, rendering generalizations difficult and often useless. Reviews also outline a lack of understanding of the direction of causality between a firm's financial performance and its social behavior: that is, whether CSP is an independent or a dependent variable in the CSP-CFP relationship (Callan & Thomas, 2009). Additional drawbacks arise from the use of different methods to measure social and financial performance, incomparability among different periods, problems in sampling procedures, and the importance of testing new mediating or moderating variables.

Although these issues indicate that the measurement process deserves careful attention and that more research is needed, I contend that a more thorough investigation of the drivers of CSP is also essential to improving the measurement process. Awareness of the drivers of CSP performance is closely linked to the identification of the domains and dimensions of CSP; therefore, it is essential for improving the measurement process. To this end, I adopt a stakeholder perspective, which is, in my view, the most suitable perspective for achieving a better grasp of the performance outcomes of CSR. As Perrini, Russo, Tencati, and Vurro (2011) outlines, a stakeholder-theory perspective allows us to understand how CSR influences and shapes financial performance.

Stakeholder Theory

From Freeman (1984) onward, stakeholder theory has gained consensus among scholars. According to Freeman (1984, p. 46), "a stakeholder in an organization is (by definition) any group or individual who can affect or is affected by the achievement of the organization's objectives." Stakeholder theory describes companies as constellations of cooperative and competitive interests with intrinsic value (Donaldson & Preston, 1995). The notion of stake is central to a stakeholder approach and refers to claimants and influencers. Mitchell, Agle, and Wood (1997, p. 859) contend that claimants "have a legal, moral or presumed claim on the firm," whereas influencers "have an ability to influence the firm's behavior, direction, process, or outcomes." These definitions reveal that the distinction is subtle, helping us understand why the concept of a stakeholder remains vague and ambiguous. A narrower definition is based on the idea that resources (time and attention, in particular) are scarce and that managers are required to focus their efforts on managing relationships with those who bring resources to the company. Proponents of this view include Clarkson (1995), who defines a stakeholder as one who bears a degree of risk as a result of investing capital into a company.

Many stakeholders play a role in the acquisition process from investment banks to advisors and from employees to customers. All of these actors, whether individuals or coalitions, have legitimate and powerful claims or stakes. The stakeholders are affected by the deal and, in turn, they affect acquisition performance. In some cases, the stakeholders' influence is based on a contract that links an individual or a company to the acquiring or merging company. This is the case with employees, suppliers, or business-to-business customers. However, a superior − often collective − interest to protect may legitimize power and influence, as in the case of a government's input into whether a deal will take place.

In this chapter, I adopt a narrow definition of stakeholders, yet I recognize that as detailed below, stakeholders may actually influence these deals in particular circumstances. In an acquisition context, adopting a stakeholder lens allows us to conceptualize these deals as radically influencing the network of the relationships between the internal and external stakeholders of acquiring and target firms. (Halinen, Salmi, & Havila, 1999). With these considerations in mind, I now move onto the analysis of acquisitions as multistakeholder deals.

ACQUISITIONS AS MULTISTAKEHOLDER DEALS

The impact of acquisitions on stakeholders is an important yet under-researched issue (Waddock & Graves, 2006). This subject relates to the examination of the effects of these deals on the society at large. The debate is polarized between the position of those who give prominence to the costs of acquisitions, especially in terms of layoffs, and those who focus attention of the benefits of acquisitions in terms of increased efficiency and competitiveness. Within the first group, some ethicists highlight hostile takeovers because they externalize some costs to noninvestor stakeholders and thereby reduce the level of innovative stakeholder practices (e.g., laid-off employees, reduced donations to local communities, or lost customers resulting from service impairment) (e.g., Chase, Burns, & Claypool, 1997). In contrast, proponents of acquisitions claim that they benefit society and stakeholders because they create more efficient markets and improve managerial performance (Chase et al., 1997).

Because stakeholders both affect and are affected by company practices, proponents of instrumental stakeholder theory believe companies develop good stakeholder-related practices because it is in their best interests from a bottom-line perspective (e.g., Donaldson & Preston, 1995; Jones, 1995). Others believe that such practices present a means of developing sound long-term relationships with stakeholder groups that are integrally based on normative or ethical considerations (Freeman, 1999).

Both views emphasize that an acquisition can be analyzed as a multistakeholder deal, with the number of stakeholders magnified over the course of the acquisition process, for the simple reason that two companies are involved (Anderson et al., 2013). The acquiring and target companies' stakeholders are almost never holding equal positions, and they often have divergent stakes. It is also important to recognize that all stakes are neither alike nor constant. For instance, during the pre-merger phase, top management and company owners play a critical role, whereas the remaining stakeholders are relatively inactive. A deal announcement expands the number of stakeholders. Some stakes are instantaneous, as in the case of investment banks interested in earning a transaction fee. Other stakes change over time. This means that some stakeholders may have different goals and can exert either more or less influence over time.

In the case of acquisitions, several contextual factors affect the influence stakeholders actually exert on acquisition performance, such as the nature of the deal (friendly vs. hostile) or the degree of relatedness between the merging parties or industries. In the case of a friendly acquisition, we expect employees to show a positive attitude toward the deal, which should produce shorter integration times and lower costs. In the case of hostile takeovers, we expect employees to exhibit negative reactions like sabotage or increased absenteeism. If the deal involves knowledge-intensive firms, scientists play a more important role than other employees because innovative performance is heavily dependent upon them (Ranft & Lord, 2000).

In related deals, especially in mature industries, acquisitions generally imply headcounts to eliminate duplication and redundancies that, in turn, negatively affect productivity.

These considerations not only reveal that stakeholders other than shareholders have interests that cannot be accounted for by shareholder value but also that their efforts to protect stakes put at risk by an acquisition can actually influence financial performance. I therefore suggest the importance of enlarging the domain of acquisition performance measurement to include nonfinancial acquisition outcomes. In doing so, I also unravel the linkages between different stakes and possible virtuous or vicious chains of effect following a merger or an acquisition (see Table 1).

In this table, I focus on shareholders, top management, employees and business consumers as primary stakeholders. Reading the table horizontally, I identify for each stakeholder the stake(s) that an acquisition likely puts at risk or provides opportunities for further development. Specifically, shareholders and top managers consider acquisitions a means to protect their respective stakes, namely shareholder value and prestige and pay. These stakes depend heavily on the other stakes included in the table. Employees and business customers may look at the deal with both positive and negative expectations, which in turn may become positive or negative behaviors during the integration process. Despite claims often made by triumphalist press releases, acquisitions bring a great uncertainty that influences the internal organizational climate and business relationships with consumers. Internally, the causes of this turmoil are found in employees' fear of losing their jobs or their colleagues and the disruption of work routines. These circumstances negatively affect the productivity by causing many, often talented, employees to leave the company soon after the announcement of the deal. Moreover, those who stay may waste time by inquiring about their work future instead of performing their daily assignments. The disruption of social ties within the target company also has implications on relationships with business and end consumers.

The merger wave within the banking industry provides an illustrative example. Many mergers have been pursued with the aim of gaining synergies from the rationalization of local branches, resulting in thousands of layoffs across the globe. In many cases, this means that consumers suddenly encounter different front line service providers at their local bank branches. Given the nature of the service, this may be traumatic or painful for many consumers. In the case of services in which front office employees mediate the relationship between the consumers and the company, it is easy to understand the trade-offs between these stakes and the performance of

Table 1. Stakeholders in M&As, Stakes, Influences on Performance, and Acquisition Outcomes.

Stakeholder	Stakes	Positive Influence on Acquisition Performance	Negative Influence on Acquisition Performance	Acquisition Outcome Metric
Shareholders	Shareholder value	Focus on performance metrics other than market performance	Excessive focus or market performance	CAR/CAAR
Top management	Prestige, pay and career prospects	Achieve synergies	Self-interest choices (Financial health and survival)	Growth, survival
Customers	Business relationship	Continue business relationship, allowing for revenue-synergies	Terminate contract	Product/service offering; Better service conditions
Employees	Retaining job; Career prospects; Pay increase; Training/learning	Commitment to the achievement of synergies	Sabotage, lower productivity	Well-being; Career advancement; Pay increase; Placement service

an acquisition. Consumers may decide to terminate their business relationship with the new entity, negatively impacting the bottom line. It is therefore possible to claim that corporate financial performance and corporate
social performance are not separate tracks, but rather intertwined and
mutually influential toward the achievement of acquisition goals.

Enlarging the measurement of acquisition performance to account for
the multiplicity of outcomes is therefore essential to identify the drivers of
financial performance in acquisitions. It is essential to recognize that
employees or customers hold stakes in acquisitions to understand how they
may actually react to protect their stakes. These reactions have financial
consequences, and may cause a longer integration processes, a decrease in
productivity, or an increase in turnover of talented people in the target
company. Any of these reactions implies lower financial performance,
regardless of the indicator we use.

With these considerations in mind, I move onto the analysis of a deal
involving two Italian banks with a particular focus on two stakeholders —
employees and business consumers — and discuss how acquisition performance measures can explain their stakes in the deal.

THE INTESA-SANPAOLO EXPERIENCE

In this section, I describe the impact of a baking industry merger on two
primary stakeholders. Consistent with the aim and scope of the chapter,
the analysis focuses on the stakes of employees and business consumers,
how they are approached, and in what manner they are realized during the
integration process.

The merger analyzed occurred in 2006 between Banca Intesa and
San Paolo-Banco di Napoli, two Italian commercial banks with established
market shares in the North and the South of Italy, respectively. The merger
took place at the end of a consolidation process that involved the global
banking industry from the 1980s. The entire industry was under pressure
for different reasons: deregulation, increasing harmonization among financial industries within the Eurozone, and increasing fixed costs due to the
adoption of information and communication technologies. All of these factors are primary drivers of the consolidation process in the banking industry. Italian banks were involved in several merger processes with domestic
and international partners: the BNL-BNP Paribas deal is just one example
of a cross-border deal in the Italian banking sector. Italian banks,

especially those operating on a regional scale, were therefore forced to merge to survive. This condition is the context in which the Intesa-San Paolo merger took place.

Given the amount of time elapsed and the associated influence of memory decay and ex post rationalization, interviews were not a meaningful means of gathering of primary data. Thus, the experience of Intesa-Sanpaolo is reported based on secondary data. I specifically analyzed strategic plans (2007−2009) that described the merger process and company balance sheets (Intesa-SanPaolo, 2006, 2007a, 2007b, 2007c, 2007d, 2007e, 2009, 2010). The aim of the analysis was to discern how the merger goals reflected the stakes of employees and business consumers. Moreover, I looked into the outcomes produced by the merger itself over the three years following the merger announcement (from 2007 to 2009). Three years is the most common time interval the M&A field, as scholars generally measure acquisition performance within this time frame (cf. King et al., 2004). As specified above, the intent is to provide an illustrative example of how acquisition outcomes are influenced by a consideration of employees and business consumers as stakeholders.

In the first strategic plan, employees' and consumers' stakes are acknowledged and tightly coupled with the new company's goals soon after the announcement of the deal. These goals are categorized into four areas, representing three primary stakeholders and one collective and superior interest: shareholders, customers, employees, and the environment and society at large (see Table 2).

Table 2. Merger's Goals and Stakeholders.

Stakeholder	Goals
Shareholders	Payout 60%
	EPS 15% per year
	New governance model
Customers	Reducing prices
	Increasing service orientation
	Improving service offering, in terms of quality and price
Employees	Human resource development
	Team building
	Career opportunity
Societal issues	Support to business community
	Sustainable development
	Promoting research and development through collaboration with University and Research centers

Source: Author's elaboration from company 2006 strategic plan.

The table demonstrates the multiplicity of goals connected to stake-holders other than shareholders. Not only did the merger intend to satisfy shareholders' aim of increased value, but it also aimed to improve conditions for employees (both in terms of pay and career advancement opportunities) and for customers (by improving service conditions and rethinking the service offering and price range). Moreover, the merger also seemed to consider societal concerns such as the development of local communities by supporting sustainable investments and research.

The declaration of the merger's motives and goals found in the 2006 strategic plan indicates that the new bank positions itself at the center of a plurality of financial and nonfinancial interests. The bank is depicted as a place where employees develop their skills and competences, where team-work is praised, and where consumers find a solution for their specific needs and receive better service conditions at lower prices. Moreover, the bank recognizes external secondary stakeholders in local communities and their intention to support them in their sustainable development programs.

The new bank expected the integration process to last two-and-a-half years, and the task force in charge of integrating the two banks to complete its assignments by the end of 2008, it is meaningful to track merger out-comes within the same time interval with regard to the stakeholders under investigation (employees and business consumers). The picture emerging from the analysis is mixed with consistency between goals and outcomes being observed for the latter but not for the former. Figures are presented in Tables 3 and 4.

As the 2008 strategic plan reports, the merger produced 15,000–20,000 headcounts, especially among more specialized employees, and many of those retained were relocated. These figures, in my view, indicate that the merger failed to consider employees' stakes. A single initiative was taken to

Table 3.   Loans Provided in 2009 (per Customer Typology).

Loans (31 June 2009) Mld euros	#	%
Individuals and families	80	18
Micro enterprises	70	15
Small and medium enterprises	115	25
Medium enterprises	45	10
Large enterprises	80	17
Public Administration and Financial Institutions	75	16
Total	470	100

Source: Author's elaboration from 2009 company strategic plan.

Table 4. Loans to Businesses (2007−2009).

Loans	2009/2008 (%)	2008/2007 (%)
Short-term loans	+ 3.4	+ 7.8
Medium-long-term loans	+ 3.5	+ 6.1

Source: Author's elaboration from 2009 company strategic plan.

mitigate the negative effects of headcounts: a placement service with financial support for employees losing their jobs. Figures regarding business consumers in the 2009 strategic plan indicate an increase of loans granted to businesses of different sizes, indicating that the merger did actually produce the stated goal of supporting enterprises in implementing growth strategies.

Taken together, these figures seem to support the traditional view that horizontal mergers produce headcounts and allow the merging companies to gain efficiency and improve their competitive position by providing a better offering to consumers. This case demonstrates that consolidation processes, such as those involving mature industries, do compromise employees' stakes. The number of layoffs represents a societal cost that is generally viewed as beneficial for the competitiveness of the merging companies.

DISCUSSION AND CONCLUSIONS

In this chapter, I attempt to provide a fresh perspective on the analysis of acquisitions and the measurement of acquisition performance. The underlying idea of this chapter is that acquisitions touch upon a variety of internal and external stakes of the merging companies. This idea builds on the premise that whether inside or outside their boundaries, merging companies are not monoliths. Both acquiring and target companies can be perceived as networks of relationships with stakeholders legitimized by a contract or another interest that requires protection. This view is a recent addition to the conventional discourse that M&As should only serve the shareholders' interests, which is reflected in the prevailing use of market-based measures for acquisition performance in premier academic journals (Meglio & Risberg, 2011). The prevailing portrait of these deals is one of a battleground where opposing shareholder groups compete for the best return and depends on the set price. This view does not do justice to the

multiplicity of stakeholders with an interest and influence on the acquisition process (Meglio, 2015). Adopting a stakeholder's lens in the analysis
of acquisitions comports with the idea that companies should be socially
responsible, a concept that has generally been ignored by acquisition scholars. Acknowledging the existence of different stakes recognizes that no single performance measure encompasses the plurality of stakes. This new
way to conceive of the multidimensionality of acquisition performance is
frequently evoked by scholars, but generally underplayed in theoretical and
empirical research. Moreover, it is important to outline that these stakes,
although different, do actually influence each other and, taken together,
determine acquisition outcomes.

Although I recognize the multiplicity of stakes in this chapter, I focus
my analysis on two stakeholders: employees and business consumers. This
choice is driven by their salience and ability to influence how an acquisition
actually performs. These stakeholders are different in many respects:
employees are internal to the companies involved in an acquisition, whereas
consumers are external. Employees have a stake to protect that we can
immediately grasp (i.e., work security and career prospects). Consumers'
stake is subtler because it relates to factors that influence buying behaviors
and how they are affected by an acquisition. In the example provided,
which refers to the banking industry, the number of loans granted to enterprises of different sizes is used to measure this stake. Although statistically
insignificant, the example indicates that acquiring companies seem to treat
consumers and employees as stakeholders when communicating acquisition
goals to external audiences. The situation changes when assessing outcomes
from their perspective and is particularly evident for employees who are
treated as a means to achieving acquisition goals, which often means layoffs and relocation.

This analysis has several theoretical implications. For the community of
management scholars, this chapter conveys the idea that acquisition performance is a multidimensional construct, meaning it should reflect the interests of several stakeholders. No single metric can do justice to the
multiplicity of stakes. For the community of stakeholder-theory scholars,
this chapter extends the idea of the importance of stakeholders beyond the
boundaries of a single firm to include the merging companies. For the community of corporate social performance scholars, this chapter contextua-
lizes the measurement of performance in the realm of an acquisition, which
is a frequent event in organizational life.

My analysis also has managerial implications because failing to take
employees' and consumers' stakes into account may produce increased

costs or reduced revenues that influence the acquiring company's bottom line. Seeing employees and consumers as stakeholders enables us to overcome the depiction of them as a means to an end. Stakeholders may actually play a relevant role in the post-acquisition context because they have relevant stakes to protect. A more thorough understanding of what these stakes look like, as well as their behavioral consequences, is instrumental to the identification of possible tools for addressing these issues. In addition, the top management team is in the best position to achieve a convergence or balance of the different stakes put at risk by an acquisition.

REFERENCES

Anderson, H., Havila, V., & Nilsson, F. (Eds.). (2013). *Mergers and acquisitions. The critical role of stakeholders.* New York, NY: Routledge.
Baden, D., & Harwood, I. A. (2013). Terminology matters: A critical exploration of corporate social responsibility terms. *Journal of Business Ethics, 116,* 615–627.
Borglund, T. (2013). The growing importance of corporate social responsibility in mergers and acquisitions. In H. Anderson, V. Havila, & F. Nilsson (Eds.), *Mergers and acquisitions. The critical role of stakeholders* (pp. 17–39). New York, NY: Routledge.
Boulding, K. E. (1956). General systems theory: The skeleton of science. *Management Science, 2,* 197–208.
Callan, S. J., & Thomas, J. M. (2009). Corporate financial performance and corporate social performance: An update and reinvestigation. *Corporate Social Responsibility and Environmental Management, 16*(2), 61–78.
Capron, L. (1999). The long-term performance of horizontal acquisitions. *Strategic Management Journal, 20,* 987–1018.
Carroll, A. B. (1979). A three-dimensional model of corporate social performance. *Academy of Management Review, 4,* 497–505.
Chase, D. G., Burns, D. J., & Claypool, G. A. (1997). A suggested ethical framework for evaluating corporate mergers and acquisitions. *Journal of Business Ethics, 16*(1), 753–763.
Ciambotti, M., Aureli, S., & Demartini, P. (2011). Italy: Demand for social responsibility in mergers and acquisitions. *Journal of Corporate Accounting and Finance, Sept–Oct.,* 45–50.
Clarkson, M. B. E. (1995). A stakeholder framework for evaluating corporate social performance. *Academy of Management Review, 20*(1), 92–117.
Cochran, P. L., & Wood, D. J. (1985). Corporate social responsibility and financial performance. *Academy of Management Journal, 27,* 42–56.
Cording, M., Christman, P., & King, D. (2008). Reducing causal ambiguity in acquisition integration: Intermediate goals as mediators of integration decisions and acquisition performance. *Academy of Management Journal, 51,* 744–767.
Cording, M., Harrison, J. S., Hoskisson, R. E., & Jonsen, K. (2014). Walking the talk: A multi-stakeholder exploration of organizational authenticity, employee productivity, and post-merger performance. *Academy of Management Perspectives, 28*(1), 38–56.

Datta, D. K., Pinches, G. P., & Narayan, V. K. (1992). Factors influencing wealth creation from mergers and acquisitions: A meta-analysis. *Strategic Management Journal,* *13*(1), 67–84.

Donaldson, T., & Preston, L. E. (1995). The stakeholder theory of the corporation: Concepts, evidence and implication. *Academy of Management Review,* *20*(1), 65–91.

European Commission. (2011). *Corporate social responsibility.* Retrieved from http://ec. europa.eu/enterprise/policies/sustainable-business/corporate-social-responsibility/index_ en.htm. Accessed on February 27, 2015.

Fowler, K. L., & Schmidt, D. R. (1988). Tender offers, acquisition, and subsequent performance in manufacturing firms. *Academy of Management Journal,* *31,* 962–974.

Freeman, R. E. (1984). *Strategic management: A stakeholder approach.* Boston, MA: Pitman.

Freeman, R. E. (1999). Divergent stakeholder theory. *Academy of Management Review,* *24*(2), 233–236.

Friedman, M. (1962). *Capitalism and freedom.* Chicago, IL: University of Chicago Press.

Griffin, J. J., & Mahon, J. F. (1997). The corporate social performance and corporate financial performance debate: Twenty-five years of incomparable research. *Business & Society,* *36,* 5–31.

Halinen, A., Salmi, A., & Havila, V. (1999). From dyadic change to changing business networks: An analytical framework. *Journal of Management Studies,* *36*(6), 779–794.

Haspeslagh, P., & Jemison, D. (1991). *Managing acquisitions: Creating value through corporate renewal.* New York, NY: Free Press.

Intesa-Sanpaolo. (2006). *Fusione per incorporazione in Banca Intesa di Sanpaolo IMI. Documento informativo.* 30 novembre/1° dicembre 2006.

Intesa-Sanpaolo. (2007a). *Struttura organizzativa del Gruppo Intesa-Sanpaolo,* Ordine di servizio, N° 1/2007, 03 gennaio 2007.

Intesa-Sanpaolo. (2007b). *Documento di registrazione.* 11 gennaio 2007. Disponibile su. Retrieved from www.intesasanpaolo.com

Intesa-Sanpaolo. (2007c). *Risultati 2006.* Comunicato stampa, Torino-Milano, 23 marzo 2007. 168.

Intesa-Sanpaolo. (2007d). *Leader Italiano di Dimensione Europea. Piano d'Impresa 2007–2009.* Presentazione, 16 aprile 2007.

Intesa-Sanpaolo. (2007e). *Approvazione dei bilanci 2006, del Piano d'Impresa 2007–2009, e della proposta di distribuzione di dividendi.* Comunicato stampa, Torino-Milano, 14 aprile 2007.

Intesa-Sanpaolo. (2009). *Crescere insieme alle imprese.* Presentazione, Milano, 03 luglio 2009.

Intesa-Sanpaolo. (2010). *Relazione su Governo Societario e Assetti Proprietari.* Milano, 15 marzo 2010.

Jones, T. M. (1995). Instrumental stakeholder theory: A synthesis of ethics and economics. *Academy of Management Review,* *20*(2), 404–437.

King, D., Dalton, D., Daily, C., & Covin, J. (2004). Meta-analyses of post-acquisition performance: Indications of unidentified moderators. *Strategic Management Journal,* *25,* 187–200.

Lee, M.-D. P. (2008). A review of the theories of corporate social responsibility: Its evolutionary path and the road ahead. *International Journal of Management Reviews,* *10,* 53–73.

Margolis, J. D., & Walsh, J. P. (2001). *People and profits: The search for a link between a company's social and financial performance.* Mahwah, NJ: Lawrence Erlbaum Associates.

Meglio, O. (2009). Measuring performance in technology-driven M&As: Insights from a literature review. In C. L. Cooper & S. Finkelstein (Eds.), *Advances in mergers and acquisitions* (Vol. 8, pp. 103–118). Bingley, UK: Emerald Publishing Solutions.

Meglio, O. (2015). The M&A performance game – a stakeholder perspective. In A. Risberg, D. R. King, & O. Meglio (Eds.), *The Routledge companion to mergers and acquisitions.* Oxon: Routledge.

Meglio, O., & Risberg, A. (2011). The (Mis)measurement of M&A performance: A systematic narrative literature review. *Scandinavian Journal of Management, 27*(4), 418–433.

Mitchell, R. K., Agle, B. R., & Wood, D. T. (1997). Toward a theory of stakeholder identification and salience: Defining the principle of who and what really counts. *Academy of Management Review, 22*(4), 853–886.

Öberg, C. (2013). Why do customers dissolve their business relationships with the acquired party following an acquisition? In H. Anderson, V. Havila, & F. Nilsson (Eds.), *Mergers and acquisitions. The critical role of stakeholders* (pp. 185–202). New York, NY: Routledge.

Okoye, A. (2009). Theorising corporate social responsibility as an essentially contested concept: Is a definition necessary? *Journal of Business Ethics, 89*(4), 613–627.

Orlitsky, M., Schmidt, F. L., & Rynes, S. L. (2003). Corporate social and financial performance: A meta-analysis. *Organization Studies, 24,* 403–442.

Perrini, F., Russo, A., Tencati, A., & Vurro, C. (2011). Deconstructing the relationship between corporate social and financial performance. *Journal of Business Ethics, 102*(1), 59–76.

Ranft, A., & Lord, M. (2000). Acquiring new knowledge: The role of retaining human capital in acquisition of high-tech firm. *Journal of High Technology Management Research, 11,* 295–319.

Risberg, A., Tienari, J., & Vaara, E. (2003). Making sense of a transnational merger: Media texts and the (Re)construction of power relations. *Culture & Organization, 9*(2), 121–137.

Scherer, A. G., & Palazzo, G. (2007). Toward a political conception of corporate responsibility: Business and society seen from a Habermasian perspective. *Academy of Management Review, 32*(4), 1096–1120.

Vaara, E., Risberg, A., Søderberg, A.-M., & Tienari, J. (2003). The construction of national stereotypes in a merging multinational. In A.-M. Søderberg & E. Vaara (Eds.), *Merging across Borders. People, Cultures and Politics.* Copenhagen: Copenhagen Business School Press.

Vaara, E., & Tienari, J. (2002). Justification, legitimization and naturalization of mergers and acquisitions: A critical discourse analysis of media texts. *Organization, 9*(2), 275–304.

Waddock, S., & Graves, S. B. (2006). The impact of mergers and acquisitions on corporate stakeholders' practices. *Journal of Corporate Citizenship, 22,* 99–109.

Wallich, H. C., & McGowan, J. J. (1970). Stockholder interest and the corporation's role in social policy. In W. J. Baumol, R. Likert, H. C. Wallich, & J. J. McGowan (Eds.), *A new rationale for corporate social policy* (pp. 39–59). New York, NY: Committee for Economic Development.

Wood, D. J. (1991). Corporate social performance revisited. *Academy of Management Review, 16,* 691–718.

Wood, D. J. (2010). Measuring corporate social performance: A review. *International Journal of Management Reviews, 12*(19), 50–84.

Zollo, M., & Meier, D. (2008). What is M&A performance? *Academy of Management Perspective, 22*(3), 55–77.

INTERACTION OF CULTURAL AND TECHNOLOGICAL DISTANCE IN CROSS-BORDER, HIGH-TECHNOLOGY ACQUISITIONS

Pankaj C. Patel and David R. King

ABSTRACT

The globalization of knowledge has driven an increased emphasis on cross-border, high-technology acquisitions where a target firm in a technology industry is acquired by a firm in another nation. However, learning depends on similarity of knowledge, and we find that needed similarity can be provided by either technology or culture. As a result, firms can learn from acquiring targets at increasing cultural distance or at increasing technological distance, but not both. We find an interaction where acquisitions made at longer cultural distances and less technological distance, and acquisitions at shorter cultural distances and greater technological distance improve financial performance. This means technological distance and cultural distance are substitutes or represent a

Advances in Mergers and Acquisitions, Volume 15, 115–144
ISSN: 1479-361X/doi:10.1108/S1479-361X20160000015007

trade-off where improved acquisition performance depends on having commonality (low distance) for one of the variables.

Keywords: Cross-border acquisitions; high-technology acquisitions; knowledge; cultural distance; technology distance; acquisition performance

INTRODUCTION

Cross-border acquisitions are increasingly important to sustaining competitive advantage (Johanson & Vahlne, 2009; Lane, Salk, & Lyles, 2001; Stahl & Voigt, 2008), but research on cross-border acquisitions has fallen behind observed activity (Collins, Holcomb, Certo, Hitt, & Lester, 2009). For example, between 1999 and 2000 40 percent of acquisitions were cross-border (Shimizu, Hitt, Vaidyanath, & Pisano, 2004), and, in 2014, over $3.4 trillion of mergers occurred globally (Mattioli & Cimilluca, 2015). Increased cross-border acquisitions are driven in part by technology advances occurring across an increasing international scope (Gelles, 2011; Light, 2011). Meanwhile, acquisitions are challenging and have an uncertain impact on acquirer performance (King, Dalton, Daily, & Covin, 2004), and cross-border acquisitions represent an even greater challenge (Bjorkman, Stahl, & Vaara, 2007; Stahl & Voigt, 2008). Considering differences in cultural distance for cross-border, high-technology acquisitions, may help to explain how firms learn from acquisitions (Collins et al., 2009; Vermeulen & Barkema, 2001) and address the need to find ways to mitigate the negative impact of cultural distance in cross-border acquisitions (Rottig, 2011; Tihanyi, Griffith, & Russell, 2005).

Cultural distance represents a salient challenge that limits transmission of knowledge (Lyles & Salk, 1996; Palich & Gomez-Mejia, 1999) where knowledge is defined as socially constructed "information" and "know-how" held in firms (Kogut & Zander, 1992). Acquisitions with cultural distance can involve "us vs. them" conflicts due to different values and practices creating inefficiencies in identifying and realizing synergies (Schweiger, 2002; Slangen & Hennart, 2008) and operational difficulties (Mowery, Oxley, & Silverman, 1996). As a result, cultural distance increases difficulties in cooperation (Bjorkman et al., 2007; Kostova & Zaheer, 1999) that hinders socialization processes necessary to exchange, recombine, and use knowledge (Nonaka, 1994; Paruchuri, Nerkar, & Hambrick, 2006). An obvious implication is that while acquisitions are often motivated by gaining socially constructed knowledge in a target that same knowledge may not survive attempts to integrate it (Ahuja & Katila, 2001; Ranft & Lord, 2000).

Despite recognized challenges in knowledge integration due to cultural differences (e.g., Aguilera & Dencker, 2004; Shimizu et al., 2004; Vaara, 2003), clear findings on the effects of cultural distance remain mixed (Bjorkman et al., 2007; Stahl & Voigt, 2008; Tihanyi et al., 2005). To address mixed findings, an inverted-U type relationship for the impact of cultural distance on knowledge transfer has been proposed (Estrin, Baghdasaryan, & Meyer, 2009; Nadolska & Barkema, 2007). However, an inverted-U relationship has drawbacks: (1) it limits the strategic options available to firms in distant cultural domains and (2) it overlooks contextual factors that may enable knowledge transfer in close or distant cultural settings. For example, culturally close targets may be easier to integrate, but have less useful knowledge. In other words, an inverted-U relationship restricts our theoretical understanding of leveraging acquisitions in closer cultural domains and managing challenges in distant cultural domains.

Maintaining a restricted outlook has practical and theoretical implications, as a focus on target firms with intermediate cultural distance may lead firms to forego valuable opportunities in distant or closer cultural domains. From a theoretical perspective, both Bjorkman et al. (2007, p. 659) and Tihanyi et al. (2005, p. 276) suggest that research examine moderator variables to detect obscured effects of cultural differences on firms. Additionally, cultural distance has been identified as underrepresented in M&A research (Shimizu et al., 2004; Slangen, 2006; Stahl & Voigt, 2008) with research needed to determine when national cultural distance may be beneficial (Gomes, Angwin, Weber, & Tarba, 2013). Further, Shimizu et al. (2004) identify knowledge transferability in cross-border acquisitions as a research need. If contingent relationships exist on the margins of cultural distance, then limiting firms to moderate cultural distance could restrict acquiring firms to resource and knowledge combinations with lower potential.

The goal of the current study is to meet identified research needs by extending the understanding of cultural distance in cross-border acquisitions by considering the contingent role of knowledge structure similarity that can range from low distance (coherent knowledge) to high distance (diverse knowledge). We build and test a contingent framework for the impact of common knowledge structures on knowledge transfer that builds on interactions of acquirer and target firm characteristics predicting performance (Harrison, Hitt, Hoskisson, & Ireland, 2001; King, Slotegraaf, & Kesner, 2008). For example, Teece, Rumelt, Dosi, and Winter (1994) identify the potential for strong organizational learning exists when market distance is high (low) and technology distance is iow (high). Therefore, firms may be able to selectively manage cross-border acquisitions based on the interaction of market and technology characteristics. Specifically, we propose that cross-border, high-technology acquisitions display improved financial performance when either culture or technology of combining firms has shorter distance to facilitate knowledge transfer.

THEORY AND HYPOTHESES DEVELOPMENT

We draw on resource based theory (Barney, 1991; Penrose, 1959) and knowledge based view (e.g., Kogut & Zander, 1992, 1996), as well as organizational learning, to propose and test a contingent relationship between cultural distance and knowledge structures that could increase the strategic options available to potential acquirers. The knowledge based view suggests that knowledge sharing is the reason for firm formation (Bresman, Birkinshaw, & Nobel, 1999; Kogut & Zander, 1996), and the transfer of resources and knowledge is a primary motivation for acquisitions (Capron & Hulland, 1999; Capron & Mitchell, 1998; King et al., 2008), including cross-border acquisitions (Bertrand & Capron, 2014; Johanson & Vahlne, 2009). However, combining knowledge during integration is critically dependent on the processes of combining capabilities (Penrose, 1959). Organizational learning examines acquiring, disseminating, and using knowledge (Dibella, Nevis, & Gould, 1996), and for acquisitions this means that some integration is required to combine knowledge (Castro & Neira, 2005; Kogut & Zander, 1992; Olie, 1994; Zaheer, Castaner, & Souder, 2011). This has led to observations that the premium paid for technology acquisitions is largely wasted without integration (Paruchuri et al., 2006), and that integration (in general) is the primary determinant of acquisition performance (Brock, 2005; Yu, Engleman, & Van de Ven, 2005). Still, the success of integration likely depends on contextual factors, and we focus on how similar culture or technology can facilitate knowledge transfer.

While all acquisitions integrate organizations that are different (Vermeulen, 2005), learning begins with having a common knowledge base and greater similarity enables higher integration due to increased familiarity (Schein, 1993; Zaheer et al., 2011). At the same time, dissimilarity of knowledge negatively impacts knowledge integration at an accelerating pace (Yang, Phelps, & Steensma, 2010), and cross-border acquisitions add national differences on top of firm and industry differences (Shimizu et al., 2004). Meanwhile, research suggestions for overcoming challenges to knowledge transfer remain limited. Existing approaches to this problem generally take two perspectives. One approach is a "process" view of knowledge transfer in acquisitions that focuses on how knowledge is integrated. Topics considered include the nature of interactions, such as the frequency of visits and meetings (Bresman et al., 1999). The other approach looks at "deal characteristics," such as organizational size (e.g., Makino & Delios, 1996; Tsang, 2002), firm age (e.g., Frost, Birkinshaw, & Ensign, 2002), decentralization (e.g., Gupta & Govindarajan, 2000), and network structure (e.g., Inkpen & Tsang, 2005) among others. While firm processes may begin to explain why some firms may be better able to transmit knowledge, neither a process perspective nor an examination of deal characteristics has provided sufficient managerial guidance. For example, simply holding more meetings offers diminishing returns, and deal characteristics are largely predetermined. For example, Cording, Christmann, and Weigelt (2010) find that 78 percent of M&A research variables are known at announcement. We add to this literature by outlining the impact of target and acquirer technology and cultural distance, as well as their interaction on acquisition performance.

Using insights on common knowledge structures as an antecedent to knowledge transfer, we develop how similar knowledge relating to either culture or technology can improve acquisition performance. Knowledge structures can be viewed as shared beliefs (Yayavaram & Ahuja, 2008) or an idea consistent with industry recipes (Hannan & Freeman, 1977) where firms dealing with similar technology develop distinct methods related to terminology and organization. For example, knowledge structures are central to transmitting knowledge (Henderson & Clark, 1990) and facilitating information processing (Williams & Mitchell, 2004), and common experience of either culture or technology may provide compatible knowledge structures needed to improve performance of cross-border, high-technology acquisitions. The degree that knowledge structures overlap may offer a source of commonality needed for knowledge transfer. Specifically, we argue that the amount of cultural and technology distance interact to influence acquisition performance. On one hand, lower technology distance will reduce adjustment costs related to greater cultural differences. On the other hand, lower cultural distance will minimize adjustment costs for integrating more distant technology. This is consistent with observations that improved acquisition performance results from searching for knowledge at different distances (King et al., 2008; Li, Maggitti, Smith, Tesluk, & Katilla, 2013; Vermeulen & Barkema, 2001). We begin by considering the direct impact of technology distance on acquisition performance.

Technology Distance

Technology distance considers the degree an acquirer and target perform research and development (R&D) in similar areas (Makri, Hitt, & Lane, 2010; Oxley & Sampson, 2004) with acquirers largely limiting their search of potential targets to firms in similar technology areas (Harrison, Hitt, Hoskisson, & Ireland, 1991; King et al., 2008; Wolpert, 2002). One reason is that lower technology distance enables an acquirer to more effectively evaluate a target's knowledge by lowering information asymmetries and the risk of adverse selection from having similar knowledge (King et al., 2008; Teece et al., 1994; Zahra, 1996). For example, Technological coherence increases knowledge interdependencies and enables search and integration (e.g., Cohen & Levinthal, 1990; Teece et al., 1994) by reducing information asymmetries (Zahra, 1996). Lower technology thereby distance implies that an acquirer can effectively interpret and understand knowledge and then identify combinations with target firm resources.

Interrelated knowledge also lowers knowledge transmission costs to facilitate integration (Cohen & Levinthal, 1990; Szulanski, 1996; Teece et al., 1994) by enabling the pursuit of complementarities "among a diversity of localized … stocks of knowledge and learning processes, processes that are kept together by organizing principles" (Foss & Christensen, 2001, p. 214). For example, Kang, Morris, and Snell (2007) found that knowledge similarity facilitates information transfer and comprehension. When technology is similar, an acquirer is better able to interpret a target firm's knowledge, as well as interrelationships among tasks, tools, and processes (Gersick & Hackman, 1990). This is consistent with research suggesting that information accumulated by an acquirer previous to an acquisition is positively associated with biotechnology acquisition performance (Higgins & Rodriguez, 2006).

At the same time, differences in knowledge increase ambiguity that can contribute to resource allocation errors and integration issues, and lower knowledge transfer (Simonin, 1999; Vaara, 2003). The challenge results not just from technology differences, but also from the path dependence in how they were developed (Penrose, 1959; Teece et al., 1994). High-technology distance relates to increased diversity of underlying knowledge associated with cognitive distance that requires greater readjustments in tasks, tools, and process interrelationships (Nooteboom, 2000; Reus & Lamont, 2009; Weick, 1979). Therefore, we predict the following:

Hypothesis 1. For cross-border, high-technology acquisitions, targets displaying greater technology distance with an acquirer are associated with lower acquisition performance.

Cultural Distance

Cultural distance relates to the similarity of acquirer and target firm national values that are deep-rooted and difficult to change (Morosini & Singh, 1994; Morosini, Shane, & Singh, 1998), and it compounds challenges in cross-border acquisitions (Athanassiou & Nigh, 2000; Verbeke & Yuan, 2007). For example, differences in national culture create difficulties for learning (Aguilera & Dencker, 2004; Brock, 2005; Brouthers & Hennart, 2007; Shimizu et al., 2004; Vaara, 2003) with differences in language, location, and culture limiting coordination and contributing to conflict (Risberg, 2001; Sarala, 2009).

Culture affects how knowledge is organized and communicated with cultural differences leading to dissimilar symbols and terminology that in turn affect sharing, communication, and integration routines for learning. For example, difficulty in knowledge integration has been found at higher cultural distances in Chinese and US joint ventures (Osland & Cavusgil, 1996), and for culturally distant subsidiaries (Hakanson, 1995; Lucas, 2006; Nooteboom, Vanhaverbeke, Duysters, Gilsing, & van den Oord, 2007). Specifically, research associates cultural distance with incompatible organizational practices that increase management difficulty as cultural distance grows (Hutzschenreuter, Voll, & Verbeke, 2011; Slangen & Hennart, 2008) due to differences between target and acquirer national values and beliefs (Morosini et al., 1998).

Different values and practices represent a real problem for gaining socially constructed knowledge with increasing dissimilarity accelerating negative impacts on learning (Yang et al., 2010). For example, one issue limiting value creation in cross-border acquisitions relates to "us vs. them" thinking due to different values and practices (Slangen & Hennart, 2008). Additionally, greater national cultural distance can heighten misunderstandings due to unfamiliarity with a foreign market (Simonin, 1999). In a meta-analysis, Stahl and Voigt (2008) conclude that cultural distance has a negative relationship with acquisition outcomes.

Meanwhile, lower cultural distance appears to offer lower adjustment costs and improved information sharing (Brock, 2005; Davidson & McFetridge, 1985). The social construction of learning and culture (Schein, 1993) makes integration easier if an acquirer and target share a similar national culture (Bauer, Matzler, & Wolf, 2016; Brock, 2005). For example, cultural similarity enables improved signaling and communication (Branzei, Vertinsky, & Camp, 2007). Therefore, we predict the following:

Hypothesis 2a. For cross-border, high-technology acquisitions, targets displaying greater cultural distance with an acquirer are associated with lower acquisition performance.

A competing perspective in published research focuses on an inverted-U shape relationship between cultural distance and firm performance (e.g., Ahuja & Katila, 2004; Bjorkman et al., 2007; Estrin et al., 2009; Morosini et al., 1998; Nadolska & Barkema, 2007) that relates to cultural distance offering both advantages and disadvantages. The disadvantages of cultural distance relating to difficulty in coordination and risk of conflict have already been discussed. An advantage of culture distance is the potential for increased learning from exposure to new ideas (Vaara, Sarala, Stahl, & Bjorkman, 2012) that complement an acquiring firm's perspective (Bjorkman et al., 2007). For example, differences in culture may help to break rigidities in an acquiring firm (Vermeulen & Barkema, 2001). This has resulted in arguments that moderate levels of cultural differences are more likely to exhibit an awareness of complementary capabilities that improve acquisition performance (Ahuja & Katila, 2004; Bjorkman et al., 2007; Estrin et al., 2009). Therefore, we examine the following competing hypothesis:

Hypothesis 2b. For cross-border, high-technology acquisitions, cultural distance has an inverted-U relationship with acquisition performance.

Contingent Relationship

Acquisitions only benefit acquirers when targets differ on important characteristics, if the underlying differences between firms are not too great to prevent learning (Vermeulen, 2005; Vermeulen & Barkema, 2001). Diverse knowledge is often needed for firms to adapt (King et al., 2008; Pascale, 1999) and acquisitions can help to restore diversity by promoting synergies across seemingly unrelated areas (Makri & Lane, 2008). We believe this diversity can be achieved through either differences in technology or differences in culture when there is enough similarity to benefit from the differences sought. We anticipate that lower technology distance can facilitate integration of more culturally distant targets and vice versa. We consider the role for low cultural distance facilitating integration of technology distant knowledge first.

We anticipate lower technology distance between an acquirer and target augments knowledge transfer with culturally distant targets. As technology becomes increasingly distant the transfer process becomes more challenging, unless culture provides the needed contextual similarity or "stickiness" (cf. Capaldo, Lavie, & Petruzzelli, forthcoming; Szulanski, 1996). The presence of similar heuristics from social norms at lower cultural distance facilitates the discussion of unfamiliar technology (Rothaermel & Alexandre, 2009).

This results from lower cultural distance requiring fewer adjustments to share knowledge (Hansen, Podolny, & Pfeffer, 2001; Kang et al., 2007; Nooteboom et al., 2007). Research involving international joint ventures supports integrating knowledge over shorter cultural distances provides a greater overlap of contextual frameworks to facilitate learning (Reuer, 2001). For example, technology sharing between culturally closer Korean and Japanese subsidiaries is often successful (Inkpen, 1996; Pak & Park, 2004). Integrating knowledge from a firm with shorter cultural distance suggests a greater overlap of institutional norms that could facilitate knowledge sharing (Reuer, 2001). Therefore, lower cultural distance may lower barriers for integrating more distant technology by making communication and coordination easier.

We now turn to considering the role of lower technology distance in enabling more culturally distant targets. Cross-border acquisitions offer access to location bound resources that involve relationships and market knowledge (Gubbi, Aulakh, Ray, Sarkar, & Chittoor, 2010; Morosini et al., 1998), and we anticipate the path dependent nature of technology and related expertise can provide a common structure for knowledge transfer between an acquirer and target. A similar knowledge structure of technology can explain technology having greater transferability across nations than other capabilities (Shimizu et al., 2004) that may also facilitate other knowledge transfer. For example, Ailon (2007) found that technology provided a common language during an Israeli acquisition of an American firm.

The preceding logic suggests that technology and culture provide independent means for learning and knowledge transfer needed to improve the performance of cross-border, high-technology acquisitions. At longer cultural distances, less technology distance improves performance, and at shorter cultural distances, more technological distance increases performance. In other words, technology and culture negatively interact or provide alternative or substituting means (Neter, Kutner, Nachtsheim, & Wasserman, 1996; Sigglekow, 2002) to achieve similarity needed to learn in cross-border, high-technology acquisitions. Specifically, two variables are substitutes when the marginal benefit of one variable (i.e., technology or cultural distance) decreases as the level of the other variable rises, or the product of their interaction is negative (Sigglekow, 2002, p. 901, 905). As a result, we propose the following:

Hypothesis 3. There is a negative interaction between technology distance and cultural distance on cross-border, high-technology acquisition performance.

METHOD

Our sample selection is theoretically driven to consider cross-border, high-technology acquisitions defined by the acquisition of a target firm in another country. Consistent with prior research we identified high-technology targets using industry codes, using the following two-digit SIC codes: 28, 35, 36, 37, 38, 48, 73, and 87 (Certo, Covin, Daily, & Dalton, 2001; King et al., 2008; Ranft & Lord, 2000). We then identified cross-border acquisitions (firms in different countries) of firms in these two-digit industries from Thomson's Securities Data Corporation (SDC) Platinum database between the years 1995 and 2006. We began our sample in 1995 to include the M&A waves related to technology and globalization (e.g., Kusstatscher & Cooper, 2005; Martynova & Renneboog, 2008) and ended it in 2006 to avoid the 2008 recession influencing our long-term performance measures. We identified an initial sample of 1,724 acquisition events completed in this time frame that resulted in majority ownership (over 50 percent control of a target firm).

Next, we collected data on patent portfolios using the Derwent World Patents Index® (DWPI^{SM}), European Patent Office, and NBER patent data Project 1976–2006 databases[1] using a name and address match at the time of acquisition. The US targets' and acquirers' patent portfolio were based on the NBER patent database and were confirmed through DWPI^{SM} database. For non-US targets and acquirers, we used name and address of patent assignee's to identify firms in the DWPI^{SM} database and European Patent Office.[2] Firm level financial information was identified from either COMPUSTAT or the Bureau Van Dijk databases. We also followed guidelines from Park (2004) to conduct international event studies by including effects of world stock market trends and exchange rate effects, in addition, to local stock market returns. While the United States remains the largest single category for the number of deals with roughly 20 percent of the total, it represents 17 percent of the value of cross-border M&A deal activity in our sample, reinforcing the importance of examining cross-border acquisitions. Based on availability of the following measures, the final sample included 1,167 acquisitions. The appendix shows the distribution of acquisitions across target countries.

Dependent Variables

Research on acquisition performance has increasingly called for multiple measures (Cording et al., 2010; King et al., 2004). Initial stock market reactions relate to a market "vote" on whether an acquisition will improve performance. As such, short-term measures can be thought of as a measure of a cross-border acquisition's potential. Meanwhile, long-term measures of performance approximate the extent that potential is realized. Both short-term and long-term measures have advantages and disadvantages, so we use a short-term and a long-term measures of performance: (1) seven-day cumulative abnormal return (CAR) $[-3,3]$ and (2) a 36-month BHAR. Again, stock market measures are adjusted for acquirer country market returns, world market returns and exchange rates (Park, 2004).

Seven-Day CAR
The standard event study methodology was used based on recommendation by Park (2004). The acquirer's predicted stock return was calculated on trading day $t = -170$ to ending day $t = -21$ to estimate daily returns and then any abnormal return was calculated using:

$$R_{ijt} = \alpha_i + \beta_i R_{mjt} + \gamma_i R_{wmt} + \delta_i X_{jt} + \varepsilon_{ijt}$$

where, firm i's return R_{ijt} in home country j on day t is based on (i) market return in country j on day t, R_{mjt}; (ii) world market return on day t; and (iii) change in currency exchange rate in country j on day t, X_{jt}. α_i, β_i, γ_i, and δ_i are firm specific estimates, and ε_{ijt} is a random error term with $E[\varepsilon_{ijt}] = 0$ and $\text{Var}[\varepsilon_{ijt}] = \sigma_{ij}^2$. For country-level market return, R_{mjt}, we use the most prominent index in respective country. Prominent indices are based on top index identified in The EAFE Index from Morgan Stanley Capital International. For the world market return, R_{wmt}, we use FTSE World market indices that captures 82–90 percent of investable equity and uses 5,000 indices worldwide. Based on Park (2004), for the exchange rates we use a trade-weighted US dollar prices based on aggregate quarterly data with 10 largest trading partners.

Next, based on Park (2004), we lag stock market returns, index returns (both country and world market returns), and changes in currency exchange rates by one day for acquirers or targets located in Australia, Japan, Korea, Malaysia, New Zealand, Singapore, and Thailand. For public holidays or missing data we use the data available for the previous day. The abnormal rate of return is:

$$\text{AR}_{ijt} = R_{ijt} - (a_i + b_i R_{mjt} + g_i R_{wmt} + d_i X_{jt})$$

Day 0 is defined as the day on which stock markets respond to news in acquirer's stock market.

The 7-day cumulative abnormal return is the sum of abnormal returns over the seven-day window $(t-3)$ and $(t+3)$ or $[-3,3]$.

BHAR

Continuing from daily abnormal returns from the CAR measure based on Park (2004), the BHAR represents the return to an investor holding a firm's stock during a given time period. We calculated returns for 36-month period after the announcements using the following equation:

$$\text{BHAR}_{ijt} = \prod_{t=1}^{T} \left(1 + \text{AR}_{ijt}\right) - 1$$

Independent Variables

Technology Distance

We examine patent portfolios of both target and acquirer firms, as patents in the same class represent similar technology (Makri et al., 2010; Oxley & Sampson, 2004). The patent portfolios are based on all approved patents in the last five years for sampled firms using IPC-4 technological classes and NAICS concordance table from the World Intellectual Property Organization (OECD, 2009; Schmoch, 2008). A set of 194,253 approved patents with complete information on technological classes were identified in both a target's and an acquirer's patent portfolios, and from these patents 736,943 citations were extracted. This creates a one-dimensional matrix representing the number of patents assigned to a target (or acquirer) in a technology class. Technological distance, one minus the technology overlap between target and acquirer firm, is represented as:

$$\text{Technology distance} = 1 - \left\{ \frac{M_{\text{acquirer}} M'_{\text{target}}}{\sqrt{\left(M_{\text{acquirer}} M'_{\text{acquirer}}\right)\left(M_{\text{target}} M'_{\text{target}}\right)}} \right\}$$

where $M_i = (M_i^1 \cdots \cdots M_i^c)$, where M_i is the matrix of patents applied or approved in technology classes $1-c$. The measure relates to angular distance between matrices of target and acquiring firm, and it ranges from zero (no overlap) to one (complete overlap). This is subtracted from 1 to measure technology distance where higher values indicate greater technology distance and smaller values indicate lower technology distance.

Cultural Distance
Based on Hutzschenreuter and Voll (2008), we use nine dimensions and scores of the GLOBE project. The measure below, in line with Kogut and Singh (1988), uses distance between target and acquirer countries, while controlling for variance in each dimension.

$$D = \sqrt{\sum_{i=1}^{9} \frac{(I_{i,\text{acquirer}} - I_{i,\text{target}})^2}{V_i}}$$

where I_i is the ith dimension of the standardized index for acquirer or target countries. Further, standardized values for each dimension were used.[3] Cultural distance was then squared to test for an inverted-U relationship.

Interaction
The interaction of technology distance and cultural distance was tested by multiplying the variables of interest (Aiken & West, 1991).

Control Variables

In recognition of having a sample with multiple countries, all currencies are converted to US dollars using trade-weighted (based on trade with ten largest trade partners) exchange rate (Park, 2004). Further, a criticism of prior research on cultural distance (Stahl & Voigt, 2008) and acquisition performance (King et al., 2004) is a lack of controls. We attempt to overcome this limitation by including variables that research suggests could influence our results. First, firms with greater technology resources may be able to overcome cultural distance (Nooteboom et al., 2007), so we control for prior knowledge stocks of acquirer and target using the natural log of total number of patents from the USPTO database during the 10-year (or, less, if either firms are less than 10 years old) prior to an acquisition event. *Second*, past experience with acquisitions may influence performance, so we control for acquirer acquisition experience in the past five years. *Third*, we measure relative size as the ratio of the natural log of acquirer and target total assets one year prior to acquisition. *Fourth*, we control for product-market relatedness based on the number of common three-digit technology classes assigned to acquirer and target firms in SDC Platinum database divided by the count of the total common technology classes shared by a target and acquirer. *Fifth*, we include acquirer R&D intensity (R&D/sales) to control for absorptive capacity that may aid capturing the benefits of ambidexterity (Cohen & Levinthal, 1990; Rothaermel & Alexandre, 2009) using three-year mean R&D intensity prior to acquisition announcement. *Sixth*, we control for acquirer experience for making prior acquisitions in a target's country for the past five years, as cultural learning through acquisition experiences in a target's country could affect acquisition outcomes (Slangen & Hennart, 2008). *Seventh*, we control for acquirer debt-to-equity (Barkema & Schijven, 2008). *Eighth*, we control for acquisition premium as paying a higher premium is associated with lower acquirer performance (Sirower, 1997). Acquisition premium is measured as the percentage difference between final purchase price of the target firm and the trading price of the target firm stock 30 days before announcement of acquisition using announcements in the *Wall Street Journal*, Lexis-Nexis Database, and Factiva Database. The percentage premium is then adjusted to a major index in the target's country over the 30-day period using the most representative country index. *Finally*, we control for year-effects (reference category 1995), and acquirer industry effects (reference category SIC code 87).

RESULTS

Table 1 shows the mean, standard deviation, and zero-order correlations among the variables. While differences in US acquisition performance are insignificant (King et al., 2004), cross-border acquisitions are often wealth creating (Shimizu et al., 2004), and our results are consistent with both findings. Premiums for high-technology firms are generally higher, and our sample's average premium of 56 percent is slightly above than the average premium paid of 40–50 percent observed over the last 20 years (Laamanen, 2007).

Since firms could engage in multiple acquisitions over the period of observation, we use OLS with the Newey-West estimators that are robust to autocorrelation and heteroscedasticity to test our hypothesized relationships, see Table 2.

Hypothesis 1 proposes technology distance is negatively related to the performance of cross-border, high-technology acquisitions. The results in

Table 1. Means, Standard Deviations, and Zero-Order Correlation.

	Mean	S.D.	1	2	3	4	5	6	7	8	9	10	11	12	13
1. Acquirer knowledge stock	5.99	13.44	1												
2. Target knowledge stock	5.65	8.35	0.16	1											
3. Acquirer prior acquisitions	11.06	13.47	0.06	0.10	1										
4. Relative size	1.57	1.40	0.13	0.10	0.05	1									
5. Market relatedness	0.31	0.36	0.11	0.10	0.03	0.06	1								
6. Acquirer R&D intensity	0.13	0.06	0.14	0.10	0.04	0.13	0.16	1							
7. Target country acquisition experience (5 years)	0.13	1.20	0.05	0.06	0.03	0.07	0.02	0.26	1						
8. Acquirer debt-to-equity	0.64	0.24	0.06	0.02	0.03	0.07	0.06	0.30	0.03	1					
9. Acquisition premium	0.59	0.26	0.16	0.15	-0.03	0.15	0.18	0.08	-0.03	-0.11	1				
10. Technology distance	0.19	0.81	0.08	0.11	0.11	0.12	0.13	0.12	0.12	0.15	0.11	1			
11. Cultural distance	0.31	0.96	0.08	0.05	0.05	0.13	0.05	0.12	0.05	0.04	-0.19	-0.09	1		
12. 7-day CAR [−3,3] (%)	0.08	1.10	0.26	0.15	0.09	0.06	0.08	-0.04	0.03	-0.00	-0.12	0.04	-0.08	1	
13. 36-month BHAR (%)	0.33	1.35	0.15	0.11	0.22	-0.02	0.03	0.04	0.04	-0.03	0.07	0.05	-0.11	0.11	1

Notes: $N = 1,167$ acquisition events.
All correlations above |0.05| are significant at 0.05 or below (two-tailed).
All correlations above |0.11| are significant at 0.01 or below (two-tailed).

Table 2.   OLS Results from Newey-West Estimators.

Variables	(1) 7-day CAR (%)	(2) 36-month BHAR (%)
Direct effects (t)		
Technology distance (H1)	0.12***	0.11**
	(0.04)	(0.05)
Cultural distance (H2a)	−0.08**	−0.115**
	(0.04)	(0.05)
Cultural distance − square (H2b)	0.03	−0.01
	(0.02)	(0.03)
Interaction effect (t)		
Technology × cultural distance (H3)	−0.40***	−0.34***
	(0.04)	(0.05)
Controls (t)		
Acquirer knowledge stock	0.02***	0.01***
	(0.00)	(0.00)
Target knowledge stock	0.01***	0.01**
	(0.00)	(0.00)
Acquirer prior acquisitions	0.01**	0.02***
	(0.00)	(0.00)
Relative size	0.04	−0.00
	(0.02)	(0.03)
Market relatedness	0.19**	0.01
	(0.08)	(0.11)
Acquirer R&D intensity	−0.08	0.61
	(0.52)	(0.66)
Target country acquisition experience	0.01	0.03
	(0.03)	(0.03)
Acquirer debt-to-equity	−0.07	−0.22
	(0.13)	(0.17)
Acquisition premium (%)	−0.38***	0.04
	(0.12)	(0.15)
Constant	−0.04	0.01
	(0.12)	(0.16)
Highest variance inflation factor	1.40	1.40
Observations	1,167	1,167
R^2	0.18	0.13
F	19.34***	13.17***
	(13, 1,153)	(13, 1,153)

Notes: Standard errors in parentheses.
***$p < 0.01$, **$p < 0.05$.

Table 2 demonstrate the opposite is true with technology distance having a positive association (at least, $p < .05$) with short- and long-term performance outcomes. These estimates suggest that technological distance provides less of a hurdle to learning than anticipated. Hypothesis 2a proposes that cultural distance is negatively associated with performance of cross-border, high-technology acquisitions, and the results in Table 2 support this conclusion. Cultural distance has a negative relationship for both measures of performance (at least, $p < .01$). The disparity between expected and actual results for technology and cultural distance suggests barriers to learning from technology distance are easier to overcome than challenges of cultural distance. In Hypothesis 2b, we examine the competing hypothesis of an inverted-U relationship between cultural distance and performance for cross-border, high-technology acquisitions. Our results do not support a non-linear relationship of cultural distance on performance ($p > 0.10$) for all measures, and we dismiss an inverted-U shaped relationship exists between cultural distance and acquisition performance.

Hypothesis 3 proposes an interaction between technological distance and cultural distance is negatively related to high-technology, cross-border acquisition performance. The results in Table 2 support a significant interaction ($p < 0.01$) for the two measures of acquisition performance.[4] Interactions presented in Fig. 1 support a negative interaction or substitution relationship between technological and cultural distance. This is consistent with improved cross-border, high-technology performance resulting from pursuing distant technology at shorter cultural distances, or similar technology in markets at longer cultural distances.

DISCUSSION

Explaining acquisition performance has been a consistent focus of management research (Haleblian, Devers, McNamara, Carpenter, & Davison, 2009; King et al., 2004). We find that cross-border, high-technology acquisitions, can improve acquirer performance. However, this depends on combining diverse knowledge with a shared knowledge base that can facilitate integration of diverse knowledge. Our findings suggest that shared technology or cultural knowledge can enable integration of culturally distant or technology distant knowledge respectively. Next, we discuss additional implications of our research for management research and practice.

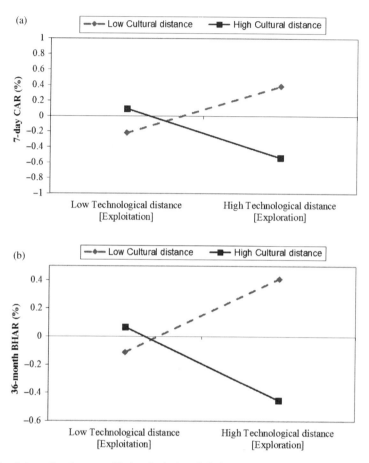

Fig. 1.   Interaction between Technological and Cultural Distance. (a) Seven-day CAR.
(b) 36-month BHAR.

Research Implications

The success of cross-border, high-technology acquisitions likely depends on
the presence of contextual similarity needed for knowledge transfer and
learning. We demonstrate the challenge of integrating unfamiliar technology and cultural knowledge are real, but it can be managed when a common foundation exists to avoid differences being too great to prevent
learning (Vermeulen & Barkema, 2001). We find needed commonality in

knowledge can be provided by either technology or culture, contributing an explanation for how firms access distant knowledge. The interaction with technology distance also offers an explanation for cultural distance offering both advantages and disadvantages (Stahl & Voigt, 2008). This also challenges research suggesting an inverted-U shape relationship between cultural distance and firm performance (e.g., Bjorkman et al., 2007; Estrin et al., 2009; Nadolska & Barkema, 2007).

Advice focusing on mid-range cultural distance (i.e., inverted-U effects) may restrict acquiring firms from considering valuable targets either at closer or farther cultural distances. A joint focus on technological and cultural distances using organizational ambidexterity addresses conflicts in existing research on cultural distance. Specifically, our results suggest that better performance is possible at both low and high cultural distance. While cultural distance has a negative direct effect on knowledge transfer, we find it can largely be overcome if an acquirer and target share similar technology. Our findings are consistent with cultural distance presenting a duality (Reus & Lamont, 2009; Stahl & Voigt, 2008). On one hand, cultural distance creates barriers to information sharing that limit integration needed to pursue strategic opportunities. On the other hand, it also promises access to unique knowledge necessary to develop strategic opportunities. We suggest that a key contingency in managing distant cultural knowledge is the extent technology may offer a substitute knowledge structure that can facilitate communication and understanding.

Our results also support knowledge sharing as a motivation for acquisitions, and we demonstrate the importance of knowledge structures on integrating technology resources. For example, accessing technology is a primary motivation for cross-borders acquisitions that depend on the ability to reconfigure knowledge stocks and redeploy resources (cf. Capron & Hulland, 1999; King et al., 2008). While cultural distances could increase information asymmetries, similarity of knowledge structures mitigate increased opacity resulting from cultural distance. We demonstrate an advantage to using cross-border acquisitions to access diverse knowledge (Bertrand, 2009) whether it is technological or local market in nature. Counter to prior findings that suggest abandoning search efforts in distant domains due to increasing information asymmetry (Datar, Frankel, & Wolfson, 2001), we suggest distant searches can be effectively managed if the search is constrained to other areas where knowledge overlaps. Implications of our findings for management research and practice are discussed next.

Implications for Practice

Research consistently cautions managers about the hazards of acquisitions as a strategic tool. However, at least in our focus on high-technology, cross-border acquisitions, it appears the challenges may be more forgiving than anticipated. The average return of 1,167 acquisitions is slightly positive across both stock market and accounting measures of performance, and the potential recognized by short-term measures of performance appear to be largely realized in long-term measures of performance. Further, the negative relationship of paying a premium in short-term measures appears surmountable as the premium paid is not significant for our long-term measures of performance.

It appears that shared knowledge structures from common technology or culture are an important mechanism mitigating cultural and technology distance respectively. During target selection and due diligence, managers can assess whether needed commonality for learning exists. This can provide managers with more nuanced decision criteria that we find is significantly associated with positive acquisition performance. The relevance of this is reinforced by inadequate due diligence having been identified as a primary reason for M&A failure (DiGeorgio, 2002).

Last but not least, it is important to acknowledge that managers should avoid focusing on targets with more intermediate cultural distance. Our results suggest that focusing on targets with moderate cultural distance from an acquirer may offer the lowest reward and still offer integration costs that further limit gains. Instead, higher gains from cross-border acquisitions likely come from distant markets with similar technology or close markets with different technology. For cross-border, high-technology acquisitions, managers need to evaluate targets on multiple criteria that exist in tension with one another and it reinforces the importance of managerial decision making. This is consistent with advice by Slangen (2006) to avoid considering cultural distance in isolation.

Limitations and Future Research

The need to make trade-offs is inherent in all research projects and several we have made may limit the generalizability of our findings. First, we examined high-technology industries where patents are relevant indicators of firm knowledge structures. Although several industries such as pharmaceuticals, electronics, and chemical industries rely on patents, attempts to transfer knowledge integration challenges in alternate industries may be significantly different. An opportunity exists for future studies to focus on product-related outcomes that could further explain acquisition performance. For example, we focus on financial performance, when our focus on high-technology targets implies additional considerations, such as the productivity or funding of R&D. For example, Erel, Jang, and Weisbach (2015) find acquirers relieve funding constraints that allows a target firm to more efficiently fund R&D. It is also possible that industries where knowledge is less codified or technology paradigms less established may require greater management intervention. This relates to another limitation of using archival data that does not observe organizational processes. We agree with Haleblian et al.'s (2009) proposal that qualitative studies focusing on process-oriented outcomes could further add to our understanding of acquisitions. For example, fine grained analysis on the process of learning in acquisitions and the influence of organizational culture using case studies or survey measures is needed to better understand knowledge transfer. Additionally, entry modes beyond acquisitions exist and our findings may not generalize to them. While Tihanyi et al. (2005) find cultural distance is unrelated to entry mode choice, replicating our results with other entry modes represents an opportunity for future research. Finally, while national cultural distance is expected to have a greater impact than corporate culture differences (Hofstede, 2001; Shimizu et al., 2004), exploring the impact of culturally different organizations represents an opportunity for future research.

CONCLUSION

We find cultural distance impacts knowledge integration and it has a negative impact on cross-border acquisition performance. However, advice for managers to focus on acquiring targets with intermediate cultural distance may overlook opportunities in both local and distant cultural domains. When similar national cultures exist, acquirers may benefit from integrating unfamiliar technology. Conversely, acquirers may benefit from culturally distant knowledge with integration facilitated by an acquirer and target having similar technology. As a result, focusing on targets with mid-range cultural distance could actually increase costs of coordination and result in lower cross-border acquisition performance. This suggests knowledge structures play a central role in managing cross-border acquisitions – an insight that advances management theory and makes more and better options available to managers.

NOTES

1. https://sites.google.com/site/patentdataproject/
2. http://worldwide.espacenet.com/advancedSearch?locale=en_EP
3. Consistent results were found with alternate specification of culture distance based on Kogut and Singh's (1988) measure based on Hofstede's cultural dimensions and Dow and Karunaratna's (2006) psychic distance measure.
4. Only final models are reported to save space. Adding the moderation effect into stepwise regression is significant and more detailed results are available upon request.

REFERENCES

Aguilera, R., & Dencker, J. (2004). The role of human resource management in cross-border mergers and acquisitions. *International Journal of Human Resource Management*, *15*, 1357–1372.

Ahuja, G., & Katila, R. (2001). Technological acquisitions and the innovation performance of acquiring firms: A longitudinal study. *Strategic Management Journal*, *22*, 197–220.

Ahuja, G., & Katila, R. (2004). Where do resources come from? The role of idiosyncratic situations. *Strategic Management Journal*, *25*, 887–907.

Aiken, L., & West, S. (1991). *Multiple regression: Testing and interpreting interactions.* London: Sage.

Ailon, G. (2007). *Global ambitions and local identities: An Israeli-American high tech merger.* New York, NY: Berghahn Books.

Athanassiou, N., & Nigh, D. (2000). Internationalization, tacit knowledge and the top management teams of MNCs. *Journal of International Business Studies*, *31*, 471–487.

Barkema, H., & Schijven, M. (2008). Toward unlocking the full potential of acquisitions: The role of organizational restructuring. *Academy of Management Journal*, *51*, 696–722.

Barney, J. (1991). Firm resources and sustained competitive advantage. *Journal of Management*, *17*, 99–120.

Bauer, F., Matzler, K., & Wolf, S. (2016). M&A an innovation: The role of integration and cultural differences—A central European targets perspective. *International Business Review.* Retrieved from http://www.sciencedirect.com/science/article/pii/S0969593114001152#

Bertrand, O. (2009). Effects of foreign acquisitions on R&D activity: Evidence from firm level data for France. *Research Policy*, *38*, 1021–1031.

Bertrand, O., & Capron, L. (2014). Productivity enhancement at home via cross-border acquisitions: The roles of learning and contemporaneous domestic investments. *Strategic Management Journal.* Retrieve from http://onlinelibrary.wiley.com/doi/10.1002/smj.2256/epdf

Bjorkman, I., Stahl, G., & Vaara, E. (2007). Cultural differences and capability transfer in cross-border acquisitions: The mediating roles of capability complementarity, absorptive capacity, and social integration. *Journal of International Business Studies*, *38*, 658–672.

Branzei, O., Vertinsky, I., & Camp, R. (2007). Culture-contingent signs of trust in emergent relationships. *Organizational Behavior and Human Decision Processes*, *104*, 61–82.

Bresman, H., Birkinshaw, J., & Nobel, R. (1999). Knowledge transfer in international acquisitions. *Journal of International Business Studies, 30*, 439–462.

Brock, D. (2005). Multinational acquisition integration: The role of national culture in creating synergies. *International Business Review, 14*, 269–288.

Brouthers, K., & Hennart, J. (2007). Boundaries of the firm: Insights from international entry mode research. *Journal of Management, 33*, 395–425.

Capaldo, A., Lavie, D., & Petruzzelli, A. (forthcoming). Knowledge maturity and the scientific value of innovations: The roles of knowledge distance and adoption. *Journal of Management.* Retrieved from http://jom.sagepub.com/content/early/2014/05/28/0149206314535442.abstract

Capron, L., & Hulland, J. (1999). Redeployment of brands, sales forces, and general marketing management expertise following horizontal acquisitions: A resource-based view. *Journal of Marketing, 63*, 41–54.

Capron, L., & Mitchell, W. (1998). Bilateral resource redeployment and capabilities improvement following horizontal acquisitions. *Industrial and Corporate Change, 7*, 453–484.

Castro, C., & Neira, E. (2005). Knowledge transfer: Analysis of three internet acquisitions. *International Journal of Human Resource Management, 16*, 120–135.

Certo, S., Covin, J., Daily, C., & Dalton, D. (2001). Wealth and the effects of founder management among IPO-stage new ventures. *Strategic Management Journal, 22*, 641–658.

Cohen, W., & Levinthal, D. (1990). Absorptive capacity: A new perspective on learning and innovation. *Administrative Science Quarterly, 35*, 128–152.

Collins, J., Holcomb, T., Certo, S., Hitt, M., & Lester, R. (2009). Learning by doing: Cross-border mergers and acquisitions. *Journal of Business Research, 62*, 1329–1334.

Cording, M., Christmann, P., & Weigelt, C. (2010). Measuring theoretically complex constructs: The case of acquisition performance. *Strategic Organization, 8*(1), 11–41.

Datar, S., Frankel, R., & Wolfson, M. (2001). Earnouts: The effects of adverse selection and agency costs on acquisition techniques. *Journal of Law, Economics, & Organization, 17*, 201–238.

Davidson, W., & McFetridge, D. (1985). Key characteristics in the choice of international technology transfer mode. *Journal of International Business Studies, 16*(2), 5–21.

DiBella, A., Nevis, E., & Gould, J. (1996). Understanding organizational learning capability. *Journal of Management Studies, 33*, 361–379.

DiGeorgio, R. (2002). Making mergers and acquisitions work: What we know and don't know—Part I. *Journal of Change Management, 3*, 134–148.

Dow, D., & Karunaratna, A. (2006). Developing a multidimensional instrument to measure psychic distance stimuli. *Journal of International Business Studies, 37*, 578–602.

Erel, I., Jang, Y., & Weisbach, M. (2015). Do acquisitions relieve target firms' financial constraints? *Journal of Finance, 70*, 289–328.

Estrin, S., Baghdasaryan, D., & Meyer, K. (2009). The impact of institutional and human resource distance on international entry strategies. *Journal of Management Studies, 46*, 1171–1196.

Foss, N., & Christensen, J. (2001). A market-process approach to corporate coherence. *Managerial and Decision Economics, 22*, 213–226.

Frost, T., Birkinshaw, J., & Ensign, P. (2002). Centers of excellence in multinational corporations. *Strategic Management Journal, 23*, 997–1018.

Gelles, D. (2011). To reach a distant workforce. *Financial Times.* August 25, p. 10.

Gersick, C., & Hackman, R. (1990). Habitual routines in task-performing groups. *Organizational Behavior and Human Decision Processes, 47*, 65–68.

Gomes, E., Angwin, D., Weber, Y., & Tarba, S. (2013). Critical success factors through the mergers and acquisition process: Revealing pre- and post-M&A connections for improved performance. *International Business Review, 55*, 13–35.

Gubbi, S., Aulakh, P., Ray, S., Sarkar, M., & Chittoor, R. (2010). Do international acquisitions by merging-economy firms create shareholder value? The case of Indian firms. *Journal of International Business Studies, 41*, 397–418.

Gupta, A., & Govindarajan, V. (2000). Knowledge flows within multinational corporations. *Strategic Management Journal, 21*, 473–496.

Hakanson, L. (1995). Learning through acquisitions: Management and integration of foreign R&D laboratories. *International Studies of Management and Organization, 25*(1–2), 121–157.

Haleblian, J., Devers, C., McNamara, G., Carpenter, M., & Davison, R. (2009). Taking stock of what we know about mergers and acquisitions: A review and research agenda. *Journal of Management, 35*, 469–502.

Hannan, M., & Freeman, J. (1977). The population ecology of organizations. *American Journal of Sociology, 82*, 929–964.

Hansen, M., Podolny, J., & Pfeffer, J. (2001). So many ties, so little time: A task contingency perspective on the value of social capital in organizations. *Research in the Sociology of Organizations, 18*, 21–57.

Harrison, J., Hitt, M., Hoskisson, R., & Ireland, R. (1991). Synergies and post-acquisition performance: Differences versus similarities in resource allocations. *Journal of Management, 17*, 173–190.

Harrison, J., Hitt, M., Hoskisson, R., & Ireland, R. (2001). Resource complementarity in business combinations: Extending the logic to organizational alliances. *Journal of Management, 27*, 679–690.

Henderson, R., & Clark, K. (1990). Architectural innovation: The reconfiguration of existing product technologies and the failure of established firms. *Administrative Science Quarterly, 35*, 9–30.

Higgins, M., & Rodriguez, D. (2006). The outsourcing of R&D through acquisitions in the pharmaceutical industry. *Journal of Financial Economics, 80*, 351–383.

Hofstede, G. (2001). *Culture's consequences.* Newbury Park, CA: Sage.

Hutzschenreuter, T., & Voll, J. (2008). Performance effects of "added cultural distance" in the path of international expansion: The case of German multinational enterprises. *Journal of International Business Studies, 39*, 53–70.

Hutzschenreuter, T., Voll, J., & Verbeke, A. (2011). The impact of added cultural distance and cultural diversity on international expansion patterns: A Penrosian perspective. *Journal of Management Studies, 48*, 305–329.

Inkpen, A. (1996). Creating knowledge through collaboration. *California Management Review, 39*(1), 123–140.

Inkpen, A., & Tsang, E. (2005). Social capital, networks, and knowledge transfer. *Academy of Management Review, 30*, 146–165.

Johanson, J., & Vahlne, J. (2009). The Uppsala internationalization process model revisited: From liability of foreignness to liability of outsidership. *Journal of International Business Studies, 40*, 1411–1431.

Kang, S., Morris, S., & Snell, S. (2007). Relational archetypes, organizational learning, and value creation: Extending the human resource architecture. *Academy of Management Review, 32*, 23–256.

King, D., Dalton, D., Daily, C., & Covin, J. (2004). Meta-analyses of post-acquisition performance: Indications of unidentified moderators. *Strategic Management Journal, 25*, 187–200.

King, D., Slotegraaf, R., & Kesner, I. (2008). Performance implications of firm resource interactions in the acquisition of R&D-intensive firms. *Organization Science, 19*, 327–340.

Kogut, B., & Singh, H. (1988). The effect of national culture on the choice of entry mode. *Journal of International Business Studies, 19*, 411–432.

Kogut, B., & Zander, U. (1992). Knowledge of the firm, combinative capabilities, and the replication of technology. *Organization Science, 3*, 383–397.

Kogut, B., & Zander, U. (1996). What firms do? Coordination, identity, and learning. *Organization Science, 7*, 577–590.

Kostova, T., & Zaheer, S. (1999). Organizational legitimacy under conditions of complexity: The case of the multinational enterprise. *Academy of Management Review, 24*, 64–81.

Kusstatscher, V., & Cooper, C. (2005). *Managing emotions in mergers and acquisitions.* Chenltenham: Edward Elgar.

Laamanen, T. (2007). On the role of acquisition premium in acquisition research. *Strategic Management Journal, 28*, 1359–1369.

Lane, P., Salk, J., & Lyles, M. (2001). Absorptive capacity, learning, and performance in international joint ventures. *Strategic Management Journal, 22*, 1139–1161.

Li, Q., Maggitti, P., Smith, K., Tesluk, P., & Katilla, R. (2013). Top management attention to innovation: The role of search selection and intensity in new product introductions. *Academy of Management Journal, 56*, 893–916.

Light, J. (2011). More companies plan to put R&D overseas. *Wall Street Journal, 22*(February), B4.

Lucas, L. (2006). The role of culture on knowledge transfer: The case of the multinational corporation. *Learning Organization, 13*, 257–275.

Lyles, M., & Salk, J. (1996). Knowledge acquisition from foreign parents in international joint ventures: An empirical examination in the Hungarian context. *Journal of International Business Studies, 27*, 877–903.

Makino, S., & Delios, A. (1996). Local knowledge transfer and performance: Implications for alliance formation in Asia. *Journal of International Business Studies, 27*, 905–927.

Makri, M., Hitt, M., & Lane, P. (2010). Complementary technologies, knowledge relatedness, and invention outcomes in high technology mergers and acquisitions. *Strategic Management Journal, 31*, 602–628.

Makri, M., & Lane, M. (2008). Responding to technological maturity: A socio-cognitive model of science and innovation in technological communities. *Journal of High-technology Management Research, 18*(1), 1–28.

Martynova, M., & Renneboog, L. (2008). A century of corporate takeovers: What have we learned and where do we stand. *Journal of Banking and Finance, 32*, 2148–2177.

Mattioli, D., & Cimilluca, D. (2015). M&A resurgence must broaden to keep rolling in 2015. *Wall Street Journal, 2*(January), R12.

Morosini, P., Shane, S., & Singh, H. (1998). National cultural distance and cross-border acquisition performance. *Journal of International Business Studies, 29*, 137–158.

Morosini, P., & Singh, H. (1994). Post-cross-border acquisitions: Implementing 'national culture-compatible' strategies to improve performance. *European Management Journal, 12*, 390–400.

Mowery, D., Oxley, J., & Silverman, B. (1996). Strategic alliances and interfirm knowledge transfer. *Strategic Management Journal, 17*, 77–91.

Nadolska, A., & Barkema, H. (2007). Learning to internationalise: The pace and success of foreign acquisitions. *Journal of International Business Studies, 38*, 1170–1186.

Neter, J., Kutner, M., Nachtsheim, C., & Wasserman, W. (1996). *Applied linear statistical models* (4th ed.). Boston, MA: McGraw-Hill.

Nonaka, I. (1994). A dynamic theory of organizational knowledge creation. *Organization Science, 5*, 14–37.

Nooteboom, B. (2000). *Learning and innovation in organizations and economies.* Oxford: Oxford University Press.

Nooteboom, B., Vanhaverbeke, W., Duysters, G., Gilsing, V., & van den Oord, A. (2007). Optimal cognitive distance and absorptive capacity. *Research Policy, 36*, 1016–1034.

OECD. (2009). *OECD patent statistics manual.* Organisation for Economic, Co-operation and Development.

Olie, R. (1994). Shades of culture and institutions in international mergers. *Organization Studies, 15*, 381–405.

Osland, G., & Cavusgil, S. (1996). Performance issues in US-China joint ventures. *California Management Review, 39*(2), 106–130.

Oxley, J., & Sampson, R. (2004). The scope and governance of international R&D alliances. *Strategic Management Journal, 25*, 723–749.

Pak, Y., & Park, Y. (2004). A framework of knowledge transfer in cross-border joint ventures: An empirical test of the Korean context. *Management International Review, 44*, 417–434.

Palich, L., & Gomez-Mejia, L. (1999). A theory of global strategy and firm efficiencies: Considering the effects of cultural diversity. *Journal of Management, 25*, 587–606.

Park, N. (2004). A guide to using event study methods in multi-country settings. *Strategic Management Journal, 25*, 655–668.

Paruchuri, S., Nerkar, A., & Hambrick, D. (2006). Acquisition integration and productivity losses in the technical core: Disruption of inventors in acquired companies. *Organization Science, 17*, 545–562.

Pascale, R. (1999). Surfing the edge of chaos. *Sloan Management Review, Spring*, 83–94.

Penrose, E. (1959). *The theory of the growth of the firm.* New York, NY: Wiley.

Ranft, A., & Lord, M. (2000). Acquiring new knowledge: The role of retaining human capital in acquisitions of high-tech firms. *Journal of High Technology Management Research, 11*, 295–319.

Reuer, J. (2001). From hybrids to hierarchies: Shareholder wealth effects of joint venture partner buyouts. *Strategic Management Journal, 22*, 27–44.

Reus, T., & Lamont, B. (2009). The double-edged sword of cultural distance in international acquisitions. *Journal of International Business Studies, 40*, 1298–1316.

Risberg, A. (2001). Employee experiences of acquisition processes. *Journal of World Business, 36*, 58–84.

Rothaermel, F., & Alexandre, M. (2009). Ambidexterity in technology sourcing: The moderating role of absorptive capacity. *Organization Science, 20*, 759–780.

Rottig, D. (2011). The role of social capital in cross-cultural M&As: A multinational corporation perspective. *European Journal of International Management, 5*, 413–431.

Sarala, R. (2009). The impact of cultural differences and acculturation factors on post-acquisition conflict. *Scandinavian Journal of Management, 26*, 38–56.

Schein, E. (1993). How can organizations learn faster? The challenge of entering the green room. *Sloan Management Review, 34*(2), 85–92.

Schmoch, U. (2008). Karlsruhe: Concept of a technology classification for country comparisons. Final report to the World Intellectual Property Organization (WIPO). Fraunhofer Institute for Systems and Innovation Research, Karlsruhe.

Schweiger, D. (2002). *M&A integration: A framework for executives and managers.* New York, NY: McGraw-Hill.

Shimizu, K., Hitt, M., Vaidyanath, D., & Pisano, V. (2004). Theoretical foundations of cross-border mergers and acquisitions: A review of current research and recommendations for the future. *Journal of International Management, 10,* 370.

Sigglekow, N. (2002). Misperceiving interactions among complements and substitutes: Organizational consequences. *Management Science, 48,* 900–916.

Simonin, B. (1999). Ambiguity and the process of knowledge transfer in strategic alliances. *Strategic Management Journal, 20,* 595–623.

Sirower, M. (1997). *The synergy trap: How companies lose the acquisition game.* New York, NY: The Free Press

Slangen, A. (2006). National cultural distance and initial foreign acquisition performance: The moderating effect of integration. *Journal of World Business, 41,* 161–170.

Slangen, A., & Hennart, J. (2008). Do multinationals really prefer to enter culturally distant countries through greenfields rather than through acquisitions? The role of parent experience and subsidiary autonomy. *Journal of International Business Studies, 39,* 472–490.

Stahl, G., & Voigt, A. (2008). Do cultural differences matter in mergers and acquisitions? A tentative model and meta-analytic examination. *Organization Science, 19,* 160–179.

Szulanski, G. (1996). Exploring internal stickiness: Impediments to the transfer of best practices within the firm. *Strategic Management Journal, 17,* 27–43.

Teece, D., Rumelt, R., Dosi, G., & Winter, S. (1994). Understanding corporate coherence: Theory and evidence. *Journal of Economic Behavior and Organization, 23,* 1–30.

Tihanyi, L., Griffith, D., & Russell, C. (2005). The effect of cultural distance on entry mode choice, international diversification, and MNE performance: A meta-analysis. *Journal of International Business Studies, 36,* 270–283.

Tsang, E. (2002). Acquiring knowledge by foreign partners from international joint ventures in a transition economy: Learning-by-doing and learning myopia. *Strategic Management Journal, 23,* 835–854.

Vaara, E. (2003). Post-acquisition integration as sensemaking: Glimpses of ambiguity, confusion, hypocrisy and politicization. *Journal of Management Studies, 40,* 859–889.

Vaara, E., Sarala, R., Stahl, G., & Bjorkman, I. (2012). The impact of organizational and national cultural differences on social conflict and knowledge transfer in international acquisitions. *Journal of Management Studies, 49,* 1–27.

Verbeke, A., & Yuan, W. (2007). Entrepreneurship in multinational enterprises: A Penrosian perspective. *Management International Review, 47,* 241–258.

Vermeulen, F. (2005). How acquisitions revitalize companies. *Sloan Management Review, 46*(4), 45–51.

Vermeulen, F., & Barkema, H. (2001). Learning through acquisitions. *Academy of Management Journal, 44,* 457–476.

Weick, K. (1979). *The social psychology of organizing* (2nd ed.). Reading, MA: Addison-Wesley.

Williams, C., & Mitchell, W. (2004). Focusing firm evolution: The impact of information infrastructure on market entry by U.S. telecommunications companies, 1984–1998. *Management Science, 50,* 1561–1575.

Wolpert, J. (2002). Breaking out of the innovation box. *Harvard Business Review*, *80*(8), 76–83.

Yang, H., Phelps, C., & Steensma, K. (2010). Learning from what others have learned from you: The effects of knowledge spillovers on originating firms. *Academy of Management Journal*, *53*, 371–389.

Yayavaram, S., & Ahuja, G. (2008). Decomposability in knowledge structures and its impact on the usefulness of inventions and knowledge-base malleability. *Administrative Science Quarterly*, *53*, 333–362.

Yu, J., Engleman, R., & Van de Ven, A. (2005). The integration journey: An attention-based view of the merger and acquisition integration process. *Organization Studies*, *16*, 1501–1528.

Zaheer, A., Castaner, X., & Souder, D. (2011). Synergy sources, target autonomy, and integration in acquisitions. *Journal of Management*, *39*, 604–632.

Zahra, S. (1996). Technology strategy and new venture performance: A study of corporate-sponsored and independent biotechnology ventures. *Journal of Business Venturing*, *11*, 289–321.

APPENDIX

Table A1. Distribution of Acquisitions.

| Target's Country | Cross-Border Acquisitions | | | | High-Tech 2-Digit SIC Codes | | | | | | | |
| | Number of deals | | Value of deals 2,000 USD | | 28 | 35 | 36 | 37 | 38 | 48 | 73 | 87 |
	Number	% deals	Value	% deals value								
Australia	37	3.17%	60,640	2.54%	5	5	3	4	5	2	6	7
Austria	6	0.51%	68,932	2.89%	1	1	1	2	0	0	0	1
Belgium	4	0.34%	96,558	4.05%		0	1	0	0	1	0	8
Canada	112	9.60%	127,756	5.36%	19	21	32	8	8	10	6	8
China	62	5.31%	31,053	1.30%	17	22	11	6	5	6	12	9
Denmark	33	2.83%	86,917	3.64%	2	4	2	5	1	5	6	8
Finland	66	5.66%	74,595	3.13%	9	10	7	10	10	6	8	6
France	66	5.66%	112,863	4.73%	6	7	10	9	9	10	5	10
Germany	66	5.66%	73,294	3.07%	9	7	10	9	9	10	7	5
Greece	22	1.89%	7,264	0.30%	2	4	4	4	1	2	3	2
Hong Kong	15	1.29%	4,153	0.17%	1	0	0	1	4	4	1	4
India	23	1.97%	67,179	2.82%	3	3	2	2	3	4	3	3
Ireland	12	1.03%	53,644	2.25%	1	0	2	1	1	3	1	3
Italy	13	1.11%	23,158	0.97%	3	4	0	2	2	2	0	0
Japan	8	0.69%	2,797	0.12%	0	1	3	1	1	1	1	0
Luxembourg	23	1.97%	15,487	0.65%	1	4	2	4	4	4	3	1
The Netherlands	17	1.46%	20,299	0.85%	1	3	4	3	1	1	4	0
Norway	15	1.29%	4,271	0.18%	0	0	4	2	4	0	4	1
Poland	18	1.54%	24,471	1.03%	3	1	4	3	4	3	0	1
Portugal	14	1.20%	47,553	1.99%	1	4	0	3	2	3	1	0
Singapore	16	1.37%	100,261	4.20%	1	1	2	2	3	2	4	1
South Africa	17	1.46%	57,341	2.40%	2	1	0	1	3	4	3	3
Spain	16	1.37%	74,340	3.12%	2	4	1	4	1	3	1	0

Table A1. (*Continued*)

Target's Country	Cross-Border Acquisitions		Value of deals 2,000 USD		High-Tech 2-Digit SIC Codes							
	Number of deals				28	35	36	37	38	48	73	87
	Number	% deals	Value	% deals value								
Sweden	17	1.46%	83,031	3.48%	3	1	3	2	3	3	1	1
Switzerland	5	0.43%	65,511	2.75%	0	3	0	1	0	0	1	0
The United Kingdom	142	12.17%	49,107	2.06%	19	14	21	15	22	22	18	11
The United States	238	20.39%	410,410	17.26%	21	43	29	32	23	21	33	36
All other countries	84	7.20%	508,661	21.32%	5	12	8	13	10	8	15	15
Total	*1,167*	*100%*	*2,385,273*	*100.00%*	*138*	*166*	*160*	*148*	*138*	*140*	*140*	*137*

Note: N = 1,167 cross-border acquisitions between 1995 and 2006.

PEERING INTO THE EXECUTIVE MIND: EXPANDING OUR UNDERSTANDING OF THE MOTIVES FOR ACQUISITIONS

Adam Steinbach, Cynthia E. Devers, Gerry McNamara and Jingyu Li

ABSTRACT

In this chapter, we review recent work examining the influence individual executive characteristics exhibit on acquisition behavior, often in service of their private interests. In doing so, we outline the findings of this limited research, explore possible alternative explanations and factors, and discuss several novel data collection and methodological techniques that scholars have advanced in the upper echelon context, in recent years. As we discuss, we believe that researchers can more fruitfully explore the underlying personal, psychological, and social factors that motivate acquisition activity, by augmenting current techniques with these methodological innovations.

Keywords: M&A; acquisitions; acquisition motives; managerial traits; managerial overconfidence; unobtrusive measures

Advances in Mergers and Acquisitions, Volume 15, 145–160
ISSN: 1479-361X/doi:10.1108/S1479-361X20160000015008

Scholars have focused much attention on determining the antecedents of merger and acquisition (M&A) behavior (Haleblian, Devers, McNamara, Carpenter, & Davison, 2009). Two distinct theoretical perspectives regarding this query – the value-enhancement view and the private interest view – are embedded in the M&A literature (Devers, McNamara, Haleblian, & Yoder, 2013). The value-enhancement perspective builds on M&A theory and research suggesting that CEOs acquire other firms because they are confident that doing so will enhance firm value (Sanders & Hambrick, 2007). Nevertheless, although this perspective is the most entrenched view in this literature, its veracity is challenged by empirical evidence that acquisitions typically do not result in positive returns to acquiring firm shareholders (McNamara, Haleblian, & Dykes, 2008). To explain this mismatch, researchers have posited an opposing view – that executives acquire primarily to enhance their own interests and, in the process, those acquisitions tend to erode firm value (Haleblian et al., 2009). Building out of the view that acquisitions are often driven by factors other than the objective assessments of value creation potential, we discuss three factors that may lead executives to champion acquisitions when the value of those acquisitions for shareholders is unclear: peer comparisons and mimetic behavior, psychological attributes, and demographic characteristics.

PEER COMPARISONS AND MIMETIC BEHAVIOR

While we would like to believe that executives champion acquisitions as a result of their assessments of the value of acquisitions for their firm, research suggests that acquisitions are, at times, pursued due to social pressures and mimetic behavior. In support, some research has revealed the importance of peer comparison for acquisition behavior. For example, studies have shown that managers appear to mimic the acquisition behaviors of firms they are tied to through interlocking directorships (Haunschild, 1993; Haunschild & Beckman, 1998; Westphal, Seidel, & Stewart, 2001). Additional evidence suggests that firms often pursue acquisitions, due to bandwagon pressures, as seen in acquisition waves (Carow, Heron, & Saxton, 2004; Harford, 2005; McNamara et al., 2008). Finally, Seo, Gamache, Devers, and Carpenter (2015) recently found that CEOs who are underpaid relative to peer CEOs engage in higher levels of acquisition activity than other CEOs, perhaps, as a means of increasing their own compensation to better align with peers' pay. Although only a few studies have examined the effect of peer comparisons in the M&A context, together, this work suggests that peer comparisons appear to generate perceptions that can motivate acquisition activity. Thus, we encourage future research that continues to explore this important antecedent.

PSYCHOLOGICAL ATTRIBUTES

In addition to peer evaluations, research has examined how executives' psychological attributes influence acquisitive behavior. First, a number of studies have examined the degree to which CEOs are hubristic or overconfident and subsequently pursue acquisitions due to their over-estimation of their abilities to extract value from acquisitions. These studies argue that executives are driven by the belief that the firm will be able to enhance firm value through acquisitions by (a) private synergy opportunities (exploiting common resources or capabilities), (b) possessing superior information that allows them to exploit emerging opportunities before their competitors can, or (c) thwarting competition by increasing market power. However, acquisitions may not generate these shareholder benefits if executives are overconfident in the value creating potential of acquisitions. Supporting this view, several studies have found support for the hypothesized relationship between CEO confidence/overconfidence and acquisition activity (e.g., Billett & Qian, 2008; Hayward & Hambrick, 1997; Ferris, Jayaraman, & Sabherwal, 2013; Malmendier & Tate, 2005, 2008; Roll, 1986).

Other researchers argue that executives may pursue acquisitions to enhance their own private interests, rather than to create shareholder value. Executives' private interests include issues such as (a) enhancing their personal wealth, (b) increasing their own power and discretion, and/or (c) diversifying their own risk. Thus, different from the value-enhancement perspective, scholars advancing the private interest view suggest that acquiring CEOs may not necessarily have confidence that their acquisitions will create long-term firm value. Private interest arguments appear to align with research showing that executive compensation policy and ownership may induce self-interested motivations to acquire. For example, studies have shown that acquiring CEOs' compensation generally increases post acquisition, regardless of how those acquisitions perform (Bliss & Rosen, 2001; Grinstein & Hribar, 2004; Harford & Li, 2007). Thus, acquiring other firms presents an attractive strategic action for CEOs even if they are not confident in those acquisitions generating returns for shareholders.

In an effort to reconcile these views, Devers et al. (2013) utilized a unique time window to examine CEOs' acquisition-specific future value creation confidence. They focused on CEOs' equity-based adjustments (changes to exercisable stock options and stock holdings) following their acquisition announcements. In doing so, they argued that if acquiring CEOs were confident in the firm value creation ability of their acquisitions, they would hold their stock and exercisable options, as opposed to sell, after announcing acquisitions. Their results confirmed that acquiring CEOs tended to sell stock and exercise options following acquisition announcements, suggesting limited confidence of those acquiring CEOs in the value creation potential of their acquisitions. These findings suggest that although CEOs with generalized confidence may acquire other firms, they may simultaneously have little confidence that those deals will enhance firm value, thereby supporting the private interest perspective.

Relatedly, researchers have examined the use of corporate communications that capture distal executive sentiment for strategic decisions, including acquisitions. For example, Graffin, Haleblian, and Kiley (2015) found that acquiring firm executives engage in impression management around their acquisitions by announcing unrelated positive information simultaneous to their acquisitions, in what they argue is a specific attempt to "offset" expectations that stakeholders may receive their acquisitions negatively. Their study provides further evidence that, in doing so, acquiring executives are not necessarily as confident regarding their acquisitions as they are commonly assumed to be. This work, coupled with the research above, advances the discussion regarding executive confidence and acquisition behavior and furthers the need for increased exploration into the underlying executive motives for acquisitions.

In sum, as we noted above, although generalized CEO confidence may increase acquisition activity, recent research appears to indicate that those same CEOs may not have high confidence in the future value creation potential of those actions. We, therefore, strongly encourage research that develops a better understanding of the role of CEO general (perhaps, trait-based) and specific (perhaps, state-based) confidence on the motivation to acquire.

Related but distinct from confidence, researchers have begun to explore the idea that CEO narcissism increases the likelihood of acquisition activity (Chatterjee & Hambrick, 2007, 2011). This research suggests that CEO narcissism is positively related with acquisition frequency and size. Narcissism also increases the variability in performance of the firm's strategic actions. Finally, CEO narcissism moderates the degree to which performance and social cues lead firms to undertake potentially risky actions, such as mergers and acquisitions, with narcissism attenuating the degree to which these actions are driven by performance cues but strengthening the effect of social cues.

Executives' risk and goal orientations have also been found to influence acquisition activity. Using unique measures, Cain and McKeon (2016) found that CEO risk propensity, measured as whether CEOs were licensed small aircraft pilots and rated high on sensation-seeking, positively influenced acquisition activity. In a somewhat similar vein, Gamache, McNamara, Mannor, and Johnson (2015) explored the influence of CEO regulatory focus on acquisition activity. Regulatory focus theory posits that goal pursuit is motivated through two independent strategic means: a promotion focus, or a sensitivity toward accomplishment and a presence or absence of positive outcomes, and a prevention focus, or a sensitivity toward security and a presence or absence of negative outcomes (Higgins, 1997; Lanaj, Chang, & Johnson, 2012). Gamache et al. (2015) showed that CEO promotion focus is positively associated with both the number and total value of announced and completed acquisitions, while CEO prevention focus negatively related to these outcomes. Interestingly, the authors also demonstrated that stock option pay attenuated the negative effect of CEO prevention focus on acquisition activity, however, stock option pay did not affect the relationship between CEO promotion focus and acquisition behavior. This work clearly suggests the need for further research exploring the role of managerial risk propensity, foci-related, or other psychological bias-driven decision making in acquisition behavior.

In addition to these attributes, other executive traits, such as Big Five personality traits (conscientiousness, agreeableness, extraversion, need for achievement, and emotional stability), temporal orientation, political orientation, affect, and core self-evaluation have the potential to influence the likelihood of pursuing acquisitions. We believe that examining the individual and collective influence of core executive psychological attributes has the potential to help us understand the choice to pursue acquisitions, the type of acquisitions undertaken, the management and integration of acquisitions, and ultimately the performance of those acquisitions.

DEMOGRAPHIC CHARACTERISTICS

Career Horizon and Age

Some limited work has shown that CEOs' are more likely to acquire other firms early in their careers than later, largely in an attempt to take advantage of the large and enduring increases to pay that follow growth through acquisitions (Yim, 2013). However, in an interesting twist, Jenter and Lewellen (2015) found that the incidence of successful takeovers is significantly increased when target CEOs are close to age 65. This work suggests that although acquisition proclivity decreases with CEO age, the propensity to be acquired increases with age. Although this work is insightful, we know little about how the life cycle of executives may influence M&A activity. Therefore, we suggest this is an area ripe for future research.

Gender

A nascent line of research has begun to focus on the question of whether and how the gender mix of corporate elites affects acquisition choices. Specifically, scholars drawing on social identity and decision making research have suggested that the diversity that arises when females are included on boards of directors of top management teams may increase acquisition-related deliberation and reduce acquisition behavior (Chen, Crossland, & Huang, 2016; Huang & Kisgen, 2013).

More recent work advances this argument by challenging the common assertion that women must think and act like men, in order to advance into the upper echelon (Ely, 1995; Johnson & Powell, 1994; Lyness & Thompson, 1997). Specifically, this work builds on gender role research to argue that women perceive far greater risk when taking on and operating in executive positions than do males. This occurs, many of these scholars argue, because audiences expect women and men to act in accordance with gender stereotypes, suggesting that men should act agentically (e.g., assertive and leader-like), while women should act communally (e.g., nurturing and caring) (Eagly, 1987; Eagly & Karau, 2002; Fiske, Haslam, & Fiske, 1991). As a result, "male" is the prototypical leader quality for most people (Ryan, Haslam, Hersby, & Bongiorno, 2011). Thus, when women display male-oriented agentic leader behaviors they violate audience expectations, which often leads women to receive much harsher judgments than their male counterparts in both success and failure contexts (Koenig, Eagly, Mitchell, & Ristikari, 2011). This research suggests that women who are also firm leaders (e.g., executives) perceive more downside risk in their positions than their male counterparts do, and, thus, act more conservatively in executive and CEO roles. In support, some recent research has shown that firms led by female CEOs engage in less acquisition-related spending and activity than male-led firms (Klein, Gamache, Devers, & Hannigan, 2015; Huang & Kisgen, 2013).

Given the relative scarcity of female executives, gender research in the upper echelon is in its infancy. However, now that the number of females taking upper echelon roles is increasing, this topic is of increasingly critical importance to management scholars and practitioners. We strongly encourage strategy scholars to continue to shed light on the role gender plays, not only in acquisition behavior, but also in strategic leadership, more generally.

We have attempted to identify several individual differences that offer fruitful opportunities for scholars wishing to advance what we know about the antecedents of acquisition behavior. We strongly encourage additional research that continues to explore how these and other characteristics (e.g., education, experience, and founder status) might work in isolation, in concert, or in conflict on acquisition behavior. Below, to facilitate this line of work, we outline several data collection and methodological techniques that we believe will help strategy researchers advance our understanding of executives' individual differences and characteristics that drive acquisition behaviors.

NOVEL DATA COLLECTION AND METHODOLOGICAL TECHNIQUES

While the above discussion highlighted the value of more fully examining the role of top executive attributes in driving acquisition activity, scholars have long recognized that effectively capturing such attributes is a challenging methodological task (Hambrick & Mason, 1984). However, recent research has identified a number of ways to measure the attributes of senior corporate leaders that are likely to have a strong influence on both the firm's likelihood of pursuing acquisitive actions as well as the aspects of those acquisitions. We discuss five methods that strategy researchers could employ, to gain insight on the managerial attributes that drive acquisition behaviors. We lay out these well-established data collection methods, with relevant examples of studies that employ them, to capture executive attributes and explore their effects on acquisition activity and other relevant strategic decisions.

Surveys and Interviews

One of the most direct methods for capturing the personal and psychological characteristics is to collect data from the executives themselves, either through surveys or structured interviews. Using this method allows researchers to collect measures of CEO and other leader attributes that have been validated by organizational psychology and organizational behavior researchers. Though this method has great potential to directly capture top executive attributes, it can also be seen as difficult, as access to and willingness of executives tend to be limited (Zaheer, McEvily, & Perrone, 1998). However, the ability to collect and leverage top executive survey and interview data can be enhanced by making participation seem more relevant or beneficial to the executives. First, researchers can leverage personal or university ties to generate an increased willingness of executives to participate. For example, Mannor, Wowak, Bartkus, and Gomez-Mejia (2015) were able to extensively interview and survey not only a sample of 84 CEOs and presidents but also individuals closest to them (e.g., TMT members, spouses, other family members) at firms with revenues of at least $20 million. Their rigorous study design (2015, pp. 16−26) allowed them to test hypotheses connecting job anxiety to strategic risk-taking, including acquisitions. To generate this sample of corporate executives, the researchers leveraged the social ties participants had with the university with which the researchers are affiliated and also through researchers' prior professional ties. This social capital was instrumental in gaining participation. McNamara, Deephouse, and Luce (2003) followed a similar logic, leveraging the social capital of the University of Minnesota, a school with which two of the researchers were affiliated, in contacting business executives in firms located in Minneapolis and St. Paul. As a result, they were able to generate a 77 percent response rate for their survey.

Second, researchers can focus on generating samples of executives from organizations that are not bombarded with requests and are more likely to be open to survey participation. For example, Simon and Houghton (2003) were able to obtain surveys and interviews of executives in small computer firms located in the state of Georgia using a two-wave study design in which they obtained this data before and after a new product launch. Importantly, rather than focus on top executives of major multi-national firms, Simon and Houghton (2003) instead chose to focus their efforts on executives of smaller firms in a narrow geographic range to obtain a sizeable enough sample to collect survey and interview data from executive decision-makers. Future researchers may benefit from a similar approach when attempting to obtain data directly from executives, including for acquisitions studies. Interestingly, in drawing on their sample of small firm executives, Simon and Houghton (2003) were able to collect data from executives in two waves, allowing them to assess the executives' confidence in an anticipated product launch as well as self-reports of launch success 18 months later. A similar approach was used by Li and Tang (2010), who used data from the Chinese government's survey of Chinese CEOs to measure CEO hubris by comparing CEOs' assessments of performance to objective performance measures, which they, in turn, found was a predictor of firm risk-taking.

Finally, researchers can use a focused, industry-specific example to increase executives' interest in participating in research, by leveraging opportunities to provide those executives potentially valuable information gleaned from that work. For example, earlier, we mentioned a study by McNamara et al. (2003) that generated a very high response rate. This study focused on a single industry, the banking industry, and, as part of an inducement to participate, the researchers promised to provide all participants with a summary of how other responding executives conceptualized the competitive structure of the industry and the major strategic issues those executives were most concerned about.

Managerial Communications

Though obtaining data on executive characteristics directly from the executives themselves and those closest to them has great appeal, particularly for construct validity, upper echelon scholars have noted the difficulties of obtaining such data, especially in large enough quantities from leaders of major corporations (Chatterjee & Hambrick, 2007). To address this issue, a number of researchers have focused on unobtrusive measures of psychological traits of executives and have demonstrated the power of these measures for examining the relationship between managerial traits and important strategic outcomes, including acquisitions. These studies typically use archival data, such as public statements and other documents issued by the firm and/or senior executives, to assess executive traits. One such example is the work of Gamache and colleagues (2015), who, by content analyzing letters to shareholders, were able to connect the regulatory focus of CEOs to their firms' acquisition behavior. Specifically, the authors detail a strong defense for the use of letters to shareholders, as a reflection of CEO characteristics, a careful construction of an appropriate dictionary for the promotion and prevention focus constructs, and the convergent and discriminant validity of their measure with a sample of undergraduate surveys (2014, pp. 1269–1271). Linguistic approaches such as theirs have gained considerable favor in strategic management research (Kaplan, 2008) with well-established procedures for their proper execution (e.g., Duriau, Reger, & Pfarrer, 2007; Weber, 1990), offering much promise for continued research on executive motivations underlying acquisition behavior and other strategic actions.

In addition to content analysis, researchers have used attributes of corporate communication and compensation to assess CEO traits. For example, Chatterjee and Hambrick (2007) used the prominence of the CEO in the company's annual report, the CEO's prominence in the firm's press releases, the CEO's use of first person personal pronouns in interviews, and the CEO's compensation relative to the second highest paid firm executive, to measure the level of CEO narcissism. They found that these elements were all highly correlated and, combined, served as a valid indicator of CEO narcissism.

Finally, the Graffin et al. (2015) study discussed above furthers an alternative methodology for capturing executive sentiment and impression management, by analyzing the release, type, and content of corporate communications obtained from archival sources. Executives frequently engage in impression management (see also Bansal & Clelland, 2004; Elsbach & Sutton, 1992; Elsbach, Sutton, & Principe, 1998; Graffin, Carpenter, & Boivie, 2011). Thus, we argue that further work examining this type of impression management behavior surrounding acquisition activity will allow scholars to develop a deeper theoretical and empirical understanding of executives' sentiments and motivations regarding their acquisition behaviors and other important actions.

Videometrics

In another "unobtrusive" measure, some strategic management researchers have begun to assess videos of executives, increasingly available in today's media landscape, as a means of capturing those executives' characteristics. Petrenko, Aime, Ridge, and Hill (2016) established a novel approach for utilizing these videos and measuring CEO characteristics using a thorough methodology of third-party ratings to validate key managerial attributes, such as CEO narcissism. They find interesting links between their video-based measures of CEO narcissism, firm CSR, and firm performance.

One of the most appealing aspects of this "videometric" approach is that it allows researchers to use well-established personality instruments from social and psychological research and apply them to executives, for which the application of these instruments has typically remained elusive. Petrenko et al. (2016) employed raters experienced in using personality assessments to rate CEOs on items from the Narcissistic Personality Inventory (NPI) as reflected in the publicly available videos of the CEOs. They found high inter-rater agreement, established consistency in CEO narcissism across time with a subsample of CEOs with multiple videos, and checked their measurement procedure using a pilot study of self- and third-party ratings of student videos and found no differences between these ratings. As a relatively new method in conjunction with the increase of publicly available videos of CEOs from various media sources, this videometric approach offers considerable promise to strategy researchers interested in capturing a seemingly limitless number of CEO and other executive characteristics for their effects on firm strategic outcomes, including acquisitions.

Personal Finances

Some researchers have also used the personal finances of executives to glean insights into their individual characteristics and traits, including in connection to their acquisition behavior. This is particularly true in capturing executives' level of confidence in their acquisitions, as studies have used the CEOs' actions pertaining to their personal equity (e.g., exercising options, selling stock) in the firm as a proxy for their confidence (see Malmendier & Tate, 2005). The argument is that if executives were confident in the value-creating potential of their firms, they would at least retain their equity moving forward. In one study, Malmendier and Tate (2008) measured CEO overconfidence by identifying CEOs who exercised their options well after the options vested. They found that these "overconfident" CEOs engaged in more value-destroying acquisitions than those who were not "overconfident." Relatedly, as noted earlier, Devers et al. (2013) showed that following acquisitions announcements, CEOs tended to exercise their options and sell their stock in the firm, suggesting their lack of confidence in the ongoing value creation potential in the acquisition. These studies suggest that closer attention to CEOs' and other executives' personal financial activity provides a strong indication of their relative confidence, particularly in relation to their firms' acquisition activity.

In addition to their confidence, other researchers have connected the personal financial actions of executives to important firm outcomes, which we argue would suggest their applicability to studies of acquisitions as well. For example, one study uses the political donations of top management teams as a proxy for the team's political orientations and connects those orientations to tax avoidance, which they argue is a form of corporate risk-taking (Christensen, Dhaliwal, Boivie, & Graffin, 2015). Further, Haynes, Campbell, and Hitt (2014) use pay comparisons of CEOs to other top executives in their teams or at benchmark firms as proxies for CEO greed. Though neither of these measures of executive characteristics has been connected specifically to acquisitions, these and other proxies identified through executives' personal financial activity likely further merit such exploration.

Experiments

One final method of data collection for strategy researchers to consider is using students in executive roles as subjects in experiments on acquisition decision making. Though this method has been infrequently used in acquisition studies, it holds potential, especially for researchers with access to more senior students, such as executive MBAs. Though there are some limitations with using experiments since they may not reflect all of the complexities or carry the same consequences as actual strategic decision making, a number of strategy researchers have successfully used experimental data to garner insights on executive preferences and decision making (e.g., Connelly, Ketchen, Gangloff, & Shook, 2015; Devers, Wiseman, & Holmes, 2007; Hitt & Tyler, 1991; Reuer, Tong, Tyler, & Ariño, 2013). Prior strategy researchers have established a strong level of generalizability of experimental and policy capturing studies by demonstrating the congruence between these studies and post hoc interviews (Hitt & Middlemist, 1979) or even actual risky decisions (Wiseman & Levin, 1996), which likely points to the usefulness of this study methodology for research on acquisitions.

One recent notable example of strategy experiments is that of Chng, Rodgers, Shih, and Song (2012), whose experimental study used MBA students to explore the combined effects of previous performance, incentives, and the decision-maker's core self-evaluation (CSE) on strategic risk-taking. In it, they find that decision-makers with high CSE engage in greater risk-taking only with greater incentive-based compensation and especially under conditions of organizational decline. The experimental method allowed them to not only administer the commonly used CSE survey items to participants but also randomly assign decision-makers to incentive- and fixed-pay conditions as well as organizational growth and decline conditions. Importantly, these conditions are unlikely to occur randomly and in such pure forms in actual firms, making experiments an appealing option for strategy researchers to measure the specific effects of different market and firm conditions. Further, these studies have the benefit of not being clouded by potential confounds that exist with studies of actual executive decisions and firm consequences. As a result, these experimental studies are able to isolate the effects of conditions and characteristics on strategic decisions and, ultimately, performance consequences.

In summary, while measuring top executive attributes is a challenging process, there are several different methods researchers can explore to get at this rich data. Doing so allows researchers to gain new insights on both the managerial antecedents that influence acquisition choices as well as the consequences of acquisitions on managerial attributes and attitudes, particularly as it relates to the psychological, demographic, and mimetic motivators of acquisition activity. Though studies employing these data collection techniques to capture executive characteristics are relatively few and far between, we fully anticipate the increasing use and publication of such techniques in the coming years, as journal editors and reviewers look for more unique and rigorous methods in strategy research. We feel that acquisition researchers can and should increasingly look to these and other similar methods to continue to explore and uncover new findings regarding the managerial antecedents of acquisition activity.

REFERENCES

Bansal, P., & Clelland, I. (2004). Talking trash: Legitimacy, impression management, and unsystematic risk in the context of the natural environment. *Academy of Management Journal, 47*(1), 93–103.

Billett, M. T., & Qian, Y. (2008). Are overconfident CEOs born or made? Evidence of self-attribution bias from frequent acquirers. *Management Science, 54*(6), 1037–1051.

Bliss, R. T., & Rosen, R. J. (2001). CEO compensation and bank mergers. *Journal of Financial Economics, 61*, 107–138.

Cain, M. D., & McKeon, S. B. (2016). CEO personal risk-taking and corporate policies. *Journal of Financial and Quantitative Analysis, 51*(1), 139–164.

Carow, K., Heron, R., & Saxton, T. (2004). Do early birds get the returns? An empirical investigation of early-mover advantages in acquisitions. *Strategic Management Journal, 25*(6), 563–585.

Chatterjee, A., & Hambrick, D. C. (2007). It's all about me: Narcissistic chief executive officers and their effects on company strategy and performance. *Administrative Science Quarterly*, *52*(3), 351–386.

Chatterjee, A., & Hambrick, D. C. (2011). Executive personality, capability cues, and risk taking how narcissistic CEOs react to their successes and stumbles. *Administrative Science Quarterly*, *56*(2), 202–237.

Chen, G., Crossland, C., & Huang, S. (2016). Female board representation and corporate acquisition intensity. *Strategic Management Journal*, *37*(2), 303–313.

Chng, D. H. M., Rodgers, M. S., Shih, E., & Song, X. B. (2012). When does incentive compensation motivate managerial behaviors? An experimental investigation of the fit between incentive compensation, executive core self-evaluation, and firm performance. *Strategic Management Journal*, *33*(12), 1343–1362.

Christensen, D. M., Dhaliwal, D. S., Boivie, S., & Graffin, S. D. (2015). Top management conservatism and corporate risk strategies: Evidence from managers' personal political orientation and corporate tax avoidance. *Strategic Management Journal*, *36*(12), pages 1918–1938.

Connelly, B. L., Ketchen, D. J., Gangloff, K. A., & Shook, C. L. (2015). Investor perceptions of CEO successor selection in the wake of integrity and competence failures: A policy capturing study. *Strategic Management Journal*. DOI: 10.1002/smj.2430

Devers, C. E., McNamara, G., Haleblian, J., & Yoder, M. E. (2013). Do they walk the talk? Gauging acquiring CEO and director confidence in the value creation potential of announced acquisitions. *Academy of Management Journal*, *56*(6), 1679–1702.

Devers, C. E., Wiseman, R. M., & Holmes, R. M. (2007). The effects of endowment and loss aversion in managerial stock option valuation. *Academy of Management Journal*, *50*(1), 191–208.

Duriau, V. J., Reger, R. K., & Pfarrer, M. D. (2007). A content analysis of the content analysis literature in organization studies: Research themes, data sources, and methodological refinements. *Organizational Research Methods*, *10*(1), 5–34.

Eagly, A. H. (1987). *Sex differences in social behavior: A social-role interpretation*. Hillsdale, NJ: Erlbaum.

Eagly, A. H., & Karau, S. J. (2002). Role congruity theory of prejudice toward female leaders. *Psychological Review*, *109*(3), 573.

Elsbach, K. D., & Sutton, R. I. (1992). Acquiring organizational legitimacy through illegitimate actions: A marriage of institutional and impression management theories. *Academy of Management Journal*, *35*, 699–738.

Elsbach, K. D., Sutton, R. I., & Principe, K. E. (1998). Averting expected challenges through anticipatory impression management: A study of hospital billing. *Organization Science*, *9*, 68–86.

Ely, R. J. (1995). The power in demography: Women's social constructions of gender identity at work. *Academy of Management Journal*, *38*(3), 589–634.

Ferris, S. P., Jayaraman, N., & Sabherwal, S. (2013). CEO overconfidence and international merger and acquisition activity. *Journal of Financial and Quantitative Analysis*, *48*(1), 137–164.

Fiske, A. P., Haslam, N., & Fiske, S. T. (1991). Confusing one person with another: What errors reveal about the elementary forms of social relations. *Journal of Personality and Social Psychology*, *60*(5), 656.

Gamache, D., McNamara, G., Mannor, M., & Johnson, R. (2015). Motivated to acquire? The impact of CEO regulatory focus on firm acquisitions. *Academy of Management Journal*, *58*(4), 1261–1282.

Graffin, S. D., Carpenter, M. A., & Boivie, S. (2011). What's all that (strategic) noise? Anticipatory impression management in CEO succession. *Strategic Management Journal, 32,* 748–770.

Graffin, S. D., Haleblian, J., & Kiley, J. T. (2015). Ready, aim, acquire: Impression offsetting and acquisitions. *Academy of Management Journal, 59*(1), 232–252.

Grinstein, Y., & Hribar, P. (2004). CEO compensation and incentives: Evidence from M & A bonuses. *Journal of Financial Economics, 73,* 119–143.

Haleblian, J., Devers, C. E., McNamara, G., Carpenter, M. A., & Davison, R. B. (2009). Taking stock of what we know about mergers and acquisitions: A review and research agenda. *Journal of Management, 35*(3), 469–502.

Hambrick, D. C., & Mason, P. A. (1984). Upper echelons: The organization as a reflection of its top managers. *Academy of Management Review, 9*(2), 193–206.

Harford, J. (2005). What drives merger waves? *Journal of Financial Economics, 77*(3), 529–560.

Harford, J., & Li, K. (2007). Decoupling CEO wealth and firm performance: The case of acquiring CEOs. *The Journal of Finance, 62*(2), 917–949.

Haunschild, P. R. (1993). Interorganizational imitation: The impact of interlocks on corporate acquisition activity. *Administrative Science Quarterly, 38,* 564–592.

Haunschild, P. R., & Beckman, C. M. (1998). When do interlocks matter? Alternate sources of information and interlock influence. *Administrative Science Quarterly, 43,* 815–844.

Haynes, K. T., Campbell, J. T., & Hitt, M. A. (2014). When more is not enough executive greed and its influence on shareholder wealth. *Journal of Management.* DOI: 10.1177/0149206314535444

Hayward, M. L. A., & Hambrick, D. C. (1997). Explaining the premiums paid for large acquisitions: Evidence of CEO hubris. *Administrative Science Quarterly, 42,* 103–127.

Higgins, E. T. (1997). Beyond pleasure and pain. *American Psychologist, 52*(12), 1280.

Hitt, M. A., & Middlemist, R. D. (1979). A methodology to develop the criteria and criteria weightings for assessing subunit effectiveness in organizations. *Academy of Management Journal, 22*(2), 356–374.

Hitt, M. A., & Tyler, B. B. (1991). Strategic decision models: Integrating different perspectives. *Strategic Management Journal, 12*(5), 327–351.

Huang, J., & Kisgen, D. J. (2013). Gender and corporate finance: Are male executives overconfident relative to female executives? *Journal of Financial Economics, 108*(3), 822–839.

Jenter, D., & Lewellen, K. (2015). CEO preferences and acquisitions. *The Journal of Finance, 70*(6), 2813–2852.

Johnson, J. E., & Powell, P. L. (1994). Decision making, risk and gender: Are managers different? *British Journal of Management, 5*(2), 123–138.

Kaplan, S. (2008). Cognition, capabilities, and incentives: Assessing firm response to the fiber-optic revolution. *Academy of Management Journal, 51*(4), 672–695.

Klein, F. B., Gamache, D. L., Devers, C. E., & Hannigan, T. (2015). *Do women at the top still shop? The influence of CEO gender on strategic investment behavior.* Oxford University Centre for Corporate Reputation Symposium.

Koenig, A. M., Eagly, A. H., Mitchell, A. A., & Ristikari, T. (2011). Are leader stereotypes masculine? A meta-analysis of three research paradigms. *Psychological Bulletin, 137*(4), 616.

Lanaj, K., Chang, C. H., & Johnson, R. E. (2012). Regulatory focus and work-related outcomes: A review and meta-analysis. *Psychological Bulletin, 138*(5), 998.

Li, J., & Tang, Y. I. (2010). CEO hubris and firm risk taking in China: The moderating role of managerial discretion. *Academy of Management Journal, 53*(1), 45–68.

Lyness, K. S., & Thompson, D. E. (1997). Above the glass ceiling? A comparison of matched samples of female and male executives. *Journal of Applied Psychology, 82*(3), 359.

Malmendier, U., & Tate, G. (2005). Does overconfidence affect corporate investment? CEO overconfidence measures revisited. *European Financial Management, 11*(5), 649–659.

Malmendier, U., & Tate, G. (2008). Who makes acquisitions? CEO overconfidence and the market's reaction. *Journal of Financial Economics, 89*(1), 20–43.

Mannor, M. J., Wowak, A. J., Bartkus, V. O., & Gomez-Mejia, L. R. (2015). Heavy lies the crown? How job anxiety affects top executive decision making in gain and loss contexts. *Strategic Management Journal*. DOI: 10.1002/smj.2425

McNamara, G., Deephouse, D. L., & Luce, R. A. (2003). Competitive positioning within and across a strategic group structure: The performance of core, secondary, and solitary firms. *Strategic Management Journal, 24*(2), 161–181.

McNamara, G. M., Haleblian, J. J., & Dykes, B. J. (2008). The performance implications of participating in an acquisition wave: Early mover advantages, bandwagon effects, and the moderating influence of industry characteristics and acquirer tactics. *Academy of Management Journal, 51*(1), 113–130.

Petrenko, O. V., Aime, F., Ridge, J., & Hill, A. (2016). Corporate social responsibility or CEO narcissism? CSR motivations and organizational performance. *Strategic Management Journal, 37*(2), 262–279.

Reuer, J. J., Tong, T. W., Tyler, B. B., & Ariño, A. (2013). Executive preferences for governance modes and exchange partners: An information economics perspective. *Strategic Management Journal, 34*(9), 1104–1122.

Roll, R. (1986). The hubris hypothesis of corporate takeovers. *Journal of Business, 59*, 197–216.

Ryan, M. K., Haslam, S. A., Hersby, M. D., & Bongiorno, R. (2011). Think crisis–think female: The glass cliff and contextual variation in the think manager–think male stereotype. *Journal of Applied Psychology, 96*(3), 470.

Sanders, W. G., & Hambrick, D. C. (2007). Swinging for the fences: The effects of CEO stock options on company risk taking and performance. *Academy of Management Journal, 50*(5), 1055–1078.

Seo, J., Gamache, D. L., Devers, C. E., & Carpenter, M. A. (2015). The role of CEO relative standing in acquisition behavior and CEO pay. *Strategic Management Journal, 36*(12), 1877–1894.

Simon, M., & Houghton, S. M. (2003). The relationship between overconfidence and the introduction of risky products: Evidence from a field study. *Academy of Management Journal, 46*(2), 139–149.

Weber, R. P. (1990). *Basic content analysis* (2nd ed.). Thousand Oaks, CA: Sage.

Westphal, J. D., Seidel, M. D. L., & Stewart, K. J. (2001). Second-order imitation: Uncovering latent effects of board network ties. *Administrative Science Quarterly, 46*, 717–747.

Wiseman, D. B., & Levin, I. P. (1996). Comparing risky decision making under conditions of real and hypothetical consequences. *Organizational Behavior and Human Decision Processes, 66*(3), 241–250.

Yim, S. (2013). The acquisitiveness of youth: CEO age and acquisition behavior. *Journal of Financial Economics, 108*(1), 250–273.

Zaheer, A., McEvily, B., & Perrone, V. (1998). Does trust matter? Exploring the effects of interorganizational and interpersonal trust on performance. *Organization Science, 9*(2), 141–159.

RELATED DIVERSIFICATION: A CRITICAL REFLECTION OF RELATEDNESS AND THE DIVERSIFICATION-PERFORMANCE LINKAGE

Martin Weiss

ABSTRACT

The linkage between diversification and performance has puzzled scholars for decades. A vast amount of empirical studies, together with the help of meta-analyses condensing diverse results, established a widely shared understanding that related diversification leads to superior firm performance. The main rationale for this finding is that relatedness within a company's portfolio of businesses allows the company to achieve synergies by sharing or transferring resources. Although the predominant importance of related diversification seems generally accepted, scholars raise severe concerns about our ability to precisely define and measure relatedness. In most studies, traditional measures of diversification such as the Berry index are used, which assess relatedness from a product/ market perspective. However, these measures face strong criticisms for their low degree of content validity. So if we doubt our understanding of

Advances in Mergers and Acquisitions, Volume 15, 161–180
ISSN: 1479-361X/doi:10.1108/S1479-361X20160000015009

relatedness, how can we agree on the performance effect of related diversification? To reassure our understanding of the diversification-performance linkage, this study critically reflects upon the underlying phenomenon of relatedness. By compiling and evaluating the different perspectives of relatedness with their heterogeneous conceptualizations and measures, this study supports the view that the multi-facetted nature of relatedness can only be captured inadequately so far. Moreover, most prior work mainly focuses on synergy potential rather than on the realization of synergies, thereby neglecting a mechanism that may have an important bearing on the performance effects of diversification.

Keywords: Diversification; relatedness; resource relatedness; resource similarity; resource complementarity; diversification-performance linkage

INTRODUCTION

Diversification represents a major opportunity for firms to grow their revenues and profits (Ansoff, 1965; Chandler, 1962). Hence, many companies seek to expand their current business by diversifying into new products and/or new markets. While increasing a firm's size through additional sales seems to be a common consequence of such strategic thrusts, the positive impact on corporate performance does not unfold automatically. In fact, the question whether diversification leads to superior performance has played a central role in research on strategic management for decades, probably being one of the most frequently investigated relationships (Palich, Cardinal, & Miller, 2000; Wan, Hoskisson, Short, & Yiu, 2011).

One pivotal mechanism to explain differences in the diversification-performance linkage is synergies, which are the most important motivation to diversify (Montgomery, 1985; Nayyar, 1992; St. John & Harrison, 1999; Zhou, 2011). Companies can benefit from economies of scale and scope that arise from sharing and transferring resources across different business units in a corporate portfolio. Therefore, the theory suggests that related diversification is superior to unrelated diversification with regard to corporate performance since a certain degree of relatedness is a prerequisite to share and transfer resources (Barney, 1991; Lubatkin & Chatterjee, 1994; Wan et al., 2011; Wernerfelt, 1984). However, despite a large number of empirical studies on the diversification-performance linkage, the findings remained inconclusive (Markides & Williamson, 1994; Neffke & Henning, 2013; Palich et al., 2000; Ramanujam & Varadarajan, 1989).

To condense this vast body of literature, Palich et al. (2000) performed a meta-analysis to examine more than three decades of research, which produced important results that received an extraordinary degree of dissemination. Aggregating all prior empirical studies, they found a curvilinear relationship between diversification and performance, shaped as an inverted-U curve. Thereby they substantiated the widespread understanding that related diversification leads to higher performance compared to unrelated diversification or firms that do not diversify.

Although some scholars raise concerns regarding this generalization, mainly due to deviating findings from their respective empirical findings (e.g., Bausch & Pils, 2009; Benito-Osorio, Guerras-Martín, & Zuñiga-Vicente, 2012), most scholars seem to follow the understanding of the inverted-U-shaped relationship. Moreover, some scholars even postulate that the identified model, claiming related diversification is the superior diversification strategy, puts an end to the discussion on how diversification and performance are linked (Neffke & Henning, 2013; Wan et al., 2011; Yang, Narayanan, & De Carolis, 2014).

Interestingly, another stream of research within the field of diversification casts serious doubts whether our existing approaches comprehensively capture relatedness. Our traditional methods to measure relatedness and, thus, related diversification evaluate the similarities of products and/or markets between different businesses. However, this provides only a weak reflection of the underlying potential to share or transfer resources (Nayyar, 1992). Further developed measures directly address the required similarity of resources, but they struggle with comprehensively including all relevant resources and providing a replicable measurement approach.

Consequently, if our ability to fully capture relatedness − and subsequently related diversification − is questioned, the conclusions on the diversification-performance linkage seem at least to be treated with caution. Therefore, it seems essential to collate the different perspectives and measures of relatedness in order to reassure our understanding of related diversification and its effects on performance.

This study seeks to contribute to our knowledge on diversification strategies by providing answers to the questions, whether we conceptually understand and have valid approaches to measure relatedness. These findings provide important value to the body of research on diversification, since they compile the different perspectives of relatedness with their heterogeneous measures. Particularly understanding resource relatedness allows for a critical reflection of a widely accepted relationship between diversification and performance.

For this aim, the chapter proceeds as follows: First, it provides the theoretical background on the diversification-performance linkage, particularly addressing synergies as the underlying mechanism and existing empirical findings. Then different approaches to assess (related) diversification will be presented. Thereby, the development from traditional and rather product/market-driven measures to resource-related measures of diversification is demonstrated. The critical reflection of all approaches with a particular focus on our ability to capture relatedness is supplemented by a discussion on the difference between similarity and complementarity in the prevailing conceptualizations of relatedness. The study ends with a discussion to conclude on our overall understanding of relatedness and, hence, the diversification-performance linkage itself.

THEORETICAL BACKGROUND

Synergies as the Underlying Mechanism of the Diversification-Performance Linkage

The reasons for a company's decision to diversify have been widely discussed in the strategy, finance, and other literature (Montgomery, 1994; Prahalad & Bettis, 1986; Ramanujam & Varadarajan, 1989; Reed & Luffman, 1986; Villalonga, 2004). The range of motives extends from economic advantages for a company, such as risk reduction, to managerial interests and beyond to external influences. Montgomery (1994) identified the market-power view, the agency view, and the resource view to be the most important perspectives for explaining why companies diversify. Throughout the literature, the realization of synergies in line with the resource-based view is regarded as the most important motive for diversification (Montgomery, 1985; Nayyar, 1992; St. John & Harrison, 1999; Zhou, 2011). Porter (1985) even took it to the extremes by arguing that a diversification strategy that is not aimed at realizing synergies has no legitimation at all.

Synergies basically refer to the "ability of two or more units or companies to generate greater value working together than they could working apart" (Goold & Campbell, 1998, p. 133). A common classification of synergies distinguishes between material and immaterial synergies (Porter, 1985). Material synergies in form of economies of scale and scope arise through the common usage of typically tangible resources (e.g., manufacturing plants or distribution channels), immaterial synergies arise from the transfer of intangible resources (e.g., technological knowledge, patents, or employees' skills) across different business units within a diversified company. Especially management synergies are regarded to be a very important type of immaterial synergies (e.g., Nayyar, 1992; Stimpert & Duhaime, 1997). They arise, according to Prahalad and Bettis (1986), if managers succeed in leveraging their superior capabilities across the different business units of a company. As a prerequisite for such managerial synergies, it is crucial that the business units share a similar dominant general management logic (D'Aveni, Ravenscraft, & Anderson, 2004; Harrison, Hall, Jr., & Nargundkar, 1993; Nayyar, 1992; Prahalad & Bettis, 1986).

Consequently, the aim for synergies in diversified firms puts a particular emphasis on their specific resource endowments. According to the resource-based view (RBV) of strategy, each company possesses a unique bundle of heterogeneous resources, which can lead to long-lasting and above-average success by creating a sustained competitive advantage (Barney, 2001). For diversification strategies, the RBV suggests that companies should diversify into businesses that require success-relevant resources, which are at the companies' disposal and which are so far under-leveraged by the company (Neffke & Henning, 2013).

Summarizing the previous arguments to shed light on the linkage between diversification and performance, synergies are the pivotal mechanism that may explain superior performance of diversified firms, but these synergies can only become effective if the different businesses are related in a sense that resources can be shared or transferred. Thus, related diversification is assumed to be superior compared to single-business firms and unrelated diversification, as companies can exploit synergies and increase their corporate performance (Barney, 1991; Lubatkin & Chatterjee, 1994; Rumelt, 1982; Wan et al., 2011; Wernerfelt, 1984).

Empirical Findings on the Diversification-Performance Linkage

For the last decades, scholars empirically analyzed the linkage between diversification and performance in search for a superior type of diversification strategy or the optimal degree of diversification. However, despite a tremendous body of research, the linkage between diversification and performance has fallen short of consensus (Neffke & Henning, 2013; Palich et al., 2000). Some found a positive linear relation (e.g., Chatterjee, 1986), some a negative linear relation (e.g., Robins & Wiersema, 1995), some a non-linear relation (e.g., Tallman & Li, 1996), and others found no relation at all between diversification and performance (e.g., Sharma & Kesner, 1996).

To condense these vast and diverse findings, several meta-analyses have been conducted (e.g., Hoskisson & Hitt, 1990; Ramanujam & Varadarajan, 1989). In this vein, the study of Palich et al. (2000) received the widest repercussions in the literature and their findings are widely assumed to be essential for our current understanding of the diversification-performance linkage (Miller, 2006; Neffke & Henning, 2013; Pehrsson, 2006b). They concluded that the relation between diversification and performance is shaped as an inverted-U curve, as they found that the overall performance increases as the company moves from a single-business firm to related diversification, but decreases when moving further to unrelated diversification where the costs of diversification outweigh its benefits. Hence, related diversification is assumed to be the optimal type of diversification, leading to the highest overall performance (Palich et al., 2000). And even though subsequent meta-analytical studies object to this conclusion (e.g., Bausch & Pils, 2009; Benito-Osorio et al., 2012), it seems as if most scholars advocate the general findings from Palich et al. and adopt the inverted-U-shaped relationship between diversification and performance (Neffke & Henning, 2013; Wan et al., 2011; Yang et al., 2014).

Interestingly, while the superiority of related diversification seems to be accepted, the understanding of what exactly is related diversification seems rather ambiguous. As the study by Palich et al. (2000) is a meta-analysis, they do not provide a specific and unequivocal definition of relatedness, but rather synthesize prior work with their respective definitions. However, the conceptualization of relatedness in prior research is afflicted with a major problem. Most studies assume that the similarity of industries within a corporate portfolio defines related diversification as they apply common measures such as the Berry index to measure the degree of diversification. Nonetheless, this view and the associated measures have faced strong criticism in the literature, as they do not seem to fully capture the underlying mechanisms that ultimately lead to the creation of synergy potential and therefore have only limited content validity (Nayyar, 1992; Robins & Wiersema, 1995),

Consequently, if we want to follow the suggestion to accentuate related diversification, we need to clarify our understanding of how to assess

relatedness. Only if we have a joint and valid understanding of the relatedness construct, we can rely on empirical findings and uphold the claim that
related diversification is the superior diversification strategy. Therefore, the
following paragraphs aim at understanding the different concepts that exist
to define and measure diversification as well as at evaluating the compre-
hensiveness and validity of our current understanding.

APPROACHES TO ASSESS (RELATED) DIVERSIFICATION

Product/Market-Related Measurement of Diversification

To understand and to measure diversification, the traditional and most
important approaches in empirical research on diversification assume a
product/market-oriented perspective on relatedness. The measurement
approaches themselves can be subdivided into quantitative-continuous
measures (e.g., Berry, 1975; Gort, 1962), also referred to as the *degree of
diversification*, and discrete-categorical measures (e.g., Rumelt, 1974;
Wrigley, 1970), also referred to as the *type of diversification* (Ilinitch &
Zeithaml, 1995; Robins & Wiersema, 2003).

Quantitative-continuous measures evaluate the degree of diversification
on a continuum from "not diversified" to "highly diversified," based on the
amount of business fields or the concentration of sales in the business fields
the company operates in (Berry, 1975; Gort, 1962). The classification of
these business fields is typically based on classification systems such as
the United States Standard Industrial Classification Code (SIC-Code).
However, these approaches had been criticized for not considering the
dimension of relatedness between the business fields of the company
(Palepu, 1985). Thus, Jacquemin and Berry (1979) developed an entropy
measure, which not only measures the degree of diversification, but also
distinguishes between related and unrelated diversification. According to
their measure, business fields are regarded as related if the first two digits
of their SIC-Codes are similar (i.e., same industry); otherwise, they are
regarded as unrelated (Jacquemin & Berry, 1979). Due to the possibility to
measure the degree of diversification as well as to categorize the type of
diversification strategy, scholars often highlight the superiority of the
entropy measure toward other measures (Hoskisson, Hitt, Johnson, &
Moesel, 1993). The entropy measure is widely used in empirical studies due

to its high degree of objectivity and reliability, which is mainly a result of using generally accepted industry classifications and relying on publicly available secondary data (Martin & Sayrak, 2003; Robins & Wiersema, 2003).

Nonetheless, quantitative-continuous measures face severe criticism in the literature, which is mostly centered on the poor content validity and, in particular, an insufficient consideration of relatedness (e.g., Farjoun, 1998; Nayyar, 1992; Robins & Wiersema, 1995). Many researchers argue that classification codes like the SIC-Code do not adequately portray the relatedness of product groups or industries (Nayyar, 1992; Robins & Wiersema, 1995) and, as a consequence, do not allow any conclusion on relatedness at all (Bryce & Winter, 2009).

Discrete-categorical measures classify companies into discrete types of diversification based on a more or less subjective analysis of the business portfolio (Robins & Wiersema, 1995). The first discrete-categorical measure was developed by Wrigley (1970) and classifies four different diversification categories: single, dominant, related, and unrelated. The differentiation between related and unrelated diversification is based on an individual assessment for each company. Except for this subjective assessment, the measure relies on the SIC-Code and, hence, faces the same criticism toward the SIC system as quantitative-continuous measures. Therefore, Rumelt (1974) developed a refined measure, which classifies companies along so-called discrete businesses, which he defines as businesses that can be operated mostly independent from each other. To attain a higher content validity for his measure, Rumelt (1974) required that these discrete businesses should be identified for each company individually, arguing that each company is unique due to its very own economic environment and history. In doing so, he deliberately added a subjective judgment at the expense of objectivity to his measure (Rumelt, 1974). The discrete-categorical measures, especially Rumelt's measure, have received broad attention in the literature as they overcome central weaknesses of the quantitative-continuous measures: They do not solely rely on the SIC-Code, but operationalize relatedness through a wider array of information and, thus, show higher content validity than quantitative-continuous measures (Nayyar, 1992; Pehrsson, 2006b; Robins & Wiersema, 1995).

However, the discrete-categorical measures are also exposed to strong criticism in the literature. Particularly Rumelt's measure is criticized for low reliability and low objectivity, which mainly stems from the subjective categorization performed by the researcher (Chatterjee & Blocher, 1992). Additionally, scholars criticize the sparse conceptualization of relatedness, which tends to overexpose product and market similarities and neglects other yet important elements of relatedness (Lemelin, 1982; Prahalad & Bettis, 1986; Stimpert & Duhaime, 1997).

Consequently, and although widely used in empirical research, most researchers agree that the traditional measurement concepts operationalize relatedness, if at all, inadequately (e.g., Stimpert & Duhaime, 1997). They only capture product and market relatedness and neglect other essential aspects of relatedness, in particular resources, which are the relevant basis for synergies (Hoskisson et al., 1993). Robins and Wiersema (2003) concluded that "the fact that the most widely used indicators of related diversification cannot be treated as reliable measures of 'relatedness' within corporate portfolios creates a real dilemma" (p. 57).

Resource-Related Measurement of Diversification

As a response to the criticism about the traditional measurement concepts, scholars in the early 1990s underwent a shift toward focusing on resources to determine relatedness in an attempt to get closer to the underlying sources for synergies. Soon after the introduction into the literature, studies investigating the effects of resource-related diversification started to offer new and important insights into the diversification-performance linkage. Over the past years scholars have conducted numerous studies addressing a wide range of different resources, such as technological resources (e.g., Miller, 2006), human resources (e.g., Farjoun, 1998), general management knowledge (e.g., D'Aveni et al., 2004), and information technology resources (e.g., Tanriverdi, 2006).

In order to provide a comprehensive overview, this study followed a twofold approach to build its sample. First, a keyword search in the EBSCOhost Business Source Complete database was performed to find articles that assess the diversification-performance linkage applying a resource-related approach. Second, prior studies summarizing the field, either as a literature review (Wan et al., 2011) or a conceptual paper (Pehrsson, 2006b), were used to identify potentially relevant studies. Once these studies had been identified, they had been read to find out if a resource-related measure was applied. Overall, 22 studies directly addressed resource relatedness. More studies address the issue of resource relatedness or are included in the aforementioned studies, but they are excluded for the purpose of this study as they apply measures that primarily capture product and market relatedness. Table 1 provides an overview of the 22 studies in which a resource-related diversification measure was developed or used.

While studying resource relatedness, all studies focus on one or more specific sub-dimensions such as managerial or technological relatedness. Even though managerial and human resources seem to be used slightly more frequent, no single sub-dimension stands out in terms of scholarly attention and its importance. This wide range of dimensions addressed in these studies lends support to the understanding that relatedness is indeed multi-facetted, leaving diversification appear even more complex than most researchers tend to acknowledge (Stimpert & Duhaime, 1997).

Table 1. Overview of Studies with Resource-Related Measurement Concepts.

No.	Article (Year of Publication)	Sub-Dimension(s) of Resource Relatedness
1.	Nayyar (1992)	Managerial relatedness
2.	Brumagim (1992)	Human relatedness
3.	Davis, Robinson, Pearce, and Park (1992)	Production relatedness; Marketing relatedness
4.	Harrison et al. (1993)	Managerial relatedness
5.	Farjoun (1994)	Human relatedness
6.	Markides and Williamson (1994)	Strategic relatedness
7.	Robins and Wiersema (1995)	Human and technological relatedness
8.	Ilinitch and Zeithaml (1995)	Managerial relatedness
9.	Brush (1996)	Relatedness in functions and relational resources
10.	Chang (1996)	Human relatedness
11.	Markides and Williamson (1996)	Strategic relatedness; Organizational relatedness
12.	Farjoun (1998)	Human relatedness
13.	Silverman (1999)	Technological relatedness
14.	St. John and Harrison (1999)	Production relatedness
15.	Tsai (2000)	Strategic relatedness; Organizational relatedness
16.	Szeless, Wiersema, and Müller-Stewens (2003)	Technological relatedness
17.	D'Aveni et al. (2004)	Managerial relatedness
18.	Tanriverdi and Venkatraman (2005)	Human relatedness
19.	Miller (2006)	Technological relatedness
20.	Pehrsson (2006a)	Relatedness in core competencies
21.	Tanriverdi (2006)	Information technology relatedness
22.	Neffke and Henning (2013)	Human relatedness

Therefore, to understand resource-related diversification, it seems crucial to specify the resources rather multidimensional instead of independently and separately (Tanriverdi & Venkatraman, 2005). However, whereas some studies (e.g., Farjoun, 1998; Robins & Wiersema, 1995) conceptualize relatedness based on more than one resource, no measurement concept so far addresses a broader set of resources simultaneously.

Another interesting finding is that even if scholars focus on the same sub-dimension of resources, they tend to apply different indicators to infer on the same dimension. For example, scholars use the occupational distribution, product knowledge, and employee's skills to measure human relatedness. Moreover, some indicators, such as the value chain stage are used to reflect more than just one dimension of relatedness (i.e., managerial relatedness and production relatedness). The multitude of indicators and the ambiguous linkages add to the already existing heterogeneity that stems from the various dimensions. Table 2 provides an overview of all indicators used in the 22 studies for all sub-dimensions of resource relatedness.

Table 2. Indicators for the Dimensions of Resource Relatedness.

Sub-Dimension(s) of Resource Relatedness	Indicator(s) for Dimension(s) of Resource Relatedness
Managerial relatedness	Expenditures on advertising, selling, R&D, and capital
	Stage in value chain
	Strengths or assets of the firm
Human relatedness	Human expertise such as knowledge, skills, ideas, and experience
	Knowledge such as product, customer, managerial, technological, and organizational knowledge
	Occupational distribution
Strategic relatedness	Customers, channels, inputs, processes, and market knowledge
Technological relatedness	Patent portfolio
Human and technological relatedness	Technology flows
Production relatedness	Plants, equipment, R&D, products, and stage in value chain
Organizational relatedness	Communication, networks, head office involvement, and centralization of strategic and financial controls
Relatedness in core competencies	Attributes of product markets, resources, and value chain
Information technology relatedness	IT-infrastructure, IT-strategy-making process, IT-vendor management, and IT-human resource management
Relatedness in functions and relational resources	R&D, promotion, and relational resources
Marketing relatedness	Customers, sales force, advertisement, promotion

To eventually measure the degree of relatedness, the scholars encounter the same dilemma as for the traditional measurement approaches. They have to select between objective measures (e.g., intensities of expenditures or patent data), which show less content validity, and more subjective evaluations (e.g., questioning executives), which is harder to replicate and limited for large scale and longitudinal studies. Even though the evaluation approach seems to better capture the complexity of relatedness, most scholars ultimately turn to more objective measurement approaches.

Overall, it has to be concluded that so far no approach to measure resource-related diversification protrudes or even gained the importance of the Berry index from the previous perspective of product and market relatedness. Notwithstanding the importance of incorporating resource relatedness into the diversification-performance linkage, only few approaches are applied in subsequent studies (e.g., Farjoun, 1994; Harrison et al., 1993; Robins & Wiersema, 1995), and most approaches are barely exploited.

Although related diversification is widely assumed to be the superior diversification strategy, it seems that we cannot comprehensively grasp what constitutes relatedness in a corporate portfolio. Most of the studies that shaped our understanding of the diversification-performance linkage apply measures following the idea of product/market relatedness. As these measures are subject to major concerns regarding content validity, the resulting findings have to be treated with caution. To improve the content validity of measuring related diversification, scholars assumed the perspective of resource relatedness. While this seems to be a promising path toward the underlying mechanism that may explain performance differences, no measurement approach prevailed to adequately capture resource relatedness. Instead, all prior studies exhibit the complexity and multidimensional nature of relatedness, which may have as many dimensions as there are resource types (Neffke & Henning, 2013).

Similarity versus Complementarity

Further adding to the difficulties to measure relatedness, another obstacle poses limits to our conceptual understanding of relatedness. We typically equate relatedness with similarity. However, scholars start to highlight the importance of complementarity, offering another facet to the puzzle.

Synergies do not exclusively arise through the transfer of similar resources, but also through a complementary set of resources (Harrison, Hitt, Hoskisson, & Ireland, 2001). Complementary resources are interdependent and mutually supportive (Milgrom & Roberts, 1995) so that the return of a resource depends on the level of returns to the other resources (Tanriverdi, 2006). Although resource complementarity as a source of synergies is well established in the literature, only few scholars have integrated it in their conceptualization of related diversification (Harrison et al., 2001). One of the few are Tanriverdi and Venkatraman (2005) who stated that "the 'resource relatedness' construct does not adequately capture the super-additive value of the resource combinations" (p. 100) and consequently addressed both, sub-additive costs (resource similarity) and super-additive values (resource complementarity) in their study. The authors found empirical support that simultaneously exploiting a complementary set of related knowledge resources (product, customer, and managerial knowledge) across the business units leads to an increase in corporate performance, whereas each of the tested knowledge categories individually did not affect corporate performance (Tanriverdi & Venkatraman, 2005).

The interplay between similarity and complementarity also becomes evident if diversification is analyzed as a process (i.e., the activities to change the composition of a corporate portfolio, for example through M&A) rather than a condition (i.e., the composition of a corporate portfolio itself). While the underlying assumption for a successful composition of a corporate portfolio is that similar resources create the potential for synergies, the motive behind changes in a corporate portfolio may take a different perspective. This is particularly the case when firms acquire other firms to get access to resources, either to secure their supply or to incorporate them. The access to resources is a frequent and important motivation of acquisitions (Capron, Dussague, & Mitchell, 1998), with the consequence that the acquiring firm searches for different and complementary resources rather than only for similar resources (Yu, Umashankar, & Rao, 2015). Speckbacher, Neumann, and Hoffmann (2014) argue from an acquisition perspective that resource complementarity leads to value that can be created by combining and integrating the acquirer's current resources and capabilities with target segment resources.

As a result, if we try to understand related diversification, we also need to clarify our understanding of relatedness itself. If we follow the main notion of equating relatedness with similarity, we may miss the additional mechanism of complementarity. Thereby, we would at least ignore another factor that creates synergies and motivates firms to diversify.

DISCUSSION

The main purpose of this study was to examine if we fully understand the crucial phenomenon of relatedness in the diversification-performance linkage. Our understanding of the advantageousness of related diversification is manifested in a meta-analytical study from Palich et al. (2000) that aggregates vast prior empirical findings. However, those prior studies mainly apply traditional measures of diversification, which − by solely focusing on product and market similarities − do not manage to fully capture the decisive resource similarities. Twenty-two identified studies directly address resource relatedness and mainly find support for a positive performance effect. Although these scholars analyze the resources as the underlying prerequisite for potential synergies more precisely, they are confronted with the multidimensionality of resource types and a variety of sub-dimensions of resource relatedness. Yet, no concept has comprehensively addressed this multidimensionality and achieved the dissemination as, for example, the Berry index − even though they have more content validity.

Consequently, we may have an idea what we assume to be related diversification, but we do not have the measures to seize it comprehensively. Further complicating these circumstances, there also seems to be a lack of conceptual clarity, whether relatedness can be equated with similarity or if complementarity needs to be included as well. This multifaceted nature of relatedness and the expectation of a valid, reliable, and objective measure give rise to the concern that such a comprehensive concept may never be developed.

Therefore, we should consider to treat our understanding of related diversification with caution. If we have limitations to point out precisely what related diversification is a conclusion on its general repercussion on firm performance seems hard to draw.

Synergy Potential versus Realized Synergies

Another criticism towards concluding on the diversification-performance linkage based on the level of relatedness stems from the discrepancy between the synergy potential, which is deduced from relatedness, and the synergies realized, which ultimately establishes the effect on corporate performance. It seems as if in most studies the prevailing assumption is that potential synergies automatically translate into realized synergies, which the potential for benefits, however, does not imply (Reed & Luffman,

1986). Hence, it is difficult to draw conclusions on the corporate performance from studies only addressing potential synergies since companies may lack the ability to realize potential synergies due to the challenges of implementation (Hoskisson & Hitt, 1988; Nayyar, 1992; Reed & Luffman, 1986).

Putting the spotlight in research on both effects, synergy creation and synergy realization, can be seen as another important path to better understand related diversification. Nonetheless, while the importance of synergy realization is widely acknowledged in the literature (D'Aveni et al., 2004; Harrison et al., 1993; Nayyar, 1992; Priem & Butler, 2001; Tanriverdi & Venkatraman, 2005), so far only few scholars (e.g., Markides & Williamson, 1996; St. John & Harrison, 1999; Tanriverdi, 2006; Tanriverdi & Venkatraman, 2005; Tsai, 2000) addressed both effects in their measurement concepts. However, even if both effects are addressed, there is usually a stronger emphasis on potential synergies instead of integrating both effects simultaneously and as equally important. In summary, the effect of related diversification may be better understood in a more precise way, if we would not only focus on the existence of resources through which potential synergies can arise, but also encapsulate that the synergy potential is realized.

Within-Industry Diversification

This critical view regarding our perspective on related diversification finds further support from a rather recent stream of research, which particularly focuses on intra-industry diversification, also referred to as within-industry diversification. Diversification within the same industry is by definition – following the product and market perspective of relatedness – related diversification, which should lead to superior performance. However, the studies in this field provide a more distinguished way to look into the performance effects of this type of diversification, often revealing strong differences (e.g., Barroso & Giarratana, 2013; Hashai, 2015; Li & Greenwood, 2004; Stern & Henderson, 2004; Tanriverdi & Lee, 2008; Zahavi & Lavie, 2013). To illustrate this perspective, one example can be drawn from the automotive industry: Ferrari, an Italian luxury sports car manufacturer, pursues a completely different production, distribution, and marketing strategy than Fiat, an automotive brand for the mass market, rather settling in lower price segments. Although both operate within the automobile industry and belong to the same company (i.e., Fiat Chrysler Automobiles), only very little potential for synergies exists.

The empirical findings from this nascent research stream are quite hetero-geneous so far (Hashai, 2015), which may be attributed to the specificities of the respective industries (Stern & Henderson, 2004; Tanriverdi & Lee, 2008). It seems as if results from research on traditional inter-industry diversifica-tion cannot be directly transferred to intra-industry diversification (Li & Greenwood, 2004). Thereby, the perspective on within-industry diversifica-tion adds precious insights toward a better understanding of related diversifi-cation, as their main findings suggest that diversifying within one industry may not necessarily lead to increased corporate performance.

CONCLUSION

In conclusion, this study shows the difficulties in research to comprehend relatedness, both conceptually and empirically, and, consequently, puts at least to some degree a question mark to our common understanding that related diversification is the superior type of diversification strategy. Related diversification is assumed to be superior based on the greater potential for synergies, for which in turn similar resources across businesses are the prerequisite. However, we either use approaches to derive related-ness that do not capture the subjacent resources or approaches that do not comprehensively address the multidimensional nature of these resources and are difficult to replicate. Moreover, an exclusive view on the required similarity of resources neglects the effects of resource complementarity, which may also contribute to the desired synergies from diversifica-tion activities.

However, it is important to note that this study is not intended to deny the notion that relatedness is a valuable condition for a company's diversi-fication strategy. It only seems critical to infer such a condition from our existing understanding and measures. It would require a more subtle and sophisticated approach enriched with information from detailed internal knowledge about the different businesses in the corporate portfolio, which is yet to be accomplished. Moreover, it appears at least questionable to simplify and conclude that synergy potential as the consequence of related-ness leads to higher firm performance, neglecting the necessity for compa-nies to realize this potential first.

In other words, we may or may not perfectly see from the outside if synergy potential exists in a diversified company. But in either case, the more prevailing question to understand if the company ultimately achieves superior performance is whether they realize synergetic effects or not.

Therefore, in both research and practice, we should rather focus on how companies execute their diversification strategies instead of trying to determine the exact type of diversification strategy and the superiority of one type over the other.

REFERENCES

Ansoff, H. I. (1965). *Corporate strategy: An analytic approach to business policy for growth and expansion*. New York, NY: McGraw-Hill.

Barney, J. B. (1991). Firm resources and sustained competitive advantage. *Journal of Management*, *17*(1), 99–120.

Barney, J. B. (2001). Is the resource-based "view" a useful perspective for strategic management research? Yes. *Academy of Management Review*, *26*(1), 41–56.

Barroso, A., & Giarratana, M. S. (2013). Product proliferation strategies and firm performance: The moderating role of product space complexity. *Strategic Management Journal*, *34*(12), 1435–1452.

Bausch, A., & Pils, F. (2009). Product diversification strategy and financial performance: Meta-analytic evidence on causality and construct multidimensionality. *Review of Managerial Science*, *3*(3), 157–190.

Benito-Osorio, D., Guerras-Martín, L. Á., & Zuñiga-Vicente, J. Á. (2012). Four decades of research on product diversification: A literature review. *Management Decision*, *50*(2), 325–344.

Berry, C. H. (1975). *Corporate growth and diversification*. Princeton, NJ: Princeton University Press.

Brumagim, A. L. (1992). Occupational skills linkages: A resource-based investigation of conglomerates. *Academy of Management Proceedings*, *1992*(1), 7–11.

Brush, T. H. (1996). Predicted change in operational synergy and post-acquisition performance of acquired businesses. *Strategic Management Journal*, *17*(1), 1–24.

Bryce, D. J., & Winter, S. G. (2009). A general interindustry relatedness index. *Management Science*, *55*(9), 1570–1585.

Capron, L., Dussague, P., & Mitchell, W. (1998). Resource redeployment following horizontal acquisitions in Europe and North America, 1988–1992. *Strategic Management Journal*, *19*(7), 631–661.

Chandler, A. D. (1962). *Strategy and structure: Chapters in the history of the American industrial enterprise*. Cambridge, MA: MIT Press.

Chang, S. J. (1996). An evolutionary perspective on diversification and corporate restructuring: Entry, exit, and economic performance during 1981–89. *Strategic Management Journal*, *17*(8), 587–611.

Chatterjee, S. (1986). Types of synergy and economic value: The impact of acquisitions on merging and rival firms. *Strategic Management Journal*, *7*(2), 119–139.

Chatterjee, S., & Blocher, J. D. (1992). Measurement of firm diversification: Is it robust? *Academy of Management Journal*, *35*(4), 874–888.

D'Aveni, R. A., Ravenscraft, D. J., & Anderson, P. (2004). From corporate strategy to business-level advantage: Relatedness as resource congruence. *Managerial and Decision Economics*, *25*(6–7), 365–381.

Davis, P. S., Robinson, R. B., Pearce, J. A., & Park, S. H. (1992). Business unit relatedness and performance: A look at the pulp and paper industry. *Strategic Management Journal, 13*(5), 349–361.

Farjoun, M. (1994). Beyond industry boundaries: Human expertise, diversification and resource-related industry groups. *Organization Science, 5*(2), 185–199.

Farjoun, M. (1998). The independent and joint effects of the skill and physical bases of relatedness in diversification. *Strategic Management Journal, 19*(7), 611–630.

Goold, M., & Campbell, A. (1998). Desperately seeking synergy. *Harvard Business Review, 76*(5), 131–143.

Gort, M. (1962). *Diversification and integration in American industry.* Princeton, NJ: Princeton University Press.

Harrison, J. S., Hall, E. H., Jr., & Nargundkar, R. (1993). Resource allocation as an outcropping of strategic consistency: Performance implications. *Academy of Management Journal, 36*(5), 1026–1051.

Harrison, J. S., Hitt, M. A., Hoskisson, R. E., & Ireland, R. D. (2001). Resource complementarity in business combinations: Extending the logic to organizational alliances. *Journal of Management, 27*(6), 679–690.

Hashai, N. (2015). Within-industry diversification and firm performance – An S-shaped hypothesis. *Strategic Management Journal, 36*(9), 1378–1400.

Hoskisson, R. E., & Hitt, M. A. (1988). Strategic control systems and relative R&D investment in large multiproduct firms. *Strategic Management Journal, 9*(6), 605–621.

Hoskisson, R. E., & Hitt, M. A. (1990). Antecedents and performance outcomes of diversification: A review and critique of theoretical perspectives. *Journal of Management, 16*(2), 461–509.

Hoskisson, R. E., Hitt, M. A., Johnson, R. A., & Moesel, D. D. (1993). Construct validity of an objective (entropy) categorical measure of diversification strategy. *Strategic Management Journal, 14*(3), 215–235.

Ilinitch, A. Y., & Zeithaml, C. P. (1995). Operationalizing and testing Galbraith's center of gravity theory. *Strategic Management Journal, 16*(5), 401–410.

Jacquemin, A. P., & Berry, C. H. (1979). Entropy measure of diversification and corporate growth. *Journal of Industrial Economics, 27*(4), 359–369.

Lemelin, A. (1982). Relatedness in the patterns of interindustry diversification. *Review of Economics and Statistics, 64*(4), 646–657.

Li, S. X., & Greenwood, R. (2004). The effect of within-industry diversification on firm performance: Synergy creation, multi-market contact and market structuration. *Strategic Management Journal, 25*(12), 1131–1153.

Lubatkin, M., & Chatterjee, S. (1994). Extending modern portfolio theory into the domain of corporate diversification: Does it apply? *Academy of Management Journal, 37*(1), 109–136.

Markides, C. C., & Williamson, P. J. (1994). Related diversification, core competences and corporate performance. *Strategic Management Journal, 15*(S2), 149–165.

Markides, C. C., & Williamson, P. J. (1996). Corporate diversification and organizational structure: A resource-based view. *Academy of Management Journal, 39*(2), 340–367.

Martin, J. D., & Sayrak, A. (2003). Corporate diversification and shareholder value: A survey of recent literature. *Journal of Corporate Finance, 9*(1), 37–57.

Milgrom, P., & Roberts, J. (1995). Complementarities and fit strategy, structure, and organizational change in manufacturing. *Journal of Accounting and Economics, 19*(2–3), 179–208.

Miller, D. J. (2006). Technological diversity, related diversification, and firm performance. *Strategic Management Journal, 27*(7), 601–619.

Montgomery, C. A. (1985). Product-market diversification and market power. *Academy of Management Journal, 28*(4), 789–798.

Montgomery, C. A. (1994). Corporate diversification. *Journal of Economic Perspectives, 8*(3), 163–178.

Nayyar, P. R. (1992). On the measurement of corporate diversification strategy: Evidence from large U.S. service firms. *Strategic Management Journal, 13*(3), 219–235.

Neffke, F., & Henning, M. (2013). Skill relatedness and firm diversification. *Strategic Management Journal, 34*(3), 297–316.

Palepu, K. (1985). Diversification strategy, profit performance and the entropy measure. *Strategic Management Journal, 6*(3), 239–255.

Palich, L. E., Cardinal, L. B., & Miller, C. C. (2000). Curvilinearity in the diversification-performance linkage: An examination of over three decades of research. *Strategic Management Journal, 21*(2), 155–174.

Pehrsson, A. (2006a). Business relatedness and performance: A study of managerial perceptions. *Strategic Management Journal, 27*(3), 265–282.

Pehrsson, A. (2006b). Business relatedness measurements: State-of-the-art and a proposal. *European Business Review, 18*(5), 350–363.

Porter, M. E. (1985). *Competitive advantage: Creating and sustaining superior performance.* New York, NY: Free Press.

Prahalad, C. K., & Bettis, R. A. (1986). The dominant logic: A new linkage between diversity and performance. *Strategic Management Journal, 7*(6), 485–501.

Priem, R. L., & Butler, J. E. (2001). Is the resource-based "view" a useful perspective for strategic management research? *Academy of Management Review, 26*(1), 22–40.

Ramanujam, V., & Varadarajan, P. (1989). Research on corporate diversification: A synthesis. *Strategic Management Journal, 10*(6), 523–551.

Reed, R., & Luffman, G. A. (1986). Diversification: The growing confusion. *Strategic Management Journal, 7*(1), 29–35.

Robins, J. A., & Wiersema, M. F. (1995). A resource-based approach to the multibusiness firm: Empirical analysis of portfolio interrelationships and corporate financial performance. *Strategic Management Journal, 16*(4), 277–299.

Robins, J. A., & Wiersema, M. F. (2003). The measurement of corporate portfolio strategy: Analysis of the content validity of related diversification indexes. *Strategic Management Journal, 24*(1), 39–59.

Rumelt, R. P. (1974). *Strategy, structure, and economic performance.* Cambridge, MA: Harvard University Press.

Rumelt, R. P. (1982). Diversification strategy and profitability. *Strategic Management Journal, 3*(4), 359–369.

Sharma, A., & Kesner, I. F. (1996). Diversifying entry: Some ex-ante explanations for postentry survival and growth. *Academy of Management Journal, 39*(3), 635–677.

Silverman, B. S. (1999). Technological resources and the direction of corporate diversification: Toward an integration of the resource-based view and transaction cost economics. *Management Science, 45*(8), 1109–1124.

Speckbacher, G., Neumann, K., & Hoffmann, W. H. (2014). Resource relatedness and the mode of entry into new businesses: Internal resource accumulation vs. access by collaborative arrangement. *Strategic Management Journal, 36*(11), 1675–1687.

St. John, C. H., & Harrison, J. S. (1999). Manufacturing-based relatedness, synergy, and coordination. *Strategic Management Journal, 20*(2), 129–145.

Stern, I., & Henderson, A. D. (2004). Within-business diversification in technology-intensive industries. *Strategic Management Journal, 25*(5), 487–505.

Stimpert, J. L., & Duhaime, I. M. (1997). In the eyes of the beholder: Conceptualizations of relatedness held by the managers of large diversified firms. *Strategic Management Journal, 18*(2), 111–125.

Szeless, G., Wiersema, M., & Müller-Stewens, G. (2003). Portfolio interrelationships and financial performance in the context of European firms. *European Management Journal, 21*(2), 146–163.

Tallman, S., & Li, J. (1996). Effects of international diversity and product diversity on the performance of multinational firms. *Academy of Management Journal, 39*(1), 179–196.

Tanriverdi, H. (2006). Performance effects of information technology synergies in multibusiness firms. *MIS Quarterly, 30*(1), 57–77.

Tanriverdi, H., & Lee, C.-H. (2008). Within-industry diversification and firm performance in the presence of network externalities: Evidence from the software industry. *Academy of Management Journal, 51*(2), 381–397.

Tanriverdi, H., & Venkatraman, N. (2005). Knowledge relatedness and the performance of multibusiness firms. *Strategic Management Journal, 26*(2), 97–119.

Tsai, W. (2000). Social capital, strategic relatedness and the formation of intraorganizational linkages. *Strategic Management Journal, 21*(9), 925–939.

Villalonga, B. (2004). Does diversification cause the "diversification discount"? *Financial Management, 33*(2), 5–27.

Wan, W. P., Hoskisson, R. E., Short, J. C., & Yiu, D. W. (2011). Resource-based theory and corporate diversification: Accomplishments and opportunities. *Journal of Management, 37*(5), 1335–1368.

Wernerfelt, B. (1984). A resource-based view of the firm. *Strategic Management Journal, 5*(2), 171–180.

Wrigley, L. (1970). *Divisional autonomy and diversification*. Cambridge, MA: Harvard University Press.

Yang, Y., Narayanan, V. K., & De Carolis, D. M. (2014). The relationship between portfolio diversification and firm value: The evidence from corporate venture capital activity. *Strategic Management Journal, 35*(13), 1993–2011.

Yu, Y., Umashankar, N., & Rao, V. R. (2015). Choosing the right target: Relative preferences for resource similarity and complementarity in acquisition choice. *Strategic Management Journal*. doi:10.1002/smj.2416

Zahavi, T., & Lavie, D. (2013). Intra-industry diversification and firm performance. *Strategic Management Journal, 34*(8), 978–998.

Zhou, Y. M. (2011). Synergy, coordination costs, and diversification choices. *Strategic Management Journal, 32*(6), 624–639.